# OROMO DEMOCRACY

# OROMO DEMOCRACY

An Indigenous African Political System

First Full Edition

## *Asmarom Legesse*

Layout & Graphic design: Laine Blata

Library of Congress Cataloging-in-Publication Data
Legesse, Asmarom.
  Oromo democracy : an indigenous African political system / Asmarom
Legesse.
      p. cm.
Includes bibliographic references, appendices and index.
    ISBN 1-56902-138-4 (hardcover) -- ISBN 1-56902-139-2 (pbk.)
  1. Oromo (African people) -- Politics and government. 2. Oromo (African
people) -- Social conditions. 3. Democracy--Ethiopia. 4.
Ethiopia--Politics and government. I. Title.
  DT390.G2 L44 2000
  360.2'089935--dc21

                                     00-009964

*In Memoriam*

**JALDESSA LIBAN**

Abba Gada of all the Borana (1960-68), a wonderful, kind and generous host

**ARERO RAMMATA**

A brilliant mind, a man of knowledge, my mentor and friend

Fig. 1.1 (Map) The Oromo of Ethiopia and Kenya

The total area of the Oromo-speaking nation is 367,000 sq. km., about as large as Germany. Their dialects are mutually intelligible across the whole region. Note the great migration of the outliers, Orma in the far South and Rayya in the far North, each a thousand km. away from the cradlelands. The population in Ethiopia has always been estimated as 40%. If that proportion holds, the Oromo of Ethiopia are now about 30 million strong, one of the largest speech communities in Africa.

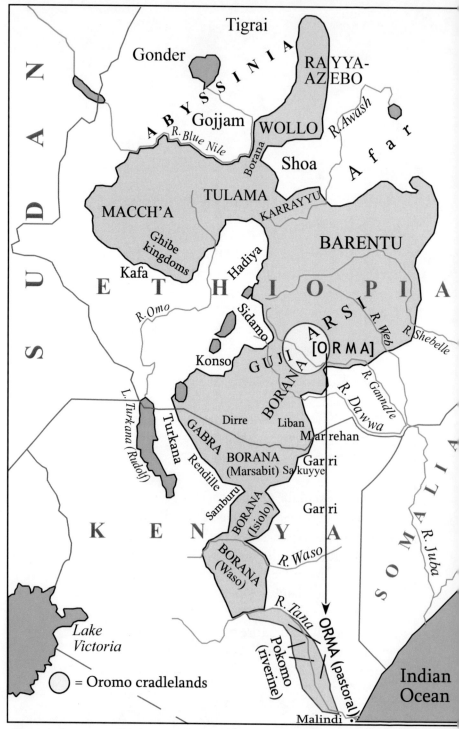

Fig 1.1 Oromo of Ethiopia & Kenya

# *Table of Contents*

## List of Figures, Tables and Maps

## List of Photographs

All the photography was done by the author with medium format cameras.

A society can live, act, and be transformed, and still avoid becoming intoxicated with the conviction that all the societies which preceded it during tens of millenniums did nothing more than prepare the ground for its advent, that all its contemporaries—even those at the antipodes—are diligently striving to overtake it, and that the societies which will succeed it until the end of time ought to be mainly concerned with following in its path. This attitude is as naïve as maintaining that the earth occupies the center of the universe and that man is the summit of creation. When it is professed today in support of our particular society, it is odious.

Claude Lévi-Strauss

We study African cultures so that they may live and grow to become the enduring foundation of a distinctive African civilization. In that process of growth, every culture has something vital to offer. Man's wider cultural identities must be allowed to grow, not by the predatory expansion of one civilization, but by the complementary integration of many diverse cultures. No human community, however humble, should be forced to give up its cultural identity without making a critical contribution to the larger reality of which it becomes a part. That remains true whether the larger reality is national culture, pan-African culture, or universal culture.

Asmarom Legesse, *Gada,* 1973

# Acknowledgements:

Many friends and colleagues have contributed toward the realization of this phase of the Oromo Democracy project. My thanks to my colleagues Mohammed Hassen, Lemmu Baissa, Abbas Haji Gnamo, Chaltu (Belletech) Dheressa, Lensa Gudina and Aseffa Jalata for much thoughtful discussion and criticism.

Donald Levine holds a special place in the evolution of my thinking about Oromo democracy. When *Gada* (1973) was in press, he invited me to the University of Chicago to offer a joint seminar in which we debated "The Amhara thesis and The Oromo antithesis," a dialectic that subsequently became the cornerstone of his *Greater Ethiopia: the Evolution of a Multiethnic Society.* The present volume is, in part, a sequel to that debate.

Two distinguished political anthropologists, Ronald Cohen and Paul Bohannan, my colleagues at Northwestern University, created the academic ambiance in which my interest in African political institutions matured. Working with them was an enriching experience.

My colleagues at Swarthmore College have been a great source of support and inspiration: Joy Charlton, Braulio Muños, Miguel Diaz-Barriga, Robin Wagner-Pacifici have made the Swarthmore experience memorable. Jennie Keith's great work on the ethnography of old age and on social borders opened up new avenues of research. Steve Piker has been a most supportive colleague and a wonderful friend: The breadth of his cross-cultural and cross-species vision was a constant source of inspiration. Swarthmore College greatly contributed to my research in terms of time off for fieldwork, funding, and the more intangible factor of a stimulating intellectual environment.

The National Science Foundation and Ford Foundation funded the field research. I am indebted to these two great institutions for their help, at a time when little funding was available for African scholars.

Special thanks to the staff of the Scholarly Programs of the Library of Congress, in Washington D.C., for their assistance, and the magnificent facilities they put at my disposal during the final preparation of the manuscript and to Habte Teclemariam for introducing me to the inner workings of the Library.

Thanks also to Sarah Emanuel Abraham who assisted me during our field trip to Marsabit: a trained anthropologist and an erudite partner, she gathered much valuable information. Many thanks to Haile

Mezghebe and his family for their hospitality and kindness during my long stays in Washington D.C.

Special thanks to Donald Levine, Alessandro Triulzi, Deborah Prindle, Bonnie Holcomb, Scott Grant, Lorraine Black and Tsehainesh Tekle for their critical comments on the manuscript and to Na'Ima Muttalib and Leah Libsekal for help in redesigning the maps.

During the preparation of the book manuscript, Kassahun Checole and Elias Amare Gebrezgheir of the Red Sea Press labored mightily to bring the book up to a publishable standard. My thanks to the Checole family for their company and hospitality throughout that period and to Tomas Mebrahtu, Philemon Mebrahtu, Menghis Ghebre, and Gebrehiwet Radi, Bisrat Zere and Gebrehiwet Libsekal for their hospitality and help with the obscure world of computers. In proofreading the final manuscript, Tekie Beyene, Zewdi Andom, and Tesfazghi Kahsu were very helpful and I thank them for it.

Since the publication of Gada, when publishers insisted that I expunge the "Postscript: An Essay in Protest Anthropology," because the editors did not like my views about some Western intellectual traditions, I experienced a variety of problems with publishers. Working on Oromo Democracy with Kassahun Checole—the founder of Red Sea Press and Africa World Press—has been a liberating experience.

Finally, I wish to acknowledge my debt to Paul Baxter with whom we have momentarily entered into an anthropological debate. It is not merely a debate between two individuals, but between two intellectual traditions that bring divergent perspectives on the same reality. Some of my current research on the political and military aspects of Gada is a response to the challenging questions he raised, and I greatly appreciate the stimulus.

The dialectics of intellectual life and the dialectics of democracy are one and the same life-giving force. Without it human thought slides into complacency, and political life into an oppressive sameness.

Asmarom Legesse,
Philadelphia, PA.,
30 December 2006

# PREFACE:

## Notes to the Limited (2000) and First Full Edition (2006)

The Oromo democracy project was launched in 1987 by four Oromo scholars—Lemmu Baissa, Mohammed Hassen, Abbas Haji Gnamo, Belletech Dheressa—and myself. The original exploratory essays were presented at the meetings of the Oromo Studies Association in Toronto, Canada, in July 1987. This book is the first published product of that project and examines the foundations of Oromo democracy. It is a study in political ethnography and ethnohistory. It will be followed by a collection of essays by all five authors to be titled *The Oromo Republic: Decline under Imperial Rule*. This symposium will explore the historic transformation of the Oromo polity and will cover several regions of Oromoland, and the role of women in history and in Gada.[1]

The study of an indigenous African democracy is a very worthwhile enterprise, because it is a rich source of ideas that can inspire and inform constitutional thinkers in Africa. On that foundation of historic and ethnographic knowledge, we can build genuinely *African democratic constitutions* that differ from the borrowed constitutions of today—*alien constitutions people do not care about and will not defend when they are violated.* That is the goal of our research and it is a theme that Oromo scholars have been pursuing for three decades (1971-2006).[2] That some of our European and American colleagues have misgivings about the wisdom of such an enterprise is painfully clear, but that should not deter us from this magnificent venture into our own "dark continent"—a continent that looks so dark to others, so brightly lit from where we stand.

Where we stand is the ancient land, Ethiopia. Part of that country is Abyssinia,[3] the other part is the area of the Horn of Africa that was annexed to Abyssinia by the powerful emperor, Menelik, during the "scramble for Africa"—a high stakes game in which Abyssinia was an important player. Throughout much of her history, Abyssinia had an ambiguous identity, because she viewed herself as a non-African nation, although she was immersed in the African cultural milieu. *Ethiopia glorified her Sabean, Jewish, and Christian heritage at the expense of her African identity.* As a result, the remaining peoples of Ethiopia, the Cushites and Nilotes, were viewed as alien and inferior.

The Oromo are the largest ethnic group in Ethiopia and one of the very largest in Africa. Historically, they were thought to be about 40% of the population. If that percentage holds, they are now probably around 30 million. They were one of the peoples of Ethiopia who were treated as aliens in their own land. The Ethiopianist establishment went along with this approach, and virtually excluded the Oromo from their purview.

This is one of the most problematic residues of Ethiopia's past on Oromo studies, and a barrier that stands in the way of fruitful intellectual discourse. I have watched the evolution of the Ethiopian Studies Association since 1962, initially as an active participant and later as an estranged and distant observer. It was not a very hospitable forum for those of us who wished to re-assess the Oromo-Cushitic role in national culture and history. That is why this book on Oromo democracy developed in the context of intense discussions at the conferences of the Oromo Studies Association in Toronto and Minnesota rather than the Ethiopian Studies Association meetings in such places as Paris, Tel Aviv, Lund, Addis Ababa or Kyoto.

### Changes in African, Ethiopian, and Oromo Studies

Coming as it did on the heels of the collapse of Empire, the global intellectual and political ferment of the 1960s and early 1970s was deeply anti-colonial in character. It gave rise to a body of literature that re-examined the intellectual relationships between the West and the former colonial world. Three particular books by anthropologists are relevant to the intellectual history we are considering here.

One was *Anthropology and the Colonial Encounter*, a symposium edited by Talal Asad;[4] the second was *Gada: Three Approaches to the Study of African Society*,[5] by this writer; a third was Donald Levine's *Greater Ethiopia: the Evolution of a Multiethnic Society*.[6] All three were published in 1973-74 at the end of the revolution of the "sixties." The Asad symposium was an exposé of the manner in which social anthropology had become the handmaiden of colonialism and pioneered new lines of inquiry divorced from that tradition. In that symposium, Wendy James wrote a searching and thoughtful paper titled, "The Anthropologist as Reluctant Imperialist," that examined the ambivalent relationship between the leading British social anthropologists and the rulers and thinkers of the British Empire in Africa.

*Gada* (1973) by this writer, was an ethnography of the Oromo of southern Ethiopia that examined how Western intellectual traditions analyzed or distorted the African cultural-social realities. It exposed aspects of African political culture, that were methodically swept under the rug, because they did not mesh with the agenda of the colonial order, and with the typologies of the anthropologists who sought to be of service to that order. It also examined the cultural, political, and social achievements of the Oromo in regard to time reckoning, historical chronology and democratic political life, which were persistently devalued and misunderstood by some ethnographers.

*Greater Ethiopia* (1974) was published soon after *Gada* (1973). In writing this book, Levine pioneered center-periphery studies in Ethiopia and, for the first time in the long history of the Ethiopianist intellectual tradition, he considered the possibility that the Ethiopian nation may be a product of the dialectic encounter between North and South, not merely a colonizing, "civilizing," or "unifying" mission by the North.[7]

This present work, *Oromo Democracy* (2001, 2006), is a sequel to *Gada* (1973). A quarter century elapsed between the publication of the two books: that, in my view, is the sort of time that is needed for a new paradigm to mature. Similarly, the Asad symposium of 1973 generated a sequel thirteen years later. Wendy James and Don Donham organized a conference that used the center-periphery perspective to re-examine Ethiopian history. The result was a volume titled *The Southern Marches of Imperial Ethiopia.*[8] In this pioneering work, the authors explored the social and cultural history of colonized societies of southern Ethiopia, paying much greater attention to reciprocal center-periphery relationships in the colonization process. They built up the perspective from the center and the periphery, using archival resources and official histories of the colonizers, as well as oral historical sources and ethnographies of the indigenous populations.[9]

The intellectual bridge between the two stages in the development of center-periphery research in the Horn of Africa, that is, between the Asad symposium (1973) and the *Southern Marches* (1986) is Wendy James—a forthright, liberal British social anthropologist who is not terrified by the concept of liberty and is willing to meet her African colleagues in their own mental universe and think with them in envisioning the future of Anthropology in Africa.[10]

The type of re-examination of basic premises that the center-periphery researchers pioneered in Ethiopia is still at an early stage of development. Levine is yet to write his sequel to *Greater Ethiopia,* a quarter of a century later. The only recent, significant and positive reaction from the Ethiopianist camp was Richard Pankhurst's *The Ethiopian Borderlands* (1977) which is a broader view of Ethiopia than was possible in the centrist tradition.[11]

Reactions from Africanists to *Gada* (1973) came in the form of an article by Karin Kalinovskaya of the Soviet Academy of Sciences in *Sovietskaia Ethnografiia,* 1977, a thorough and scholarly commentary. Next came an article-length review by Christopher Hallpike, and a short review by Paul Spencer—both critical and thought provoking.[12] This is wholly understandable since the language in which the book was written was not the language of compromise: It was intended to provoke intellectual discourse, not put it to sleep. By contrast, the commentary of French colleagues was much more constructive: An example is Marc Abèles' article-length discussion of Gada titled "Générations et royautée sacré."[13] It compares the Oromo institutions with sacred kingship in other parts of South Ethiopia, where sacred kings and elected leaders form the two forces that are balanced against each other. The parallels with Oromo democracy are of great interest.

In these and other respects my research runs parallel to the work of Claude Lévi-Strauss, Edmund Leach, Victor Turner, Max Gluckman, Gunther Schlee, Marc Abèles, Patrick Menget, Jacques Bureau—fertile domains that are yet to be fully exploited. By contrast, I find myself swimming upstream when dealing with the dominant conservative tradition in British political anthropology.

The post-colonial dialogue with this latter tradition is not yet over. Those who believe that colonialism is a dead horse that should be spared from further beating are eager to sweep the colonial experience under the rug, as Paul Baxter has done in fifty years of research and writing. The time has come to dissociate political anthropology from its deeply biased colonialist, centrist, royalist, or Hobbesian linkages. Here and there, our discipline is showing evidence of being transformed into modestly objective science that takes into account the perspectives of the conquerors and the conquered. Nevertheless, a great deal of the intellectual residue of the colonial era is still with us, and will probably continue to be for decades, until researchers make a concerted effort to eliminate the vestiges of this unfortunate phase of human history when half of the world was reduced to a state of near slavery. Unlike center-periphery authors, some British academics sleep-walked through the revolution of the 1960s and 1970s: it made little difference in their thinking about Africa. For conservative Englishmen, the end of empire was obviously traumatic—a phase of history that is best forgotten. Their attitude stands in stark contrast with that of their liberal countrymen, who celebrated the liberation of Africa. It is the conservative, not the liberal heritage that dominated British political anthropology.

The greatest change occurred in the thinking of Oromo scholars writing about their own culture and re-thinking Ethiopian history from their own perspective. Among the many writers whose work deals with Oromo democracy are Dinsa Lepisa Aba Jobir,[14] Lemmu Baissa, Mohammed Hassen, Tesemma Ta'a, Abbas Haji Gnamo, Chaltu (Belletech) Dheressa, Aseffa Jalata, and Abdullahi Shongolo.

The work of Mohammed Hassen, as reflected in his book *The Oromo of Ethiopia*, and in his many subsequent essays on Oromo ethnogenesis is a significant turning point in Ethiopian studies. He is the first modern historian to write the history of a Cushitic people of Ethiopia using their indigenous chronology (Gada) as one of the critical frameworks for his analysis.[15] The result is a highly informative re-interpretation of the genesis of the Oromo nation—including Macch'a, Tulama, the Ghibe Kingdoms and Barentu—and their interaction with the kingdoms of Shoa, Gojjam, and the Turko-Egyptian rulers of Harar.

Lemmu Baissa and Tesemma Ta'a wrote on the great confrontation between Macch'a war chiefs and Abyssinian colonizers, in the last quarter of the 19th century. They examined how, prior to this confrontation, internally-generated changes were taking place, whereby the Oromo war chiefs *(moti)* were engaged in large-scale land acquisition, how they used that wealth to build up their power at the expense of the traditional elected leaders, and how that brought about a decline of the democratic institutions. It is these new war chiefs who then confronted the Gojjamite and Shoan armies. In the end, some of the new leaders made a pact with Menelik and continued to function in the greatly expanded empire, where they retained a small measure of political autonomy, and secured some protection from extreme exploitation.[16]

Abbas Haji's work on the history of the Arsi is another highly instructive study of how the Arsi waged war against the armies of Ras Darghe and Emperor Menelik. In this devastating confrontation, the Arsi demonstrated the effectiveness of Oromo military organization.

The National Assembly *(Ch'affe)* and clan councils *(Qitt'e)* of the Arsi were heavily engaged in mobilizing the warriors and organizing a resistance that kept the emperor's army at bay for more than a decade. The study reveals that the Oromo did indeed have an effective military organization, and were able to resist the imperial army using nothing but their cavalry and traditional weapons, at a time when the emperor had a massive army equipped with modern firearms.[17]

Other Oromo researchers are pushing the frontiers of knowledge in many areas. Some have made a special effort to write eye-witness accounts of the Gumi Gayo general legislative assembly that is held in Borana every eight years. This is one of the most important political events in the life of the Oromo. The writers are Tari Jarso, Jatani (Mebatsion) Ali, Gollo Huqqa, and Abdullahi Shongolo.[18] The evidence they have gathered is precious and can serve as the basis for analyzing Oromo legislative history.

Father Lambert Bartels holds a special place in Oromo studies. His book, *Oromo Religion,* is authentic ethnography at its finest, based on a lifetime of work among the Macch'a. Not only religion but many aspects of social structure are elucidated by the primary evidence he presents. His account is so faithful, that it reflects even the conflicting views of his informants, and captures some aspects of the *cognitive dialectics underlying Oromo democracy* and Gabaro/Borana relationships.

Another source of change in the study of Oromo institutions comes from two Italian scholars, Alessandro Triulzi and Marco Bassi. Triulzi, a historian, has contributed three seminal papers relevant to Oromo institutions: one on the breakdown of Gada in the late 19th century among the Northern Macch'a,[19] another on the character of the Borana/Gabaro dual organization appropriately titled "United and Divided,"[20] and a third on Makko Bili, the great Oromo lawmaker.[21] He has also made an exhaustive search of the published and unpublished works of Antoine d'Abbadie—an important contribution to Oromo studies. Triulzi's approach is a type of highly disciplined and rigorous scholarship that makes excellent use of historic accounts of the institutions, such as the highly informative works of Massaja and d'Abbadie, and illuminating documentary and oral-historic data he gathered himself.

Marco Bassi is an anthropologist who conducted field research among the northernmost Borana in Kenya and in the Borana heartlands in Ethiopia. His book is titled *I Borana: Una societa assembleare dell' Etiopia* (The Borana: A Society of Assemblies in Ethiopia).[22] He presents primary observational data on the clan councils but not the Gada assemblies. As such, his work is an important contribution to some hitherto unexplored areas of Oromo political life. Unfortunately, he chose to focus his *field* research entirely on the kinship system and to leave out the Gada institution: He never visited the Gada Assembly or any senior Gada leaders at work. Hence, he has no personal experience of the Gada institution and has no business making sweeping statements about it, based, as they are, on zero days of participant observation.

Aneesa Kassam has written the only modern eye-witness account by an anthropologist of the Gada Mojji rituals in Kenya. It is rich in factual, observational detail and gives us new insights into the Gada institution and its ritual-political cycles. Jan Hultin has written on the problem of political inequality in Macch'a Oromo society: he examines the process of marginalization of men from Gada *(ilman jarsa, garba)* due to the under-aging process. He analyzes the linguistic and status parallels between them and the assimilated aliens *(Gabaro).*[23]

Special credit is due to Karl Eric Knutsson who re-focussed our attention on the Qallu and the relationship between the Gada and Qallu institutions. His work on Macch'a and Borana anticipates the multi-institutional and pan-Oromo analysis that runs through the entire length of this book.[24]

Finally, we should also acknowledge those writers who claim that Oromo have no political, judicial, or military institutions. Their work too is relevant to our project because it has provoked a debate that has yielded some dividends. We hope and trust that such debates will continue to animate Oromo studies.

### The Debate with Baxter

By far the most judgmental among the European scholars is Paul Baxter who spent much time advancing the *negative thesis* that Oromo institutions, such as Gada, have no political or practical functions. As such, his judgment strikes at the very heart of our thesis on Oromo democracy and must, therefore, be examined with some care. The chapter below on "Warfare, Gada, and Age-regiments: Point and Counterpoint" is partly devoted to this task and deals with some of the more contentious issues he raised.

This book on Oromo democracy is a study of the interface between ethnography and history that re-examines the same historical materials examined before, such as Bahrey's chronicle on Gada warfare, but does so with a deeper understanding of the structure of Oromo institutions. The task, in short, is to write a historical note on Oromo political institutions that is constrained and informed by the structure of those institutions. It is, however, not much more than a footnote to the rich histories offered by Triulzi and Mohammed Hassen, two historians who are exploring the critical interface between ethnography and history.

In *Age, Generation and Time*, Baxter attempts to explain the differences between our approaches as arising from the fact that he is a "comparative Africanist" and I, an "Ethiopianist." That, however, does not begin to explain the divergences. There is more comparative analysis in my work than in his and I am critical of both the Africanist and Ethiopianist traditions.[25] I am not an Ethiopianist by training, by professional association, or intellectual inclination.[26] The anthropologists who have had the greatest influence on my thinking have never set foot on Ethiopian soil.[27] Nearly all my published work, starting from my very first essay on the subject, examined Oromo institutions in a comparative African context.[28] My ethnography on Borana has been reviewed and debated more in Anthropological and Africanist literature than in Ethiopianist journals.[29] I have conducted as much field research in Kenya as in Ethiopia.[30] The methodological aspect of my research compares three intellectual traditions: British case analysis, French structuralism, and American empiricism.[31] That is what the "three approaches" in the sub-title of *Gada* (1973) are all about. All that does not add up to a profile of a committed member of the Ethiopianist establishment.

## Cultural Burdens of the Scholar

Scholars who use one vocabulary to talk of Western institutions and another to examine African institutions create an unbridgeable intellectual chasm in comparative research. A science that switches codes in examining varieties of the same domain and then spends much time debating its vocabulary is, indeed, a dismal science. In the study of democracies in non-Western societies, political scientists, such as Arend Lijphart and Gabriel Almond, have done more credible work in comparative political anthropology than the anthropologists themselves, mainly because they do not seem to carry the kind of intellectual deadweight inherited by the anthropologists from their colonial predecessors.[32]

Over and above the value-laden lexicon and taxonomies of anthropology, there is also the problem of an even more blatant type of value judgment that mars the literature on African political life. If one scholar overvalues Oromo cultural achievements and another devalues them, if one habitually looks at the world through the eyes of the dominant society and another through the eyes of the oppressed groups, they both suffer from their cultural perspectives. The foghorns have now been sounded on both sides[33] and one hopes it will have a salutary effect on the quality of the research that emerges, once the fog clears.

Scholars who say there is no such thing as an indigenous Oromo "democracy" or "government" should ask themselves whether they are concerned about the applicability of the concepts of "government" and "democracy" to Oromo institutions on serious, clearly articulated, cross-cultural, scientific grounds or because they like to think that democracy is a unique Western invention that should not be lumped together with the institutions of "inferior societies." Scholars who draw parallels between Western and African democracies must also ask themselves "Are we trying to boost nationalist egos by telling people that their cultural achievements parallel those of Western democracies or is there, in fact, an adequate scientific basis for making the comparison?"

On this issue we should, I believe, stop posturing, cut out the patronizing language, examine each perspective as a testable thesis, not a manifesto, and let the evidence speak for itself.

### The Qallu Institution and Dual Organization

In addition to the age/generation organizations that are widely discussed in the literature, Oromo also have two other institutions that form the basis of their democracy but were badly neglected by researchers. These are the Qallu institution and the dual organization or, more specifically, the moieties.

In the first half of the sixteenth century, the Oromo nation as a whole was divided into two great moieties called BARETTUMA and BORANA. With regard to Oromo moieties, the following thesis is presented:

(1) The ancient moieties were politically poised against each other and competed with each other for the top gada office of Abba Gada. (2) The moieties had their own separate cradlelands and shrines for Muda pilgrimages, but they also participated in the same political-military system: They were at once "United and Divided" to use Triulzi's characterization of the Borana-Gabaro relationship. (3) The thesis also suggests that in some cases, such as Borana and Orma, the moieties were replicated from the parent society. In other cases, such as Macch'a,

they were broken up during the great migration and were rebuilt, thus re-establishing ritual and political balancing that is a central feature of Oromo political life.

Most historians assume that the BARETTUMA and BORANA were two "tribes" that separated sometime in the 16th century or earlier and went in different directions, ultimately occupying two disparate regions in Ethiopia: BARETTUMA in the east and BORANA in the west. That is a widely held view in the literature. Evidence if offered indicating that this premise is untenable. BARETTUMA and BORANA are not tribes but moieties. Two moieties cannot migrate separately without changing their character as interacting, balanced, and adversarial entities. That remains true whether the moieties are exogamous or not.

Please note that the names of the ancient moieties—BARETTUMA and BORANA—are capitalized to distinguish them from the same terms that appear as the names of different branches of the Oromo nation, as in the case of the Barentuma of Harar or the Borana of southern Ethiopia, and as moieties or sections within branches, as in the Barettuma moiety in Orma or the Barentuma section of Tulama.

## Purposes and Methods

After reading this book, the reader will, I hope, realize that Oromo democracy does indeed exist; that it is a polycephalous system of government, and that it is based on division of labor between the different institutions. If this book achieves any of these goals, it will have served its purpose. It is worth noting, however, that the division of labor is not highly differentiated *within* institutions, as indicated in *Gada* (1973), and much better defined *between* institutions—an important focus of the present study.

With regard to method, the first approach that was employed is the technique of historic/ethnographic parallels to reconstruct socio-political systems of earlier centuries, by analogy with the institutions of the most conservative and least altered societies now extant. Secondly, the center-periphery approach was employed to show how colonial rule influenced Oromo institutions and how the institutions reacted, often creatively, to the colonial impetus.

It is also worth remembering that although there is much kinship between the perspective adopted in this book and center-periphery research, it goes beyond that approach in looking at the Oromo polity not only as the periphery of empire but also in its own right and in relation to other democracies. The study deals with all branches of the

Oromo nation and identifies features inherited from the parent society, and those that evolved or were borrowed subsequently. In this regard our approach has much in common with comparative historical linguistics and derives analytical ideas from that discipline, particularly those concerning the procedures employed in determining the traits in the daughter societies that can be attributed to the parent society, or those that must be relegated to lower branches of the ethno-historic tree or to borrowing and influences from neighboring societies.

## Chapters and Topics

**Chapter 1,** titled "Oromo Democracy in an African Context," examines the way Ethiopianist and Africanist scholarship dealt with Oromo political and military institutions. Since British Social Anthropology has had very important things to say about Oromo institutions, and other African political systems of the same kind, we also discuss this intellectual tradition.

**Chapter 2,** on "Oromo Warfare, Gada and Age-regiments: Point and Counterpoint," examines how Gada served as the organizational basis of Oromo wars in the early phases of their territorial expansion and how the society developed a non-generational age-based system to serve as a subsidiary institution to Gada. Baxter's views on Gada, age-sets, warfare, and government are discussed and the underlying methodological and philosophic bases are exposed.

**Chapter 3,** titled "The Oromo Polity: The Key Institutions," is a description of the four principal institutions that make up the political system, their relationships with each other and the division of labor between them. Gada, the dominant institution, is given special attention and a brief account of the entire life cycle is presented. It is assumed that readers will consult *Gada* (1973, revised in 2007) for fuller treatment of the subject. The two books, *Gada* (1973) and *Oromo Democracy* (2000, 2006), are intended to be read as companion volumes. One complements the other in critical areas.

**Chapter 4,** on "The Dual Organization and the Qallu Institution," is an examination of the moieties and the Qallus who represent them. Special attention is given to how moieties are balanced against each other in ritual and political activities. The moiety replication and re-building thesis is presented to show how moieties were torn apart and rebuilt as the nation expanded and how assimilated aliens were integrated into the moiety structure, creating new space for them within the rebuilt moieties or along the Oromo/Gabra parameter.

Chapter 5, titled "Principles of Oromo Democracy: Explorations in African Constitutional Thought," is the culminating stage of our study. All the institutions are presented as elements of one and the same democratic political system. It includes analyses of eighteen basic principles underlying the Oromo polity and comments by a Borana elder on each principle. The National Assembly *(Gumi or Ch'affe)* is not presented in any one chapter. It takes center stage in the analysis of the Oromo constitution, chap. 5, but, as the over arching institution to which all others are subordinated, it is discussed throughout the book.

Chapter 6, titled "Conclusion: Retrospect and Prospect" is a reassessment of Oromo democracy. It identifies the main strengths and weaknesses of the institutions. It also examines the role they have played and the greater role they might play in the societal evolution of a democratic Ethiopian nation.

## Sources: Ethnographic, Oral-historic and Archival

In addition to the rich resources gathered by my predecessors, my colleagues and my students in Oromo studies, the primary information I have employed consists of different types of data:

(1) *Ethnographic data* I obtained through 5 years of participant-observation and interviews in Ethiopia and Kenya; (2) *Oral history* data gathered from Oromo elders in Ethiopia and Marsabit, Kenya between 1962 and 1984; (3) *Archival materials* obtained in Kenya and London in 1984; (4) *Follow up* data gathered in 1995 from Borana and Arsi elders in Ethiopia; (5) A short *field trip to Orma,* in Kenya, in 2006.

My earliest field data were based on interviews with Oromo elders in Ethiopia, mainly Macch'a, Arsi and Guji-Borana in Western, Eastern and Southern Ethiopia respectively. The findings are titled "Oromo Field Notes, 1961." This body of exploratory information was collected largely for the purpose of selecting the most appropriate fieldwork site for the study of the Gada System. On the basis of that year-long part-time inquiry, I selected Borana, Ethiopia, for intensive field study.

The timing of my fieldwork had far reaching consequences. The occurrence of the Gada transition rites at the end of my first year of field work (Summer of 1963) was entirely coincidental. However, three of my subsequent field trips to Borana were planned to coincide with critical events: in 1971, to see the Gada rites of passage a second time; in 1973, to observe to total solar eclipse in Marsabit, Kenya; and again in Marsabit, in 1979, to see Gada Mojji rituals. I have, thus, observed

Gada rites and ceremonies—once by chance, twice by design—over a period of twenty five years.

The main body of information presented here is based on extensive observation, surveys, and in-depth interviews with Borana elders and political leaders in Southern Ethiopia recorded under the title of "Borana Field Notes, 1963-1971." I was in Ethiopia in 1973-74 to carry out a survey of Addis Ababa. During that year I gathered some oral historic data. I left Addis Ababa one week after the Emperor's abdication. Thereafter, during the Dergue era, the focus of my research shifted to the Boran and Gabra of Northern Kenya, where I conducted three years of ecological field research between 1976 and 1984, recorded as "Kenya Boran Field Notes, 1976-1984. The results are to be published under the title of *A Pastoral Ecosystem: Field Studies of the Boran and Gabra of Northern Kenya.* Part of my work in Marsabit was devoted to in-depth oral history. It was obtained from a group of Boran (as well as one Konso, and one Sakuyye) elders, recorded as "Marsabit Elders: Oral-Historical Records of the Oromo of Northern Kenya, Marsabit, 1984." The most recent data on the Oromo constitution were gathered in 1995 in Ethiopia and are recorded as "Conversations with Galma Liban, 1995." The interviews were concerned with Gada, warfare, and the principles of Oromo democracy. Similar interviews I conducted, at the same time, with an Arsi elder are recorded as "Conversations with Haji Idris Mahmoud, 1995." The two names given here are pseudonyms.

While this book was in press I visited the lush green territory of the Orma along the banks of the Tana River in Kenya, the only part of the Oromo nation I had not seen. The result is a set of impressions, photographs, interviews referred to as "Preliminary Orma Field Notes, 2006." Aided by Hilarie Kelly's rich ethnography and extensive personal communications I was able to integrate Orma into my analysis of Oromo ethnogenesis, and made adjustments on the national map.

There is a significant amount of archival documentation in this book. It is derived from two main sources: the oral-historic evidence cited above which was cross-checked with the Kenya National Archives and the Public Records Office in London. Of the royal chronicles of Imperial Ethiopia the most useful was Pereira's *Chronica de Susenyos,* parts of which were translated from Portuguese into English by this writer's research assistants. The reign of Susenyos is one particular period when Amhara and Oromo histories become deeply intertwined.

**The limited (2000) and full editions (2006) compared**

Readers should note that the limited edition was a preliminary printing of 200 copies. The full edition incorporates significant changes made as a result of feedback from colleagues, deeper analyses of the institutions, new data from many part of Oromo nation. The changes are these:

(1) On insight gained form Galma Liban, the Gada Cycle was altered to reflect new findings regarding the distinction between *rites of passage* and *political transition ceremonies*. The outer part of the spiral was left out because the issue of the *ilman jarsa* or "prematurely retired population" is not discussed in any detail here as it is in *Gada* (1973, 2007). The Gada Cycle is offered in two forms (English & Borana) and it is more complete. (2) The *regimental organization* described on page 48 of both editions is different. In the first edition, I described the pattern that would obtain if the war took place in first half of the gada period i.e. before circumcision. Since the most important wars occur after this event, a different organization is presented in this edition: after the circumcision of GADA (VI) there are *two different lubas in the Raba grades: junior and senior, simultaneously* (a critical fact that is completely missed by Pecci and Bassi). (3) Much of the text in the second edition was altered significantly, so that it reflects more closely the facts as they were recorded in the works of other students of Oromo culture and in my 1995 field notes—part of which were then still not transcribed from tape. (4) The English text was made less redundant, closer in meaning to the Oromo original for which it stands. (5) The chapter on Dual organizations was changed to include Macch'a, Tulama, Arsi, Barentu, Orma. (6) The bibliography was completed and the index expanded. (7) Photographs taken by this writer during fieldwork periods were added, with captions that contain significant, now historic, information.

# NOTES

1. The book will cover major parts of the Oromo nation including Macch'a, Tulama, Barentu, Arsi, and Borana.

2 Lemmu Baissa, "The Democratic Political System of the Oromo (Galla) of Ethiopia and the Possibility of its Use in Nation-Building" (M.A. thesis, George Washington University, 1971); Dinsa Lepisa Aba Jobir, "The Gada System of Government" (LL.B. thesis, Addis Ababa University, 1975).

3. "Abyssinia" is the indigenous name for the ancient kingdom of north-western Ethiopia. The name, in its original form, was *Habashat* equivalent to Amharic *Abesha,* Tigrinya *Habesha.* For the Amharic and Tigrinya speakers of Ethiopia it is still an ethnic term of self-designation. It is older than the country's assumed name "Ethiopia" by at least a millennium. Writers who claim that Abyssinia is a demeaning term do not know what they are talking about. It is still in use, in ordinary speech, among the Amharic and Tigrigna speakers in Ethiopia and Eritrea in spite of what the racist fascist regime in Italy did, in the late 1930s, to give it a negative connotation.

4. (New York: Humanities Press, 1973).

5. (London, New York: Free Press-Macmillan, 1973).

6. (Chicago: University of Chicago Press, 1974).

7. *Ibid.,* chap 8-11.

8. (Cambridge & New York: Cambridge University press, 1986).

9. A paper titled "Ethiopian Colonists" by this writer was presented at that conference but was not published in the proceedings. Instead it evolved into a much larger paper titled "Borana: under British and Ethiopian Empires" to be published in *The Oromo Republic,* forthcoming.

10. Wendy James, "The Anthropologist as Reluctant Imperialist," in Talal Asad, ed. *Anthropology and the Colonial Encounter* (New York: Humanities Press, 1973); and Wendy James, "Kings Commoners, and the Ethnographic Imagination in Sudan and Ethiopia," in *Localizing Strategies: Regional Traditions in Ethnographic Writing,* ed. Richard Fardon (Edinburgh: Scottish Academic Press, 1990.

11. (Lawrenceville, NJ., Asmara, Eritrea: Red Sea Press, 1997).

12. Christopher Hallpike, "The Origins of the Borana Gada System: A Discussion of '*Gada: Three Approaches to the Study of African Society*', by Asmarom Legesse" *Africa, Journal of the International African Institute,* London, 46 (1976) 48-56 and *Age, Generation and Time*, eds. Baxter et al (New York: St. Martin's Press, 1978).

13. Marc Abèles, "Générations et royauté sacré chez les Galla d'Éthiopie," in *Production pastorale et societé.* Cambridge: Cambridge University Press, 1976.

14. I regret that I possess only an illegible version of Dinsa's thesis and received it too late to be able to make use of it in writing this book. All my attempts to meet him in Addis Ababa, in 1995, failed.

15. Mohammed Hassen, *The Oromo of Ethiopia: A History 1570-1860* (Trenton, N.J.: Red Sea Press, 1994).

16. Lemmu Baissa, "Gada Government in Wallagga: The Rise of War Chiefs and the Shoan Conquest," paper originally presented in the Oromo Studies Association, Toronto, Canada, 1987. Tesemma Ta'a, "The Political Economy of Western Central Ethiopia: From the Mid-16th Century to Early 20th Centuries," (Ph.D. diss., Michigan State University, 1986).

17. Abbas Haji, "Les Oromo-Arssi: continuité et évolution des institutions d'une societé éthiopienne," (Thèse de doctorat de l'Université de Paris I, Pantheon-Sorbonne, 1990).

18. The most substantial of these papers has been published by Abdullahi A. Shongolo titled "The Gumi Gaayo Assembly of the Boran: A Traditional Legislative Organ and its Relationship to the Ethiopian State and the Modernizing World," *Zeitschrift für Ethnologie* 119 (1994): 27-58. The other writers were kind enough to send me their manuscripts which will, in due course, be placed in archives.

19. "The Gudru Oromo and their Neighbours in the two Generations before the Battle of Embabo," *Journal of Ethiopian Studies,* 13, no. 1 (1975): 37-63.

20. "United and Divided: Boorana and Gabaro among the Macha Oromo in Western Ethiopia," in *Being and Becoming Oromo,* ed. P.T.W. Baxter. (Lawrenceville, N.J.: Red Sea Press, 1996), 251-264.

21. "The Saga of Makkoo Bilii: A Theme in Mac'a Oromo History," *Paideuma* 36 (1990): 319-327.

22. (Milano: Franco Angeli, 1996)

23. Aneesa Kassam, "Ritual and Classification: A Study of the Booran Oromo Terminal Sacred Grade Rite of Passage," *Bulletin of the School of Oriental and African Studies,* 62,3(1999):484-583. Jan Hultin, " 'Sons of Slaves' or 'Sons of Boys,' the Premise of Rank Among the Macha Oromo," *Proceedings of the 8th International Conference of Ethiopian Studies* (University of Addis Ababa, 1988), 809-818.

24. Karl Erik Knutsson, *Authority and Change: A Study of the Kallu Institution among the Macha Galla of Ethiopia* (Göteborg: Ethnografiska Museet, 1963).

25. A simple reading of my "Postscript: An Essay in Protest Anthropology," in *Gada* (1973) should leave no doubt about my intellectual roots. The essay is deeply critical of both Africanist and Ethiopianist intellectual traditions.

26. In my entire career I have attended only two meetings of the Ethiopian Studies Association.

27. These are E.E. Evans-Pritchard, Claude Levi-Strauss, Edmund Leach, Victor Turner, Philip Gulliver, John W. M. Whiting and A. Kimball Romney. None of these thinkers have had any association with Ethiopian studies. I have also studied the work of senior European scholars such as Enrico Cerulli and Adolf Jensen because of the wealth of ethnographic and analytical ideas they offer concerning the Gada System. It is a body of primary evidence, published in Italian and German, which Baxter completely ignores, but instead cites (1978:156) three incidental amateur British ethnographers as "intelligent non professional observers." This is petty academic parochialism.

28. See my "Class Systems Based on Time," *Journal of Ethiopian Studies* 1 (1963):1-19, which compares the Oromo of Ethiopia with the Jie of Uganda, the Maasai of Kenya, and the Konso of Ethiopia.

29. My principal work, *Gada* (1973), received little attention in the *Journal of Ethiopian Studies*, but it was reviewed in eight international journals including three article-length reviews.

30. I did one year of part-time and two years of full-time fieldwork among the Borana of Ethiopia and three years full time field research among the Borana and Gabra of Kenya, in addition to making several shorter field trips to both areas.

31. In mainland Europe and the United States, I suspect that more people have read *Gada* for its comparative methodological analyses, than its substantive content. Some of my British colleagues read the methodological material with deep misgivings. The exception was Prof. Edmund Leach, a brilliant social anthropologist, who gave me eight pages of penetrating hand-written confidential comments on the methodology and ethnography in *Gada*. He gave me his thoughtful

comments, with both of us seated, alone, inside the magnificent King's College Chapel, Cambridge University. I was given a choice of holding the discussion either in a pub—to Meet Prof. Leach's colleagues—or the historic chapel—for a tête-à-tête. I chose the latter. For those comments and the welcome, I am deeply grateful. Prof. Leach's attempt to arrange a meeting for me with Prof. Levi-Strauss, in Paris, failed.

32. See in particular Arend Lijphart's *Democracies: Patterns of Majoritarian and Consensus Government in Twenty-One Countries* (New Haven: Yale UP, 1984) and *Democracy and Institutions: the Life and Work of Arend Lijphart,* ed. M. L. Crepaz et al (Ann Arbor: Michigan UP, 2000).

33. In my "Essay in Protest Anthropology" in *Gada* (1973) and in Baxter's essay in *Age, Generation and Time* (1978).

---

### *The Lallaba Ceremony, 1963*    →

This is the grand event when the newly elected leaders of the luba were proclaimed. The young luba sat in the foreground. They laid down their spears signalling the end of the election contests. Their fathers were seated behind them holding up their ceremonial staffs *(ororo)*. Each one of the fathers of the candidates had to individually bless the winners, one by one, including those who defeated their sons—if they were not successful. A new fire was lit with firesticks, to signal the new era. The fire was then taken door to door to every household. Until new gada leaders are elected and proclaimed eight years later, they keep the fire burning. They do so by borrowing fire from neighbors and refraining from lighting a new one.

Fire thus serves as the symbol for transition from one gada period to the next, just as bonfires symbolize transition from one year to the next in the Maskal celebration of the Ethiopian Orthodox church. The two customs are cognates, but the Cushitic custom has greater antiquity.

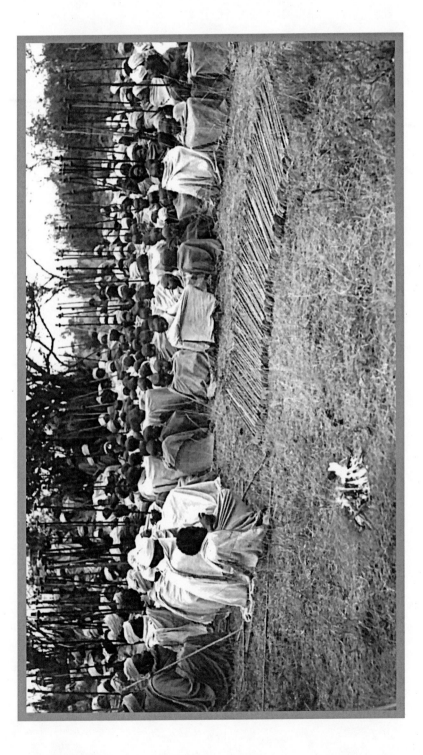

# Chapter 1

# OROMO DEMOCRACY IN AN AFRICAN CONTEXT

## A Critique of Africanist and Ethiopianist Scholarship

This book is dedicated to the study of the democratic traditions of the Oromo people of Ethiopia, and how those traditions changed in response to internal and external pressures. There is adequate ethnographic evidence on which to base the analysis of the traditional political system, as well as documentary and oral-historic resources that reveal the pattern of transformation of the institutions over time. The attempt to examine these institutions in the wider Ethiopian or African context, however, runs into major intellectual barriers, and the problems are as much in the Ethiopianist as in the Africanist intellectual traditions.

## The Barriers in Ethiopian Studies

On the whole, Ethiopianists treated Oromo studies as a superfluous and barely tolerated appendage of Ethiopian Studies. Their primary focus was the Semitic-speaking populations of Northern Ethiopia and their cultures, languages, literature, history, and archaeology.[1] Specifically, it was presumed that, prior to their incorporation into the expansive Christian Kingdom, the Oromo had no political institutions of their own, other than the monarchic or quasi-monarchic institutions that the empire created or legitimized. This body of research was conducted from an Orientalist rather than Africanist perspective, which tended to dissociate North Ethiopian civilization from its African roots and from those populations of Ethiopia whose cultures are entirely African in character. One of the most surprising consequences of this distortion is that Ethiopian literature is classified in the US Library of Congress under "Hebraica," as if Ethiopian languages were a branch of Hebrew. It is also worth noting that Ethiopian studies are taught as part of Middle Eastern or Oriental studies at the famous Istituto Orientale of Naples.

Edward Ullendorff, a leading British linguist and Ethiopianist, a man who held the only chair in Ethiopian studies in the British university system and one of the founders of the Ethiopian Studies Association in Ethiopia and Europe, made the following, now infamous, statement on the subject: "The Gallas [Oromo] had nothing to contribute to the civilization of Ethiopia; they possessed no material or intellectual culture, and their social organization was at a far lower stage of development than that of the population among whom they settled."[2] Referring to the era of the princes that followed the Oromo migrations, he adds, "[The Oromo] were not only the cause of the depressed state into which the country now sank, but they helped to perpetuate a situation from which even a physically and spiritually exhausted Ethiopia might otherwise have been able to recover far more quickly."[3] He describes the Oromo migrations as "the gathering momentum of *tidal wave* which, by sheer force of numbers, was utterly irresistible. Abyssinians...were swallowed up in this vast immigration."[4]

Other Ethiopianists also reflect similar deeply held views of Oromo culture and history, in contrast to the culture and history of the peoples whom they consider to be "true" Ethiopians. Thus,

Huntingford, who has made significant contributions to Oromo historical studies, adopts an entirely Abyssinian perspective in approaching Oromo ethnographic and historic materials. Deriving his data from the work of earlier observers, he presents the population of Ethiopia as consisting of the following (Huntingford, 1955):

| | |
|---|---|
| Ethiopians | 32.6% |
| Galla [Oromo] | 42.7% |
| Sidama | 10.1% |
| Somali | 6.0% |
| Negroids & Nilotes | 6.6% |
| Afar | 2.0% |

The belief that two thirds of the people of Ethiopia were not Ethiopians is very strange indeed, but it was the perspective adopted by the Ethiopian establishment and transmitted effectively to Ethiopianist scholars. In fact, it is the Cushitic and Nilotic Ethiopians who are the indigenous peoples of Ethiopia, and the Abyssinians who are, in part, immigrants from across the Red Sea.

---

**A more fundamental error that Huntingford committed in his Oromo research is the exclusion of the Borana of southern Ethiopia from his ethnographic survey of the Ethiopian Oromo.[5] That is a little like trying to understand the language, culture and history of the English speaking world without reference to England. The exclusion of the Borana may have been justified seen from an *Abyssinian imperial perspective.* The Borana do indeed stand on the extreme periphery of Ethiopia. However, it is wholly unjustified when viewed from the *perspective of Oromo history and ethnography* which was, presumably, Huntingford's mandate. He was after all writing an ethnographic survey of the Oromo, not of Ethiopia. Within the Oromo world, the position of the Borana is central, since it is one of two cradlelands from which the Oromo nation evolved.**

---

So also was Beckingham's and Huntingford's translation and analysis of Bahrey's *History of the Galla* (1593) limited because they ignored Borana ethnography. Bahrey—the Ethiopian monk who wrote the first history of the Oromo in Ethiopic (Ge'ez) while the great migration was in progress—does not begin to make sense until we put him in the context of Borana institutions. (See pages 154-158, below.) In this instance, we can see quite clearly that the problem does not only concern the focus of the writer on the *center* or the *periphery* but also the validity of the research program itself. Whether the investigators place themselves mentally at the center, on the periphery, or whether they view the historic situation from *both perspectives* makes a substantial difference for scholarly inquiry. In Ethiopianist research, the centrist perspective is dominant. It is maintained even when it leads to erroneous conclusions.

There are many traditional Abyssinian historians, such as Aläqa Tayyä Gäbrä-mariam or Blatta Həruy Wäldä-Səllassie, whose thoughts are a direct reflection of the dominant culture. They have discussed Oromo history in the context of Ethiopian history and their perspective falls squarely at the base of the intellectual tradition we are examining here. A fairly typical example is Aläqa Tayyä who devotes a chapter to Oromo history in his book *Yä Ityop'ia Həzb Tarik* or "History of the People of Ethiopia." Writing during the era of Emperor Menelik, he describes, with satisfaction, the Oromo populations in Damot [Gojjam] and Wollo who penetrated the Christian highlands, abandoned their language and adopted Amharic.[6] However, in all the regions where the Oromo have demographic dominance and/or relatively high cultural-linguistic autonomy, he sees nothing but waste, rot and devastation. He says that there is clear evidence that "the country today occupied by the Galla from Harar to Balaya Borena and from Kefa to Rayya-Azebo was in ancient times a Christian country."...[Today the territory is left with] "the ruins of cemented walls of palaces, fragments of sacred objects, plates, dishes, crosses, crowns, staves, sistrums and other items of the respected churches [the remains] of what were [once] towns, all broken up, buried and decayed by the earth, and excavated in our era of Menelik II in many regions of the Galla country. Furthermore, investigations of cave after cave have revealed church robes...eaten by insects and torn by bats, and sacred objects and books which were...hidden when the Galla plundered them."[7]

There is a certain amount of pseudo-archaeological thinking in this account that attributes the destruction of Ethiopian churches to the devastation brought about by Oromo migrations, when, in fact, many of the remains may simply be the contents of churches destroyed in other wars that occurred at the same period of history, such as the wars of Imam Ahmad (alias "Gragn"). The latter waged a jihad that targeted the churches. It is also worth remembering that Oromo leaders who converted to Christianity built Orthodox churches rather than destroying them.

Many other Ethiopianists adopt the same perspective of seeing Ethiopia as consisting of "true Ethiopians" contrasted with a whole group of residual peoples who are on the periphery of the Ethiopian core and whose main contribution to Ethiopia is thought to have been a destructive one. In particular, the Oromo migrations are often seen as a kind of "natural disaster" that fell upon Abyssinia, not a human activity guided by intelligent thought. Favorably quoting Atsmä Giorgis, Mesfin Woldemariam, an Ethiopian geographer, says, "If the Amharas in Gojjam and Dembia and the Tigreans did not confront them with sufficient strength and stop them, the Gallas, like a *flooding river,* would have spilled over Egypt."[8] He says that the end of the Galla menace came about when Menelik "assimilated them by making them share power and through intermarriage."[9] He adds that "Galla movement as a nomadic, destructive and *purposeless force* had ceased completely," as a result of Menelik's efforts.[10]

The images which Aläqa Tayyä and Professors Huntingford, Ullendorff, and Mesfin presented in the above passages are not uncommon in Ethiopian studies. The misfortune of these authors is that they did not beat around the bush, as some of their contemporaries did, but put their prejudiced views down in black and white for future generations to contemplate.

From a *historic perspective,* the Oromo migration was not a formless "flood," or a "tidal wave," nor was it a "purposeless force," but a disciplined movement of people with an effective military organization. The great migration did not go across the whole of Ethiopia by the "sheer force of numbers" but as a result of a campaign which, in its early stages (1522-1578), was coordinated on a scale that staggers the imagination. At the core of that military organization stood the Gada and Moiety systems—two institutions that spanned the entire Oromo nation in the 16th century. From a *geographic perspective,* the Oromo are not marginal to the Ethiopian nation. They are at its very core. The capital city is in the heart of Oromo country and the Oromo nation occupies a cross-shaped territory whose intersection is at the center of Ethiopia. Take out Oromo land and what remains is four pieces of territory with no land bridge linking them, like Kashmirs and Pakistans with massive India wedged between them.

A large amount of Oromo vocabulary and the associated cultural ideas have become part of Amharic culture. Oromo developed a powerful method of incorporating aliens into their society and have taught the rest of Ethiopia some crucial lessons about the political uses of a broad-based assimilationist ethic, as opposed to the type of elite assimilation practiced by the Ethiopian royalty. Oromo have thus made a significant contribution to national integration. The very concepts of individual and communal adoption are concepts that were borrowed from Oromo language into Amharic. Remarkably, the Oromo word *guddifeccha* for "adoption" has been written into the Ethiopian civil code with a meaning that is somewhat narrower than the Oromo original.[11] This is one of the rare instances when Abyssinian culture acknowledged, at least lexically, its indebtedness to Oromo culture. As Tesemma Ta'a has suggested, both individual and communal adoption were significant factors in the history of the Oromo "and might partly explain the rapidity as well as the dynamics of their expansion throughout the length and breadth of the Ethiopian plateau."[12]

There is no doubt that the most important ideas about the assimilation of aliens were borrowed by Amhara from Oromo, not vice versa. As evidence, we might cite an interesting lexicographic point. The Amhara do not have a word that means "Amharization." There is only an English word for it, invented by sociologists such as Donald Levine. By contrast, the Oromo do have a word for Oromization: it is *Oromsu* (v.t. "to Oromize," Borana) and *Oromoomu* (v.i. "become Oromo," Tulama). Borana use the term *Oromsu* to refer to the assimilation of total aliens into *their* society. On the other hand, Borana who assimilate another Oromo people or the allied peoples use the word *Boransu,* (v.t. "to Boranize").[13]

The difference between Oromo and Amhara assimilation is not only a function of *scale* or *conceptual framework*. They also differ in their basic *strategies*. Whereas Oromo assimilate other societies and culturally recognize their indebtedness to those they have assimilated, Amhara rarely make any such recognition. For example, Emperor Haile Sellassie's Oromo ancestry was completely scrubbed from his biography and autobiography. The Shoan dynasty was in the habit of marrying their enemies after they had conquered and baptized them. Within one generation, that fact was deleted from the genealogy. The assimilé changed not only his name, but the name of his Oromo parent as well.

For the Amhara nobility, it is quite possible to incorporate aliens and their descendants into their ranks, while rejecting the very society from which the assimilé originated. Consider, for instance, the following document produced by one of Emperor Menelik's contemporaries. In a little book by Hailämariam Särabyon titled *Təmhrtä Mängəst,* "A Lesson in Government" we learn that Menelik declared Lij Iyyasu to be his heir. In that speech, he said that the purpose of his life was to unify his people. However, by "his people" he meant the Amhara and did not include "the Galla" (Oromo) in his conception of the nation.

በሃገራችን ዙሪያ እስላምና ጋላ በዛ፡ ዙሪያውንም'ን ከበበው፡ እኛም ሳንናውቅ ጎንደር ተቃጠለች። ይህ ሁሉ ስለ መለያየት፡ አንድ ስላለመሆን ነው።

> Around our country the Muslims and Galla [Oromo] have proliferated; they have surrounded us, without our knowledge Gondar was set on fire; all this [has happened] because we are divided, we are not united.[14]

In short, he expresses his thought about the Oromo menace, at the same time that he passes the throne to a man who is the son of an Oromo king and his own grandson. By adopting this ambivalent attitude, Menelik sealed the fate of Lij Iyyasu, his heir, who was later violently dethroned by the Shoan nobility under the leadership of Ras Tafari, the future Emperor Haile Sellassie. They accused Lij Iyyasu of having Muslim loyalties. In Wollo, Muslim and Oromo were one and the same, and both were a threat to the Shoans.

The rest of his statements in the speech leave no doubt that when he says "my country" he means Shoa or, at best, Amhara. Thus, after listing all his conquests he says: **ከድፍን እትዮጵያም ሁሉ የኔ አገር ከበረ፡ ባለጠጋም ሆነ።** "And from the whole of Ethiopia, my country was honored, it became wealthy." To say, as the apologists of the Solomonid dynasty do, that Menelik's purpose was to *"unify Ethiopia,"* is revisionist history that bears only a faint resemblance to the truth. Menelik does speak of "unity" but he means the unity of the Amhara and, most assuredly, does not include the Oromo among the people he thinks should be united against external threat.

The Oromo were the threat and Menelik made little attempt to in-corporate them into the nation, aside from the *token assimilation* he resorted to at elite levels.

Hence, one notable difference between Oromo and Amhara as-similation is that the Oromo gradually grant full citizenship to the peoples they assimilate, a fact that steadily swells their numbers from generation to generation. Their success derives from the fact that they give ample elbow room to the assimilated aliens who are allowed to: (1) *Merge completely* and claim common ancestry with their Oromo hosts; (2) *Retain their identity* and become new corpo-rate entities (clans) inside Oromo society; (3) *Form an alliance* with the Oromo hosts and duplicate Oromo institutions for themselves. These are the three different strategies of assimilation available to aliens at different stages of becoming Oromo.

By contrast, Amhara assimilation is limited to elite levels and is half-hearted in approach. Menelik's ambivalence toward his own grandson and heir is pervasive in Amhara culture. Assimila-tion opens the door a crack; it does not fling it wide open. There is always a trail of evidence pointing to the assimilé's alien descent that can be brought to the surface, whenever it becomes necessary to slam the door shut, and turn against an assimilated ally.

It is clear that the Oromo introduced to Ethiopia the strategy of *mass incorporation of aliens*, a strategy that emperors Susenyos and Menelik attempted to use occasionally. This is a proposition I had presented in *Gada* (1973) and in a joint seminar with Donald Levine at the University of Chicago, soon after the publication of *Gada*.[15] The proposition re-appears in greatly elaborated form in Levine's *Greater Ethiopia: The Evolution of a Multiethnic Society,* where he revises his earlier thesis of *Amharization* as the driving force behind national integration and considers the possibility that the Oromo may have been key players in the formation of the Ethiopian nation. He presents the model of an *Amhara thesis, an Oromo antithesis,* and an *Ethiopian synthesis. Gada* (1973) furnished most of what he conceived of as the "Oromo antithesis."

Between the perspective presented by Ullendorff, Huntingford, Tayye, and Mesfin, on the one hand, and Levine's final position in *Greater Ethiopia,* on the other hand, there has been a significant paradigm shift. Levine pioneered center-periphery research in Ethiopian studies, before that style of analysis took off and became an alternative approach to Ethiopian studies. Understandably, however, Levine's attempt to re-think some of the basic premises of Ethiopian studies was greeted with a royal scowl by critical segments of the Ethiopianist establishment, but it was welcomed by the people of the Ethiopian periphery who saw themselves included in the nation's history for the first time. The book is a major treatise and represents a turning point in Ethiopian studies. It will probably be so recognized once the dust settles. One major deficit in Levine's thesis is that he presents the "Ethiopian synthesis" as having already happened. In reality, it was social change in progress, which veered off from its original course, when national integration was re-invented in the form of "ethnic federalism" by the present regime.

## The Barriers in African Studies

Another source of difficulty in Oromo research derives from the fact that Anglophone scholars, who wrote extensively about African political systems, showed a strong and abiding interest in African monarchies and chiefdoms, but very little interest in, and much contempt for, indigenous African democracies. They huff and puff indignantly whenever the word "democracy" is used to describe an African institution, suggesting that the concept is their own exclusive patrimony, and Africans should not claim it as being in any way associated with their cultural heritage.[16] This is an aspect of Western ethnocentrism that is still prevalent today.

It is part of a much wider and older problem in the Africanist literature. We will begin by looking at the comparative evidence from Eastern Africa, before going deeper into the manner that academic scholarship has treated Oromo institutions. The monarchic bias in history, ethnography, and political science is manifested in Ethiopian studies as it is in African studies. It is a general problem of European scholarship on Africa, and it does not make much sense until we examine it in this larger context.

The development of these attitudes in African studies is deeply rooted in the colonial past. We will, therefore, examine how the colonizers viewed African political institutions, and how those views resonated with the basic premises of political anthropology.

## COLONIALISM AND THE MONARCHIST PERSPECTIVE

As the European colonists penetrated Africa and began to impose their alien rule, they were engaged in the business of devaluing African political institutions, in order to legitimize the corresponding colonial institutions. In general, the more centralized a traditional polity is, the easier it is to link it with the colonial hierarchy, appended, of course, at the bottom or the lower end of that hierarchy. Indirect rule works best with kingdoms and chiefdoms, sultanates and emirates, but it is not easily established in democratic societies.[17] Indeed, the very notion of indirect rule was developed in an effort to bring such rulers as the Sultans of Sokoto, the Emirs of the Fulani (Nigeria) and the Kabakas of Buganda (Uganda) into the fabric of the British empire and to use their institutions as a vehicle for administration under the guidance of British officers.[18] It was difficult to imagine a colonial chain of command with Her Britannic Majesty, Victoria, at the top and an African democracy at the bottom. It would be a totally incongruous mix.

Lord Lugard, one of the architects of British colonial policy in Africa, says in a book titled, *Representative Government and 'Indirect Rule' in British Africa,* that there are two types of African society: one type consists of "advanced nations" who have traditional centralized government, that is, kingdoms and chiefdoms. Those were the institutions selected for the construction of indirect rule. He contrasts these with what he calls "primitive Africans" who have no government, but only have "patriarchal rule" at the level of the family. These "primitive Africans" can only be incorporated into the British Empire by helping them to learn about proper government and the rule of law under British tutelage.[19] If not, they could be governed by "foreign agents" but he disapproved of such "direct rule" because it had no legitimacy, and destroyed what little sense of the rule of law these "primitive Africans" might have had. It was also a drain on the British treasury, for Lugard was always mindful of the cost of colonial ventures to the British taxpayer.

More importantly, we learn from this work, *Representative Government* (1882)—later expanded into *The Dual Mandate in British Tropical Africa*—that he had developed a crude typology of

African political systems. Remarkably, Lugard's model is directly derived from the work of Thomas Hobbes, *The Leviathan* (1651). The typology also anticipates the dual classification of monarchies and stateless societies that Fortes and Evans-Pritchard were to establish nearly sixty years later (1940). Their typology was to cast a shadow on political anthropology that endured until the present.[20]

Why did the British colonists favor monarchies and why were they so contemptuous of decentralized or democratic political systems? In part is was a product of conservative British political theory which the colonists took with them to Africa. In part, it was also a pragmatic choice: even if a bond were to be established by treaty with elected African leaders, there is no guarantee that their successors would abide by the commitments made by the leaders. Each generation of such leaders is accountable to the people who elected them, and the relationship between them and the colonizer would have to be re-negotiated again and again.

Secondly, the fact that the societies rely heavily on assemblies for political leadership, meant that there is no one individual who can serve as the link between the colonial rulers and their subjects. These are some of the reasons why colonial administrations were so persistent in their attempts to undermine African democracies, and had to find more suitable substitutes for them. In some areas, such as Kenya, where a ruthless form of direct rule was the order of the day, colonial administration was established by simply *planting chiefs* where there were none. Typologically, Kenyan colonial administration was at the opposite end of what Lugard proposed. It stood on the extreme periphery of British colonial practice, more akin to the administrations of *settler societies* such as Rhodesia, than to those of Ghana or Uganda.

As would be expected, the conduct of chiefs who were appointed to govern democratic societies, such as Gabra and Borana, did not mesh with British ideas of proper colonial government. They behaved as *representatives* of their people, which is Lugard's idea of good government, not as hired hands, spies and tax collectors of the government, which is the settler colonists idea of good government. The  problem was that these "chiefs" were in the habit of discussing with their communities the orders handed down by colonial rulers. The directives were sometimes accepted, sometimes rejected. That created situations that bordered on "insubordination." Examples of such mismatches occur among the Igbo in Nigeria and the Gabra in Northern Kenya.[21] In these situations official British contempt for African democratic societies became firmly established and the academics picked up those attitudes and gave them respectability and a pseudo-scientific aura. Their very democratic conduct was taken as evidence of "unruly behavior," demonstrating that they are "ungovernable" because they "lacked proper forms of leadership." This process of intellectually and academically undermining African democracies continues right up to the present time, a half century after the demise of the empires in whose service the attitudes were originally developed. We can at least understand the practical motives for these attitudes when expressed by colonial authorities, but there is no justification for such attitudes today, other than the inertia of old habits.

In the colonial world, the pragmatic thinking that led to these attitudes is quite clear. Kings and chiefs could be made to serve the colonizer in perpetuity with offers of benefits, titles, gifts, legal and economic privileges and, most importantly, the legitimization of their authority in the new colonial order. Some of these rulers were knighted and others were made members of various "Orders of the British Empire." Honorifics were thus a useful currency employed by the colonial governments to buy off the local rulers. The practice was most appropriate from the perspective of British thrift, for it cost virtually nothing to give out or validate such titles.

Like Britain, the Christian Kingdom of Ethiopia also became a colonial empire in the late 19th century, and the methods that were employed were the same, in some respects, but different, in other respects. Abyssinian monarchs did not send out or sponsor explorers who "discovered" new territories, nor did they use commercial or missionary vanguards to get a foothold in newly 'discovered' territory. However, they had another variety of "explorers" who served as the harbingers of Abyssinian imperial rule. I refer to this as the "shifta vanguard"—a society of adventurers, brigands, hunters, plunderers and traders who softened the ground for the conquering army. They were more like Francisco Pizarro than Frederick Lugard in their approach. They began their careers as hunters and outlaws, and ended up on the gallows, if captured, or as officers of the imperial army and colonial governors if they were "reconciled" with the administration. The latter practice horrified their British counterparts because the officers of Northern Kenya found themselves negotiating about border matters with the very men they were hunting earlier as bandits. During the early decades of the 20th century, historians of the NFD use the words "Tigre" and "Shifta" interchangeably because most of the shifta were Tigrayans, although later the term lost its ethnic reference and became a generic label for outlaws as other ethnics joined them in the lucrative plunder.[22]

The Christian Kingdom employed the same kind of honorifics as the British Empire to reward the leaders of the colonized populations. The titles they bestowed were no less ostentatious than those of their British counterparts. There was a hierarchy of 15 military ranks and 13 civilian ranks below the level of royalty.[23] Many of the Oromo leaders who served the Emperor, or those who submitted to imperial rule without much struggle were fitted into this hierarchy. They were given such titles as *Grazmach* (commander of the left guard), *Kagnazmach* (commander of the right guard), *Fitawrari* (commander of the front guard), *Ras* (head of an army) or even *Negus*, "king," the final title given to Ras Gobana, that represented mid- to high-level ranks in feudal-military hierarchy. At lower echelons, they were also given the role of *balabbats* or "intermediaries" between their people and the colonial authorities.[24] Paradoxically, Lord Lugard's concept of "indirect rule" had a more hospitable environment in Ethiopia under Menelik than in the Kenya of Lord Delamere.

The hierarchic and authoritarian structure of Feudal Ethiopia was very handy in re-organizing the colonized populations and getting them in shape for total submission. In a most revealing essay titled, "Feudalism in Heaven and on Earth," the Ethiopian historian, Taddese Tamrat, writes that the omnipotent kings of Ethiopia were surrounded by a multitude of functionaries, "each of whom was proportionately represented in sacrality and omnipotence of the central court, just like the multitude of angels, demi-gods and spirits in heaven." He quotes a book of King Zera Yaqob as saying "The children of the royal house take much pride in being the son [sic] of a king saying, 'we are of the blood of the royal house.' The children of the princes also take great pride saying, 'we are the mighty princes.' . . . and all the children of chiefs … trumpet saying 'we are the children of chiefs' and they say to those who are not the children of chiefs 'you shall not rank with us,'... 'stand away.'"[25] It is not possible to overstress the sharply ranked character of Abyssinian society. It is very sad to realize that some European and American academics melt when they hear the unmitigated arrogance of the Ethiopian nobility. Even if they rationally condemn such conduct as "authoritarian," it becomes a cathected object that is celebrated vicariously.

On the exalted summit of the empire sat the "king of kings" or "emperor" whose role was defined by an eminent Ethiopian court historian in the following words:

> The emperor's power over his dominions is boundless; it prevails in the spiritual or secular realms,  he raises people to high posts or demotes them, he gives or withholds, he imprisons or releases, he cuts, kills, or forgives, he has these and similar powers.... Viewing him as the representative of God, the people willingly accept all his commands.... *People shudder at the mention of his name.*  None fail to honor contracts made in his name. So greatly honored is the monarch that if one shouts 'Stop in the name of the king!' not only people but even running water comes to a halt.[26]

That is a profile of "the sovereign" that would absolutely delight Thomas Hobbes, since the sovereign, in his view, must be able to *terrify* and *inspire awe* in order to command the loyalty and obedience of his naturally unruly subjects. (*Leviathan*, 1561, 2006, p. 93)

### The Royal Seduction and Mythological Legitimacy

There is a long history of Abyssinian writing that celebrates the glory of the kings of Ethiopia, and seeks to establish that the laws of Ethiopia are the laws of God and are, therefore, not subject to challenge by their own people or by other kingdoms. In this body of literature, the most critical piece is the origin myth contained in the *Kibre Negest*, "The Glory of Kings," a medieval document that is devoted to the demonstration of the divine origin of the Ethiopian kings.[27] The myth says that the first Ethiopian king, Menelik I, was born of a clandestine encounter between King Solomon of Israel and the Queen of Sheba (Saba, Makeda) queen of Ethiopia. Menelik grew up in Ethiopia and, as a young man, went to Jerusalem where he was recognized by his father.  He returned to Ethiopia  accompanied by the first-born sons of the nobles of Israel and founded the Solomonid dynasty.  He stole the Ark of the Covenant (the Tabernacle of Zion) from his father and took it to Ethiopia. The Ark subsequently became the core symbol of Ethiopian Christianity and is believed to still exist in the ancient Church of Zion at Axum.

The myth prophesies that the kings of Ethiopia are destined to become the defenders of the true Christian faith, that they will destroy all the enemies of Christ, and establish God's kingdom on earth. With some measure of humility the text prophesies, in the final chapter, that the world will not be ruled by the Ethiopian kings alone, but jointly by the King of Rome (i.e. Constantinople) and the King of Ethiopia. The two will meet in Jerusalem, destroy the Jews who rejected Christ, and "divide between them the earth from the half of Jerusalem ...."[28]

It is doubtful that there are any ruling dynasties in Christendom that have created as divine a pedigree for themselves as the Solomonid dynasty of Ethiopia. They are the cousins of Christ—the son of God. Indeed, the last member of the dynasty, Ras Tafari, whose crown name is Haile Sellassie, "the power of trinity," was raised to the status of "the living God," by the Ras Tafarians. Whether they are seduced by such myths and glorious pedigrees or not, most societies cannot resist the kind of mythological heavy artillery put forth by the Ethiopian monarchy.

A great many people are awed by the language of the Kibre Negest, including some Europeans and Americans, who hail from democratic cultures, but become weak at the knees when they are in the presence of the pomp and grandiloquence of royalty—a fact that leads one to suspect that their democratic culture is only skin deep, or that they use double standards in judging the worth of political institutions, one to be applied at home and the other in foreign lands (i.e., Locke and Mills at home, Hobbes firm hand for the natives). Such double standards allow them to reject all traces of autocratic thinking in their own societies, while celebrating extreme forms of absolute monarchy in their colonies or in Ethiopia.

In the case of the *conservative* British writers, it would seem that there is no question of double standards, since they never claimed to have abandoned their monarchist heritage. Nevertheless, they too must answer the question as to why they celebrate absolute monarchy abroad, while they go to such great lengths to constitutionally constrain monarchy at home. Perhaps they do so under pressure from their *liberal* countrymen, but otherwise yearn for the glorious days of absolute monarchy.

### *The ox that has no brain*

Not only foreign observers but also some leaders of the colonized populations in Southern Ethiopia were won over by the mystique of Abyssinian monarchy. High ranking Oromo war chiefs, such as Ras Gobana Dhacch'i, who served the Ethiopian emperors, were completely sucked into the feudal hierarchy, and enslaved by their craving for higher and higher rank. What is appropriately referred to as "Gobanism" in Oromo studies is this phenomenon of Oromo chiefs who helped Menelik to colonize their own people.[30]

Oromo scholars are mindful of how this type of Trojan Horse was used in the imperial conquests. Awareness of this historic phenomenon, however, is not limited to academic or scholarly circles. Commenting on Ras Gobana's eagerness to ingratiate himself with Menelik at the expense of his own people, an Arsi elder said to this writer: *Qotiyyo qalbi hinqabu, harka kolase arraba,* "The ox has no brain, it licks the very hand that emasculated it."[31] His views testify to the fact that there is a renewed understanding of the tactics that were employed to subjugate the independent Oromo territories. That aspect of the Abyssinian colonial strategy was quite effective, so long as the imperial mythology endured, but has since lost its mystical powers during the Marxist-Leninist revolution and the subsequent assassination of the last Emperor and his cabinet by the communist dictator Col. Mengistu Hailemariam: an angry Amhara of dubious Amhara descent. He committed the final act of regicide which terminated the centuries old Solomonid dynasty. The raising of consciousness by the communist revolution was further consolidated by the popular liberation fronts that brought down the communist military junta. The resulting environment of political consciousness is now pervasive in Oromo society and in the rest of the Ethiopian South.

The promise of full acceptance by the Abyssinian royal establishment was the tool that kept the Oromo war chiefs and their descendants tied to the colonial state for decades. But the ultimate tool employed by Abyssinian rulers was the use of elite political marriages between their women and the leaders of the new colonies. The most powerful traditional or emergent rulers of these territories were permitted, or more likely ordered, to intermarry with the Abyssinian royal house, thus greatly weakening the ethnic boundaries at the top echelons of the imperial hierarchy, and permanently attaching the local leaders to the royal lineage. In this manner, the emergent dynasties of Macch'a and the powerful Yejju dynasty of Wollo were bonded by marriage with Shoan royalty.

The culture of Abyssinian imperialism—the royal mythology, the colonial build up of hierarchy and status, the elaborate systems of rank, the new patterns of privilege and stratification resulting from the distribution of conquered lands and the allocation of newly acquired serfs among the conquerors—was all fundamentally anti-democratic in character. If we compare the authoritarian posture which the Abyssinians maintained in the colonies with those of the British Empire we find that there were many remarkable similarities, and a few significant differences, between them.

## European and African empire builders: reflection and mutual admiration

In the Ethiopian colonial order, the accumulation of wealth was directly tied to the conquest state: Using public office to amass personal wealth was an entirely legitimate activity. Indeed it was the only legitimate way of accumulating property, that is, through fiefs *(gult)* and land grants *(rist)* in the conquered territories, given by the monarch or the feudal lord to his supporters and soldiers. It was also acquired in the form of ivory, gold, and slaves obtained by the shifta vanguard, as well as land expropriated in the colonization wars, cultivated for the members of the conquering army by the newly acquired serfs *(gebbar)*. These were honorable ways of building up one's wealth and status. By contrast, property accumulated through investment and trade was treated as ill-gotten gains, subject to onerous levies by the feudal establishment. *The Idea of Usury* (q.v. B. Nelson) was as much a part of Ethiopian feudal ethic as it was of its European feudal counterpart.[32] These values clashed with the market-oriented modernization the Ethiopian emperors—Menelik and Haile Sellassie—were attempting to introduce.

A most poignant demonstration of this cultural dilemma which Ethiopia faced was revealed during the creeping coup d'état that brought down the Solomonid dynasty. It is important to remember that when the communist military junta forced Emperor Haile Sellassie to abdicate, on 12 September, 1974, it was not because they thought he was "corrupt," as the Western press claimed, but because he had become a "merchant." As evidence, they flashed some receipts on the television screens showing that he had actually received money from a beer company and a bus company he owned.[33] What he had done was quite legitimate from a capitalist perspective. But from the perspective of Ethiopian feudal values—which reduces the  merchant class to a caste-like estate—the information that was revealed left him mortally wounded.[34] Curiously, the feudal and communist aversion to "profit" and "usury" merged into a crude amalgam in the new pseudo-communist ideology.

Aside from Ethiopian attitude about the acceptable method of accumulating wealth, which was worlds apart from the rampant capitalism of the Victorian era, and is more feudal than capitalist in its roots, Ethiopia developed a colonial culture that partly mirrors the British system.[35] Abyssinian colonists despised the culture of the peoples they governed and they were more contemptuous of the democracies than they were of the kingdoms and chiefdoms. They also attempted to consciously emulate the conduct of the British gentlemen of the colonies, with the hope of winning their recognition as peers in the imperial quest.[36] Thus, one colonial order drew strength and legitimacy from the other. This reciprocal relationship had its roots back in 1896, at the Battle of Adwa, where Menelik destroyed an Italian colonial army. Thereafter, he too had a "sphere of influence" in the Horn of Africa. The British in Northern Kenya knew that Emperor Menelik could mobilize a huge army at any time to defend his "effective occupation" of newly acquired territories if not his "sphere of influence" beyond those territories.

Ethiopia under Menelik was recognized as an expansive colonizing nation, even if the European colonists in the region hated the thought of having to compete for territory with an African monarch on terms of equality. They were acutely aware of the fact that Ethiopia, in the late 19th century, was rapidly becoming a colonial power: sotto voce, they acknowledged that fact and took it into consideration in their calculations about the partitioning of the Horn of Africa. It did not pay to confront Ethiopia's massive army, when they could get the job done more cheaply, and with negligible loss of lives, by crushing smaller nations elsewhere in Africa.

How conscious British colonial officialdom was of Ethiopia as a significant player in the partitioning of Africa is expressed well in the biography of Lord Delamere, the founder of Kenya Colony. The biographer, Elspeth Huxley, says "The Abyssinians had caught a severe attack of the prevailing imperialist fever" and that they were "the only Africans to join in the scramble for Africa."[37] She adds that, later in his life (1923), Lord Delamere began to resent the fact that Ethiopia was a member of the League of Nations and thus an "equal partner" with Britain, and suggested that it would be the height of irony—a veritable farce—if Ethiopia sat on the Council that regulated the British Mandated Territories (later Trust Territories), that is, former German colonies handed over to Britain to administer on behalf of the League of Nations at the end of the First World War.[38] The irrational contempt expressed by Delamere and the settler colonists toward the Ethiopian crown is disparagingly described in the Foreign Office archives as "the Nairobi Mind," (David Napier Hamilton, 1974, p. 366)

By contrast, the British at home had a soft spot in their hearts for the recent Ethiopian emperors, especially the last emperor—Haile Sellassie—who spent his years of exile in the 1930s in Bath, England. That encounter and the royal mystique of the Solomonid dynasty, which is grander in its claims than anything Britain could ever conjure up, helps to explain why the British granted Haile Sellassie the highest honor in the British orders of chivalry—the Order of the Garter. The honor was periodically given only to a few people in the entire history of the order, going back to the year 1348 A.D., when it was first established.[39] *There is no doubt that there was some measure of cultural resonance between Abyssinian and British royalist thought and their respective passion for honorifics.* Each society used the other as a mirror in which it saw its own face reflected and from which it drew vicarious legitimacy.

Menelik's messages to the other colonial powers reveal that there was little doubt in his mind as to the character of his enterprise. In one famous circular he sent to the great powers, he indicates his intention to "restore the ancient frontiers of Ethiopia as far as Khartoum and to Lake Nyanza beyond the lands of the Galla [Oromo]."[40] The message suggests that he had his eyes on a vast region of Africa that later became the Anglo-Egyptian Sudan and the Uganda Protectorate. This territory lies far beyond the Ethiopian periphery, and it is quite likely that neither Menelik nor any of his imperial predecessors had ever seen it. The image of an Emperor and his advisors, sitting around a table with a map of Africa, trying to carve up the continent into pieces destined for conquest, bargaining with other powers using frontier peoples as pawns in their colonial games, is an altogether familiar image in the courts of European monarchs of the Victorian era, but it is probably a most unusual image in the courts of African kings.

If there is any doubt in the minds of our readers about the colonial character of Ethiopia under Menelik, there was no doubt in the minds of Menelik's war chiefs. They called the periphery of the empire by the distinctive name of *dar ager* and they called their expansionist program *ager maqnat*, literally, to "straighten out a [new] country," from which we get the derivative phrase *qign ager*, which unambiguously means "colony." It is the same phrase that was later employed by Emperor Haile Sellassie, in his new guise as African liberator and a founding father of the Organization of African Unity, to refer—with moral indignation—to European colonies in Africa. Somewhere along the line, the African colonizer had turned into an African liberator, but a great deal of history had to be swept under rug in order to bring about that metamorphosis. *Many of our most respected colleagues in Ethiopian studies were instrumental in re-writing history to validate the born-again Emperor.* These are the very same historians and social scientists who criticize scholarly studies of the potent transformations now taking place in the Oromo nation, claiming that they are objective scholars who do not meddle in such "politics."

### The Monarchic Factor in Colonialism

As the colonizer, be he African or European, embarks on his imperial enterprise, his own monarchic roots have great relevance to the task at hand. He approaches his subjects with far greater respect, if the people he colonizes have the rudiments of monarchic tradition. He is like fish out of water, if he lands in a part of Africa where there are no kings, chiefs, sultans or emirs and the people he encounters are devoid of the trappings of royalty and nobility. The psychological problem that such societies pose for the monarchist colonizer is that his newly acquired subjects are temperamentally ill at ease in the presence of conspicuous displays of rank. Instead of being awed by it, they view it as a form of fatuous arrogance and its rituals as a parade of feathered and over-decorated clowns.

The most important reason why the British colonists were so impressed with Buganda and looked down upon the Maasai, why the Abyssinians had a modicum of respect for the kingdom of Abba Jifar, but had little regard for the democratic Arsi or Borana was because the monarchic institutions of the colonizer employed the same cultural currency, the same ideas of status and honor, the same values of royalty and nobility, and the same attachment to honorifics as the subjugated kingdoms, but had little in common with the democratic societies. That is how the kingdoms of Buganda and Jimma became "protectorates" and enjoyed some economic and political autonomy, while the democratic populations such as the Maasai, the Arsi and the Borana were dispossessed, their land was treated as "game reserves" or "state domains" and, in the case of the Arsi, the population was decimated.

When a population militarily resisted the colonial conquest, however, their culture made no difference: they were all pillaged, destroyed, and enslaved or sold into slavery. That was certainly the case with the kingdom of Kafa in Southwest Ethiopia, a well organized state, which had awesome fortifications and a powerful army. Kafa put up a fierce resistance against the Abyssinian colonizers. Nevertheless, the kingdom was destroyed, in spite of the fact that the Abyssinians fully appreciated their monarchic culture. The Arsi-Oromo were another people who resisted the Shoan conquest, and paid a heavy price for it. This defensive war was one of the bloodiest in the colonial era. An estimated six thousand victims were massacred in one battle; the mutilation of prisoners was conducted on a massive scale, and one of Menelik's generals cut off the right hands of 400 victims in one day.[41] In these instances, we see that the monarchic society such as Kafa or the democratic society such as Arsi are in the same boat—the common factor being the fact that they had the effrontery to resist the imperial army.

The anti-democratic bias of the British colonists has its counterpart in the Abyssinian colonial order, and the motives are not significantly different in the two cases. If Menelik recognized the authoritarian elements in Oromo society, including kings such as Abba Jifar, hereditary Qallus such as Afalata Dido, and the emerging "dynasties" of war chiefs in Wallagga such as those of Bakare Godana, Jote Tullu, and their descendants, but totally failed to recognize the elected leaders of all the Oromo populations including those of Arsi, Guji and Borana—it is not because the former had "government" and the latter did not. It is because the authoritarian institutions were intelligible and useful, the democracies were not.

One key fact that needs to be emphasized is that the Abyssinian colonial government was much less effective than its British counterpart. Whatever damage it did to indigenous democracies was moderated by its inefficiency. In the absence of modern communication networks, the sheer distance between center and periphery in the Ethiopian empire prohibited the degree of micro-management the British were able to impose on the Oromo of Northern Kenya.

> **It is ironic, therefore, that Ethiopia introduced a system of indirect rule in Borana, while the British colonial administrators were intent on creating "chieftaincies" in the conquered territories. Before the newly invented chiefs could be installed, however, the indigenous democracies had to be put down militarily, intellectually, and ethically. The academic depreciation of democratic institutions of societies such as the Oromo is politically consistent with that agenda. The claim that such a society has no government left the field wide open for the colonial and post-colonial administrations to create a government for them—to fill the void, as it were. It gave them *carte blanche* to govern as they saw fit, without any obligation to respect, honor or build upon existing institutions.**

The misfortune of the Arsi was that they were so close to the center of the expansive Christian Kingdom, that the emperor could raid their territory whenever he wished. It took many campaigns to break the Arsi resolve to resist the imperial conquest. The advantage of the Borana—who lived along the Ethiopia-Kenya border—was that they were far from the center of the empire. As such *the Borana could move across the international boundary whenever one or the other colonial regime became insufferable.* Thus, they were able to retain some measure of autonomy from both regimes during the decades when the colonial scramble was in progress.[42]

## British Social Anthropology on African Political Systems

British scholars have made substantial contributions to the study of African political systems. However, they are not evenhanded in their approach to different types of political institutions. High on the agenda of British researchers was the study of African monarchies. It was a type of political system Lord Lugard, the architect of British African colonial policy, placed on top of his agenda.[43]

Perhaps the richest body of information in political anthropology concerns the nature of African monarchy. It is a field in which British social anthropologists have no peers. They have produced some of the deepest analyses of African kingdoms such as those of the Shilluk and Azande of the Sudan (Evans-Pritchard),[44] the Bunyoro of Uganda, (Beattie)[45] the Zulu of South Africa and the Barotse of Zambia (Max Gluckman),[46] the Swazi of Swaziland (Hilda Kuper),[47] and the Ashanti of Ghana (Rattray)[48] in addition to the sweeping comparative studies such as A.M. Hocart's *Kings and Councilors* written in the grand tradition of James Frazer's *The Golden Bough.*[49] Against the background of this vast body of literature on monarchy, it is truly amazing that there is no comparable writing on African democracy. We cannot assume that such institutions did not exist in Anglophone Africa merely because the British—scholars and colonial officers alike—had difficulty acknowledging their existence.

In spite of the anti-democratic bias exhibited by British social anthropologists, it would be unfair to suggest that they ignored all aspects of democratic conduct in their African research. They often delved deeply into complex, ambiguous, subtle and occasionally dialectical aspects of political life, that reveal that even the most centralized and authoritarian kingdoms in Africa contain some elements of constraint on power, checks on the abuse of political authority, and balancing mechanisms.[50]

### Kings at bay

British social anthropologists write of African kings who must look askance at their mothers as they dispense justice and hand down decisions. Queen mothers were important figures in their own right. Should the king misbehave, the queen mother was appealed to and her word could not be readily dismissed. They write of councils of electors who have the right to make and unmake kings. Such kings were sometimes elected from a group of contenders through a variety of competitive or deliberative strategies. They write of dual kingdoms such as that of the Shilluk of Southern Sudan in which half of the land represented the spirit of kingship, and the other half represented the human king-elect, and the two halves stood in political opposition to each other. On the occasion of the investiture, there was a mock battle between them; the spirit of kingship was victorious and captured the king. He was, thereby, "possessed" by the spirit of kingship, and transformed into a sacred being.[51] We read about sacred drums, royal stools, and other regalia considered to be objects imbued with of the spirit of kingship, that is, the sacred element of kingship which lives on through the centuries, as human kings come and go. Hence, the human king becomes only part of the office, while the other part is held by the custodians of the royal paraphernalia, where the spirit of kingship resides. They wield considerable moral authority balanced against the king's political and military power.[52]

Thus, British social anthropologists have brilliantly studied and analyzed an extensive array of democratic elements that occur *within the framework of monarchy.* As they conduct these studies, they are approaching the subject from the vantage point of their own indigenous and most intriguing political culture. It makes sense for them to study democracy from this perspective because that is how democracy emerged in Britain—not as a revolutionary alternative to monarchic absolutism, but as a slow and complex transformation of monarchy itself.

From the time that the Barons of England forced their king, John, to sign a contract called the "Great Charter," in 1215 AD, until the "Glorious Revolution" of 1688, the British re-worked their institutions endlessly.[53] It was a long history of wars, civil strife, and forced abdications. Unlike the American and French revolutionaries, the British did not *think* their way to democracy. Parliament, king, and the estates used threats, force, excommunication, banishment and other such tools of "collective bargaining" to arrive at the *compromise of compromises* that ultimately became the British "constitution." It took them nearly half a millennium to establish a constitutional monarchy and a parliamentary democracy based on the first Bill of Rights in the history of Europe. The final product is a system that is steeped in subtlety and paradox and refuses to treat authoritarianism and egalitarianism as distinct rational options—as the heirs of the American (1776) and French (1789) revolutions tend to do—but treats them as the antipodes of a single polity, falling back on the former when the need arises and aspiring to the latter when the higher ethical code requires it, shedding that ethical code when colonizing other societies, but invoking it when dealing with the "civilized" world community, to which they are bound by international covenants.

## *Omission of democracy in British Social Anthropology and in its typology of African political institutions*

It is clear that British political anthropology systematically ignored the full-blown African democracies in Africa, that is, those that did not treat democracy as an annex to monarchy. Because their writings tower over the field of political anthropology, the greatest among them, men like E.E. Evans-Pritchard, cast a very long shadow indeed. A half-century after they wrote their original treatises, they continue to influence anthropological research in Africa. Whatever they included in their typologies became the agenda of political anthropology; whatever they left out remained beyond the purview of researchers. Generations of researchers from Europe, the United States and Africa followed in their footsteps.

The classification of African political systems created during the late colonial era by Evans-Pritchard,[54] the founder and dean of British political anthropology, was in keeping with the basic cultural attitudes we have already described. In his model there were two fundamental types of African political institutions: monarchies (and chiefdoms) on the one hand and "stateless societies" on the other.[55] A fully democratic system of government has no place in this taxonomy. Evans-Pritchard and his colleague, Meyer Fortes, simply did not consider the possibility that there might be democratic societies in Africa that differ materially from stateless societies, i.e., those that have no rulers, no chiefs, no kings and were thought to live in a state of near-anarchy. These are the primordial humans of Hobbes (and Lugard) who have "government" only at the level of the patriarchal household, whose dominion is "paternall and despoticall," but quite unruly above that level.

One wonders if such societies would have played as important a role in Evans-Pritchard's thinking had he not stumbled upon the

Nuer, the proud tall people of Southern Sudan who insisted on treating him as an equal, and harassed him to the point where he had to re-think his fundamental assumptions. How serendipitous was this particular turn that political anthropology took? It is useful to remember that Evans-Pritchard decided to study the Nuer only after his entry into Ethiopia was rendered impossible by the Italian invasion of the country in 1935. His original plan was to study the Oromo of Ethiopia. We must wonder then what would have happened to political anthropology if he had come face with Oromo Democracy. Would the paradigm of political anthropology have been Zande Autocracy versus Oromo Democracy? Had he applied his great intellect to Oromo studies, it would have been a great service to humankind, but quite useless for the British empire, since the Oromo were not, in the main, British subjects and their institutions too democratic to be of any practical use for colonial administrations.

The great French savant, Antoine d'Abbadie, who was steeped in Oromo culture, and had no ax to grind on behalf of colonial regimes, went away with precisely that kind of insight. After living in Ethiopia for many years and learning about Oromo institutions first hand, he came to the conclusion that the options confronting humankind were not *monarchy* versus *anarchy*, but *democracy* versus *despotism*, a fundamentally different polarity that makes democracy and the role of *liberty* in human life a central, not peripheral, issue.[56] Curiously, however, liberty—which plays such a dominant role in the development of Western political thought—plays hardly any role at all in British studies of African political life, thought and behavior. By contrast, even conservative British political philosophers, such as Edmund Burke, ventured out into that dangerous domain, at a time when the British empire was still on solid ground. There is more on liberty in his work, than in any of the political ethnographies on Africa.

British anthropological writers rarely worry about "how democratic" or "how free" an African society is: their principal concern is with "how orderly." There are no great books in British social anthropology dealing with the question of *"freedom"* in African cultures.[57] There is, on the other hand, an entire library of books dealing with *law and order*, the forces of formal and informal *social control*, and the administration of *justice*.[58] It is, I believe, this deep concern with "law and order" and with the presence or absence of "proper *authority figures"* which led Evans-Pritchard and his many followers to have such great admiration for various forms of *"centralized government,"* but to adopt a negative attitude toward decentralized systems of government they call *"acephalous,"* which is Greek for *"headless."*

Underlying this polarized perspective there is an enduring *Hobbesian illusion* that equates law and order with the sovereign power of kings and implies that democratic societies are always on the verge of descending to the *state of nature*, where every man was at war with every other man.[59] It is an illusion because the achievement of "law and order" is as likely to occur in a democratic as in a monarchic environment. The king and "all the king's men" can be heinous characters in royal garb, just as the president and "all the president's men" can behave like a criminal gang. Oromo society with its complex laws, long legislative tradition, and effective methods of checking the abuse of power, maintained orderly government and succession to political office for four centuries, while many "civilized" nations were going through centuries of insurrections and civil wars. How deep this sense of order is among Borana can be gleaned from the fact that *homicide*—within their society—is virtually unknown. What society in the West, democratic or not, can claim as much?

### Deficit Ethnography

British Political anthropology, did not only ignore indigenous African democracies, it also focused its attention on what the decentralized political systems *lacked*. The fact that scholars dwelt on the "missing elements" in these "headless" societies, inhibited inquiry into the sources of political *authority* in those systems. Most of the studies inspired by Evans-Pritchard's work on the Nuer focused on what they thought was missing in these systems: lack of centralized *power*, lack of *leadership* that has any control of *resources*, lack of a *hierarchy*, the lack of methods of *law enforcement*, lack of a proper *territorial organization*, in short, the lack of *"government,"* narrowly conceived.[60] The weakness of this approach lay in the fact that it was not possible to arrive at an adequate understanding of alien political institutions by *elimination* alone, that is, by trying to understand what they are missing.

We can illustrate the point with the following example: if I tell you that a stranger I saw was wearing *no hat, no jacket, no trousers, no underwear, no socks, no shoes,* you might very well be inclined to think that he was *stark naked.* But you would be committing an error. He may in fact be fully clothed. He may be wearing a type clothing you would not expect to see, something like the Ethiopian all-purpose *ghabi*—a warm toga-like cotton outfit that can cover the entire body from head to toe. Students of acephalous societies commit the same kind of fallacy as they try to define unfamiliar institutions by examining their presumed deficits.

An entire generation of anthropologists attempted to duplicate and enlarge upon Evans-Pritchard's brilliant insights in many parts of Africa. Examples of this type abound in *African Political Systems,* edited by Evans-Pritchard and Meyer Fortes, and in *Tribes without Rulers,* edited by Middleton and Tait. The essence of these analyses is the "without." This is the phenomenon that we might label "*deficit ethnography.*" It consists of a list of features considered necessary for orderly political life, which we then tick off to see if they are present or absent in the society under investigation.

Over and above the extreme intellectual paucity of such a *negative hypothesis,* it is also an ethnocentric viewpoint. It tells us more about our culture than the culture under study, since the check-list that we carry in our minds is, in the main, a parochial cultural artifact. Such an approach fails to show how societies achieve an orderly way of life without the conventional trappings of centralized government. In the case of acephalous societies, we are merely told that they have a pattern of endemic feuding and *regulated or ritualized conflict* within them that works as a kind of "balancing mechanism," and produces some semblance of order.[61] We learn nothing about the internalization of *moral norms*—the regulator people carry in their heads—that causes them to abide by laws, rules and norms without law enforcement agencies cracking whips over their heads. We learn nothing about *legitimate political authority,* as opposed to the *organized violence* which we call "political *power.*"

Students of segmentary societies never bother to tell us that the same kinds feuding, bargaining and conflict management that exist in acephalous systems also exist at the core of Western democracies. They prefer to compare them with the "peace in the feud" that exists in criminal organizations and adolescent gangs[62] rather than the pattern of endemic ritualized feuding, collective bargaining and alternative methods of dispute settlement employed by organized labor and industrial capitalists, the political party in office and the loyal opposition, and in the many forms of political association that vie for dominance in liberal democracies. By making one type of comparison and not the other the scholar contributes to the trivialization and delegitimization of African democracies.

### Monocephalous, Acephalous, and Polycephalous Systems: A More Inclusive Typology

The Oromo polity is neither a centralized political system, headed by a king or chief, nor is it "acephalous" "headless," or "stateless," that is, lacking all forms of institutionalized political leadership. It is, most assuredly, not an "ordered anarchy." The Oromo are one of the most orderly and legalistic societies in Black Africa and many of their laws are consciously crafted rules, not customarily evolved habits. The Oromo polity has three heads. The leaders of these institutions are recruited in different ways and have different functions. In other words, their political system is neither *monocephalous* (one head), nor *acephalous* (no head), but a type of polity I would like to refer to as *"polycephalous"*—with different *kinds* of leaders whose powers are *separated* by custom and law.[63] The Oromo political system is very different from the kingdoms and chiefdoms in Africa, nor do they have much in common with the so-called "stateless societies" known to anthropology. Hence, a democratic society such as the Oromo has no place at all in Evans-Pritchard's taxonomy.

We are, therefore, justified in asking why Evans-Pritchard and his colleague Meyer Fortes completely left out of their typology in *African Political Systems* one of the great varieties of government that occur in ancient and modern times and across all the language families of humankind? Was it really because they could find no evidence of democratic institutions in Africa? Did they consider these institutions to be so different from their Western equivalents that they could not examine them under the same intellectual rubric? Was it any more valid to compare African and European monarchies, than it was to compare African and European democracies?

I suggest that both types of institutions were equally divergent from, or comparable to, the European prototypes. However, since monarchy was in decline in most of Europe, and the transition to democracy had become the epitome of Europe's highest political aspirations, admitting that some varieties of democracy were firmly planted in Africa in the 16th century, when in fact they were not fully established in Britain, the United States and France, until the 17th or 18th centuries, and in some parts of Europe until the end of the 20th century, would have made the ideological premise of the "civilizing mission" somewhat implausible. The idea, further, that African democracies may have had some constitutional features that were more advanced or more effective than their European counterparts was, and still is, considered to be quite heretical.

## OROMO DEMOCRATIC INSTITUTIONS

The Oromo have developed their own variety of democratic political organization that has endured for at least four centuries of *recorded history.* It is based on elected leadership in each generation and orderly succession from one generation to the next. This central aspect of their political life unfolds within the framework of several institutions that assist the leaders to fulfill their respective tasks. But the institutions also help to constrain the leaders when they abuse their authority. There is adequate historic evidence showing that the Oromo had a highly developed democratic political-legal system during the past five centuries and that the system has endured among the Borana in Southern Ethiopia until the present time.[64] It also continues today as a variety of village- and clan-level democracy in other parts of the Oromo nation such as Arsi, Macch'a and Tulama and most of the Kenyan Oromo: Boran and Orma.

Most observers would probably agree that such conduct, at the grass roots level, is universal in Oromo, even where the macro institutions were altered or destroyed. Here, we focus only on the larger institutions and ignore village-level or clan-level democracy with the hope that others will continue the inquiry where we left off.

We begin our examination of Oromo Democracy with a non-technical capsule presentation of the three principal and one subsidiary institutions that are the building blocks of their political system. These institutions are the generational system (Gada, "the rulers"), the moiety organization (Qallu, "electors and ritual leaders") and the National Assembly (Gumi). There is also one other institution that exists only in some parts of Oromo country and has a special role in the political order. This is the age-organization (*hariyya*, "the war-riors") which furnishes the fighting force in all military campaigns. Before the age organization came into being, the military functions were managed by the generational organization *(Gada)*. In any case the Abba Dula or "war chief" leads the nation in times of war.

The only purpose of the English glosses we have used here is to help the reader recognize each of these four institutions by refer-ence to one prominent activity. Furthermore, the abridged profile is presented in layman's language: it is a prelude to the more accurate and more comprehensive descriptions that will be presented later. Neither the glosses nor the simplified descriptions should be taken as "definitions" but merely as mnemonic devices—tools that can help the reader to remember each institution and to easily grasp the ethnographic accounts and analyses that will follow.

### Gada: "the rulers"

The Gada System is a system of gada classes *(luba)* or segments of genealogical generations that succeed each other every eight years in assuming political, military, judicial, legislative and ritual responsi-bilities. A "generation" is forty years long and there are five segments or gada classes within it. Each gada class—beyond the first three grades—has its own internal leaders *(hayyu adula)* and its own assem-bly *(ya'a arbora)*. The leaders of the luba become leaders of the nation as a whole when they come to power as a group in the middle of the life course—a stage of life called "gada" among the southern Oromo and "luba" in other parts of Oromo country. The class in power, GADA (VI), is headed by an officer known as Abba Gada or Abba Bokku in different parts of the Oromo nation, terms that mean "father or leader of the institution" or "bearer or owner of the symbol of authority" respectively. The leaders and their generational cohort go into partial retirement at the end of their eight-year term of office.[65]

### Hariyya: "the warriors"

The age-set system *(hariyya)* is a subsidiary institution that works as a supportive organization under the authority of the gada assemblies: it is organized strictly on the basis of age. Structurally, it has nothing to do with genealogical generations. Age-sets and gada classes are *cross-cutting social categories:* one is not a sub-set of the other. Age-sets have their own councilors *(hayyu hariyya)* who lead the group in times of peace—mostly in social and ritual activities. They also have elected regimental leaders *(abba ch'ibra)* who lead them in times of war. Age-sets are well developed among the Borana but exist only as an informal association of age-mates or companions *(hiriyya)* in other regions.

### Qallu: "the electors and ritual leaders"

The Qallu are the hereditary leaders of the two Borana moieties and the moieties are the "societal halves" of the Oromo nation. Moieties cut across the age and gada classes. The two most senior Qallu are the ritual leaders to whom the Oromo come on pilgrimages to receive their blessings. All the electoral and many of the national ritual activities are governed by the moiety assemblies headed by the Qallus. In Borana today, there are two principal Qallus at the head of the Sabbo and Gona moieties, just as there were two Qallus or "Abba Mudas" at head of the BARETTUMA and BORANA moieties of the Oromo in the past.[66] Until recent decades, people from many parts of Oromo territory went back to the cradlelands of the Oromo in Southern Ethiopia. They are located in a small area in northeastern Borana and southwestern Arsi (see Fig. 4.2 and the frontispiece map). Oromo pilgrims went to the Qallus of the Borana (heirs to the ritual leadership of the ancient BORANA moiety) and to the Arsi (heirs to ritual leadership of the ancient BARETTUMA moiety). Thus the Qallu institution became the ritual force that kept the roots of the ancient moiety system alive and the pilgrimages were the branches linking the far-flung communities to those roots.

### Gumi: "the National Assembly"

The Gumi is made up of all the gada assemblies and gada councils of the Borana—active and semi-retired—who meet, as a single body, once every eight years. It is comparable to the great assemblies recorded in the history of other parts of Oromoland such as the Ch'affe of the western (Macch'a), central (Tulama) and eastern (Barentu-Arsi) Oromo. This assembly stands above all other Oromo institutions: It reviews all unresolved cases of conflict. It also evaluates the activities of the gada class in power, revises the existing laws and proclaims new laws. Over a period of four centuries of its history, the Gumi has made some *fundamental changes* in the laws that govern Oromo society.

* * *

This brief description of the key elements of the Oromo polity is intended to serve as a generalized profile of the system as it exists today in Borana, and as it also probably existed—minus the age-sets—in earlier centuries when the Oromo nation as a whole were divided into two great moieties cross-cutting the gada classes. These are the two organizational principles—moiety and Gada— that appeared in Bahrey's account of the Oromo nation in the 16th century and it is the very same organizational system that emerged in Domenico Pecci's study of Borana in 1941, Karl Eric Knutsson's study of Oromo institutions in 1967 and my own studies of the Borana socio-political system in 1973.[67]

Our understanding of the Oromo nation as a whole is based on historical evidence as well as ethnographic analyses of the system, as it has survived until the present time among the most conservative branch of the Oromo nation, mainly the Borana of Southern Ethiopia, where there are two moieties cutting across the gada classes, and the two systems operate as alternative bases of political action.[68] John Hinnant gives a full account of the Guji institutions, Gada and Qallu. However, Guji exhibit some very unusual features. It is, thus, difficult to include them in our present analyses.[69]

One of the coordinate institutions, Gada, is also present, albeit in scrambled form, in the works of Paul Baxter: scrambled, because it is a systemic institution in the hands of a scholar who believes that all systems are the unreal product of obsessive minds, such as those of the Borana and the French. As he puts it "It is as if Boran had a Gallic obsession to impose a seemingly logical set of constructs over the higgeldy-piggeldy of daily life." Their great weakness is that they are "intellectually tidy."[70] Implicit in this approach is the belief that the Gada System, which is a true system, is unreal and thus not worth studying, as a system.

Two anthropologists—Eike Haberland and Paul Baxter—have written ethnographic accounts of Oromo institutions that differ materially from the accounts presented in this book, because they do not view Gada and Qallu as *interdependent institutions* and do not consider the possibility that the four institutions we have described may be closely related facets of one and the same political system.[71] *Relationships among the four institutions plays virtually no role in their ethnographic studies.* Even when the society has boldly articulated laws that define these relationships, they are ignored. In this book, one of our primary objectives is to examine the *reciprocities* and patterns of *mutual regulation* that exists among institutions—a critical feature of their democratic life.

## NOTES

1. As a simple example of this phenomenon one might cite G.W.B. Huntingford's *Historical geography of Ethiopia* (Oxford: Oxford University Press, ca 1989) that has hundreds of pages of documentation of historical place names in Northern Ethiopia and barely mentions the Oromo moieties (BARETTUMA and BORANA) and the places where they turn up in the historic records.

2. Edward Ullendorff, *The Ethiopians: An introduction to Country and People* (London: Oxford University Press, 1960), 76.

3. *Ibid.*, 76.

4. *Ibid.*, 75-76, (italics added).

5. G.W.B. Huntingford, *The Galla of Ethiopia, the Kingdom of Kafa and Janjero* (London: International African Institute, 1955) and C.F. Beckingham and G.W.B., Huntingford, *Some Records of Ethiopia*, (London: Hackluyt Society, 1954) in which the relevant sections are the introduction and the chapter on Bahrey's "History of the Galla."

6. Tayyä Gäbrä Mariam, *The History of the People of Ethiopia,* trans., ed. Grover Hudson and Tekeste Negash (Uppsala: Center for Multi-ethnic Research, 1987), 65, emphasis added. The source employed here is the Amharic text titled *Yä Ityop'ya Həzb Tarik.*

7. *Ibid.*, 67, (this author's translation).

8. Mesfin Wolde-Mariam, *An Introductory Geography of Ethiopia,* (Addis Abeba: Berhanena Selam Press, 1972), 16, (italics added).

9. *Ibid.*, 17.

10. *Ibid.*, 1, (italics added).

11. *The Civil Code* (*Yä Fətha Bəher Həgg*), vol. 2, chap. 11.

12. Tesemma Ta'a, "The Political Economy of West Central Ethiopia: from the Mid-16th Century to the Early 20th Centuries" (Ph.D. diss., Michigan State University, 1986), 53.

13. In contrast to the verb "to Americanize," in the United States, there is no verb that means "to Britishize" in the United Kingdom, only the verb "to Anglicize," which refers to language, not people. The lexicon reflects the underlying reality in the two nations: one multiethnic, the other ethnically insular, but linguistically wide open. The British have done with their immense lexicon, what the Oromo have done with neighboring societies. Both are instances of boundless assimilation.

14. Hailämariam Särabyon, *Təmhərtä Mängəst* [A Lesson in Government] (in Amharic) (Addis Ababa, n.p., n.d.)

15. Asmarom Legesse, *Gada*, 9.

16. This is reflected in all the works of Paul Baxter and of those who follow in his footsteps such as John Hinnant and Marco Bassi.

17. See for instance the paper by Helen Lakner, "Colonial administration and social anthropology: Eastern Nigeria 1920-1940," in *Anthropology and the Colonial Encounter,* (1973), 127-132.

18. Frederick D. Lugard, *The Rise of our East African Empire,* vol. 2, (London: Frank Cass, 1968); and Margery Perham, *Lugard,* 2 vols, 1968 reprint.

19. Frederick D. Lugard, *Representative Government and "Indirect Rule" in British Africa* (Edinburgh: Blackwood, 1882), 21, 23-44.

20. *African Political Systems,* eds. Meyer Fortes and E.E. Evans-Pritchard (London: Oxford University Press, 1940).

21. See the remarkable career of Qalla Rasa, who was chief of the Gabra and Borana of Marsabit at the turn of the 20th century, as an example of the clash between the colonial administration and a chief appointed by the colonists to govern the democratic Gabra and Borana. This is discussed in my essay "Borana under British and Ethiopian Empires," in *The Oromo Republic*, (forthcoming).

22. KNA, Kittermaster, O-in-C, NFD to Chief Secretary, Nairobi, Feb. 26, 1919; KNA, Bamber, D.C. Moyale to HBM's Minister, Addis Ababa, Jan. 25, 1919, pp. 10-11.

23. Mahtämä-Səllassie Wäldä-Mäsqäl, *Zəkrä Nägär,* (in Amharic) 641 ff., (this author's translation).

24. This office was essentially a new title invented for colonial purposes. It had nothing to do with the same term employed in Northern Ethiopia where it meant "one who has a father," that is, wellborn.

25. Taddese Tamrat, "Feudalism in Heaven and on Earth: Ideology and Political Structure in Medieval Ethiopia," *Proceedings of the Sev-*

*enth International Conference of Ethiopian Studies*, Lund, 26-29 April, 1982, 195-96.

26. Mahtämä-Səllassie, *Zəkrä Nägär,* 52 (this author's translation, italics added).

27. *Kibre Negest, The Queen of Sheba and her only son Menyelek (I)*, trans., ed. E.A. Wallis Budge (London: Hopkinson, 1922).

28. *Ibid.*, 225-227.

30. For a discussion of the Gobanist phenomenon see Lemmu Baissa, "The Decline of Gada Government in Wallagga," paper presented at the Oromo Studies Association conference in Toronto, Canada, 1987.

31. Asmarom Legesse, "Conversations with Haji Idris Mahmoud," Addis Ababa, 1995.

32. Banjamin Nelson, *The Idea of Usury: from Tribal Brotherhood to Universal Otherhood,* (Chicago: U. Chicago Press, 1969). I have discussed this matter in another essay titled "Post-Feudal Society, Capitalism and Revolution," *Leo Froebenius Symposium* (Dakar, Senegal: Deutche UNESCO Commission, 1975). See also Mahtämä-Səllassie, *Zəkrä Nägär,* 107 ff.

33. Tape recordings by this writer of the radio broadcasts by the Dergue made on the occasion of the forced abdication of Emperor Haile Sellassie, on 12 September 1974.

34. Asmarom Legesse, "Post-feudal society, Capitalism, and Revolution," *Leo Froebenius Symposium (*Dakar, Senegal: Deutche-UNESCO Commission, 1975).

35. See, for instance, the conduct of Dejjazmach Aseffa, the son of Ras Lulsegged, and his encounter with British officials after he arrived in the frontier with a contingent of 2500 soldiers. Arnold Hodson, *Seven Years in Southern Abyssinia* (Westport, Conn,: Negro Universities Press, 1970), 249 ff. There is ample evidence in the archival literature and in Arnold Hodson's book indicating that each group of colonists mimicked the other. For instance, the N.F.D. administration tried to establish an alliance with the Ethiopian shifta when the power of the central government was at its lowest ebb during the reign of Lij Iyyassu, a procedure they had roundly condemned in Ethiopia in previous years (*Ibid*, p. 176-177). Conversely, the Ethiopian district administration in Borana province mimicked the idiom and conduct of British colonists when it suited their purpose.

36. Hodson, *Seven Years*, 183.

37. Elspeth Huxley, *White Man's Country: Lord Delamere and the Making of Kenya,* vol. 1 (New York: Praeger, 1967), 38-39.

38. *Ibid.*, 102, (55).

39. Anthony Sampson, *Anatomy of Britain* (Liverpool: Hodder and Stoughton, 1962), 293.

40. Heinrich Scholler, "Letters Exchanged between the Ethiopian and German Emperors," *Proceedings of the Fifth International Conference of Ethiopian Studies* (Chicago, University of Illinois, 13-16 April, 1978), 504.

41. On the Arsi massacres see Abbas Haji, "Les Oromo-Arsi," p. 175, 179 and Abbas Haji, "The History of Arssi 1880-1935," (B.A. Thesis Addis Ababa University, 1982), 41-42.

42. For a revealing account of the process by which Borana were able to escape from repressive administrative practices of either the British or Abyssinian rulers, see KNA: PC/NFD2/2/1, Marsabit Handing Over Report, Sharpe to Bailword, 1930, pp. 11-12.

43. Frederick Lugard, *The Dual Mandate in British Tropical Africa,* (Edinburgh: Blackwood, 1922).

44. E.E. Evans-Pritchard, "The Divine Kingship of the Shilluk," in E.E. Evans-Pritchard, *Social Anthropology and other Essays (*New York: Free Press, 1964), 192-212; E.E. Evans-Pritchard, *The Azande: History and Political Institutions* (Oxford: Clarendon,1971).

45. J.H.M. Beattie, *The Nyoro State* (Oxford: Oxford U.P., 1971).

46. Max Gluckman, "The Rise of the Zulu Empire," *Scientific American* (1960): 157-68; Max Gluckman, *The Judicial Process among the Barotse of Northern Rhodesia* (Manchester: Manchester U.P., 1953).

47. Hilda Kuper, *An African Aristocracy: Rank Among the Swazi* (Oxford: Oxford University Press, 1947).

48. R. S. Rattray, *Ashanti Law and Constitution* (Oxford: Clarendon Press, 1929).

49. A.M. Hocart, *Kings and Councilors*, ed. Rodney Needham, foreword by E.E. Evans-Pritchard (Chicago: University Press, 1970).

50. For a review of such practices see John Beattie, "Checks on the Abuse of Political Power in African States," *Sociologus* 9 (1959): 97-115.

51. Evans-Pritchard, "Shilluk," 192-212.

52. Rattray, Ashanti Law; K. Oberg, "The Kingdom of Ankole in Uganda," in Fortes and Evans-Pritchard, *African Political Systems*, 121-162; and Beattie "Checks on Abuse," 97-115.

53. George Burton Adams, *Constitutional History of England* (New York: Henry Holt, 1938), chap. 5-17.

54. Meyer Fortes and E.E. Evans-Pritchard, *African Political Systems* (Oxford: Oxford University Press, 1940).

55. *Ibid.*

56. Antoine d'Abbadie, "Sur les oromo: grande nation africaine," *Annales de la societé scientifique de Bruxelles* 4 (1880): 167-192. Henri Foidevaux, "Antoine Thomson D'Abbadie," *Dictionnaire de Biographie Française* (Paris: Librairie Letouzey, 1933), 36-42.

57. Among British social anthropologists, Max Gluckman is the exception who proves the rule. He devoted much attention to cross-cutting ties that give people room for individual choice and thus room for liberty. However, even the symposium with the promising title of *Freedom and Constraint*—a festschrift written mostly by Gluckman's students—fails to do justice to the theme of freedom. See in particular the overview of Gluckman's work by Don Helderman, "Some Contributions of Max Gluckman's Anthropological Thought," in *Freedom and Constraint: A Memorial Tribute to Max Gluckman*, ed. M.J. Aronoff (Assen: Van Gorcum, 1976), 7-14.

58. One great example of such studies is Max Gluckman's, *The Judicial Process among the Barotse of Northern Rhodesia* (Manchester: Manchester University Press, 1953) and the symposium by Hilda and Leo Kuper published a decade later titled *African Law: Adaptation and Development* (Berkeley: U. California Press, 1965).

59. See, Thomas Hobbes, *Leviathan*, chapter xviii. Although Evans-Pritchard rejects the approach of the "political philosophers"—because they are said to deal with how people ought to behave, not how they do behave—the philosophical assumptions underlying his work on African political systems is, in fact, tied to one particular thread in the development of British political philosophy, i.e. the conservative tradition, whose assumptions are adopted to the exclusion of the entire liberal tradition of John Locke and his followers. In regard to political and legal anthropology, the intellectual line of descent from Hobbes, to Maines, to Lugard, to Evans-Pritchard, to Baxter will be examined in a forthcoming essay. It is a parochial tradition because it is utterly British. It is doubly parochial because it is British with an ultra-conservative complexion.

60. *Tribes Without Rulers,* ed. J. Middleton and D. Tait, with preface by E.E. Evans-Pritchard (New York: Routledge, *circa* 1958, 1967).

61. Evans-Pritchard, *The Nuer*; and Fortes and Evans-Pritchard, "Introduction" to *African Political Systems*, as well as a host of writers follow Evans-Pritchard's style of analysis of "stateless," "acephalous," and "segmentary" societies.

62. Paul Baxter, "Introduction," to *Age, Generation and Time*, 3-4.

63. The word "polycephalous" is mentioned in Middleton and Tait's *Tribes without Rulers*. As used by Jean Buxton the term refers merely to the multiplication of chieftaincies within the same society, not separation of powers between different institutions.

64. Hinnant, "The Gada System of the Guji of Southern Ethiopia," (1977); Torry, "Subsistence Ecology among the Gabra (1973).

65. The Oromo prefix *Abba* is often translated as "Father of" which is not always correct. It carries another meaning of "owner of" as in *Abba barch'uma ennu*? "Who is the owner of the chair?" Hence, we translate the word variously in different contexts: *abba lafa,* land owner, *abba warra,* head of family, *abba dula*, war chief, *abba bokku*, bearer of the symbol of authority. It is the second meaning, "owner of," that appears in the Ethiopian royal horse names, imperial *noms de guerre* that are derived from Oromo equestrian traditions. It is never used in that sense in Amharic.

66. There are also three lesser Qallus belonging to a particular clan, called Matt'arri, who have no electoral functions and no significance in terms of pan-Oromo ritual integration.

67. Karl Erik Knutsson, *Authority and Change* (Göteborg: Etnografiska Museet, 1967) and Asmarom Legesse, *Gada*, 1973.

68. There are elements of dual organization in most of the other Oromo populations, including, Gabra, Arsi, Tulama, and Macch'a. For an examination of dualisms in Oromo societies see especially Lambert Bartels' *Oromo Religion*, Alessandro Triulzi's "United and Divided," Haberland's *Galla Süd Äthiopiens*, Knutsson's *Authority and Change*, and G.W.B. Huntingford's *The Galla of Ethiopia*.

69. John Hinnant, "The Guji: Gada as a Ritual System," in *Age, Generation and Time*, ed. P. Baxter and U. Almagor, 207-244.

70. Baxter, "Boran Age-Sets and Generation-Sets," in Baxter and Almagor, eds., *Age, Generation and Time*, p. 165.

71. Eike Haberland, *Galla Süd Äthiopiens* and *Age, Generation and Time*, ed. P. Baxter and U. Almagor.

### Madha Galma, Abba Gada of all the Borana, 1952-60:

He led the biggest military campaign of the 20th century, as a war chief *(Abba Dula)*, while he was still in the senior warrior grade (RABA DORI Vb). He mobilized and commanded eleven age-regiments, and a cavalry, of which 400 were armed with rifles. In 1950, he fought a victorious war against the Marrehan Somali, who had invaded Liban. He was neither an orator nor a politician, but what he lacked in political skills he made up for with his valor. Viewed as a hero by his people, he nonetheless shunned all praise and adoration, in keeping with Borana ethics *(borantitti)*. Shown here—*ororo* staff in hand, a symbol of the gada class, and wearing the blue checkered turban *(rufa)* of the senior councilors *(Adula)*—in his fifties, as a semi-retired elder, continuing to serve as one of the presiding officers *(Abba Sera)* of the Gumi Gayo national convention.

*Chapter 2*

# WARFARE, GADA, AND AGE-REGIMENTS

## Point and Counterpoint

Baxter is a distinguished scholar who has dedicated a major part of his career to Oromo research. He is a devoted supporter of the Oromo Studies Association and a friend of the Oromo nation. At the same time, he has probably done more to devalue and delegitimize Oromo institutions than any other scholar has done. That is a contradiction that students of Oromo culture have had to live with for decades. He comes to this contradictory position not directly but on a circuitous path that links him with the colonial era in Northern Kenya. He did his field research in Marsabit while British colonial rule was still intact. He celebrates traditional "centralized governments" as bearers of the burden of "law and order," in contrast to what British social anthropologists have referred to as "stateless societies," which are presumed to be lawless and had to be forcibly brought under Pax Britannica, after their "warlike and anarchic" institutions were replaced by more amenable officers.

The concept of stateless or acephalous society probably had some validity when it was first formulated by Evans-Pritchard, to account for the extraordinary segmentary lineage system of the Nuer, at the core of which there was a fairly orderly pattern of conflict management, that served as their method of maintaining order in the absence of any of the formal institutions of government. That mode of analysis was repeated many times since Evans Pritchard's work. Baxter treats Borana as if they were a stateless people in spite of the fact that they have four indigenous institutions each with its own head, each charged with different responsibilities—including, warfare, dispute settlement, law making, and law enforcement. In other words, he has tried to fit a square peg in a round hole, but had to do a lot of hacking on the peg to make it fit. Putting Borana in the same category as the Nuer, as varieties of the same type of social system, is one of Baxter's more basic errors. He claims that Borana have no government, no military organization, and no method of enforcing their laws. He adds that the Borana do not and did not have military commanders, who headed a military organization, now or in pre-colonial times.[1]

Despite the fact that they have neither kings nor chiefs, Oromo are not "stateless." They have produced one of the most remarkable political systems, effective legislative and judicial institutions and, by African standards, an elaborate military organization. They had all that in the 16th century, and continuing, in varying degrees, until they fell under Ethiopian and British rule in the late 19th century and, in the case of the Borana, until the time of our fieldwork—Baxter's in the 1950s and mine in the 1960s.

The Borana are one and same people who live on both sides of the Ethiopia/Kenya border. Their name "Boran(a)" has a terminal vowel which is optional: in Kenya, scholars habitually drop it, in Ethiopia they do not. We will adopt this usage to indicate clearly who we are referring to: "Borana" for Ethiopian, "Boran" for Kenyan, and "Boran(a)" for either or both. The presence of Boran and other Oromo-speaking populations in Kenya is one reason why British social anthropology came to be relevant to Oromo studies, and why Baxter did a study of the Kenya Boran. That is also why this writer crossed over to Kenya to continue research into Boran society, when Ethiopia fell under a communist dictatorship in 1975—a regime that was hostile to scholarly research. Baxter's study was a general ethnography, a dissertation submitted to Oxford University, never published. Mine focussed on the Gada System, but also covered kinship and the Qallu institution. It was a dissertation submitted to Harvard University and published two years later.

Baxter has attempted to describe two of the institutions outlined above in fragmentary fashion at different stages of his career. None of these studies are satisfactory, judged by the most rudimentary criteria of field research.[2]

(1) His account of the Gada System (1954) is inadequate in that he has little understanding of major sections of the eleven-grade life cycle. (See the Gada Cycle, p. 123.) He mentions the first grade, DABBALLE(I), under the wrong designation of *Ijolle Guduru*, referring to their hairstyle. He focuses on the senior warrior grade (RABA), but pays little attention to the stage when the members of the gada class are in power (GADA VI) as leaders of the whole society. He ignores the subsequent stages of partial retirement (YUBA VI-XI), when they perform important legislative functions in the National Assembly *(Gumi)*. The three grades he is most aware of are grades I, Vb, XI all belonging to the same *gogessa* (i.e. genealogically related classes that are on same axis on the Gada Cycle). All three—but especially XI—were relatively more active in Kenya during the time his fieldwork. He was there in the last two years of a gada period, soon after the Gada Mojji (XI) handover ceremony, and Madha Galma was in the senior warrior grade waging the biggest Borana war in the 20th century, which Baxter was completely unaware of, though it happened two years prior to his fieldwork. For obvious reasons, therefore, his emphasis is on the final retirement ceremony (XI), which he considers to be the "culminating" stage of the life cycle. This is a skewed picture of the institution where the stage of greatest authority (GADA VI) is left out and terminal stage of the life cycle is elevated to great heights.[3] He believes that Abba Gada is not the office of the leader of the whole Gada institution, but the title of a man elected from among the Raba warriors (a fictitious election procedure is described). In fact, the Abba Gada is elected 21 years earlier by the Qallus (moiety ritual leaders), through electoral contest.[4]

According to Baxter, before and after the RABA grade (V), the men are said to be *"waiting" for long stretches of their lives,* Thus, the missing grades in his ethnographic record (II-IV & VI-X) become blank pages in their life histories.

(2) Similarly, his analysis of the age-set system is inadequate: he claims that it has no political or military, only social or ritual functions, but also fails to describe those presumed functions.

In this chapter, we will comment on Baxter's writing on the age organization and the Gada System, but not on the Gumi Gayo National Assembly or the moieties (represented by the Qallu houses) since he has no primary data on these institutions.

### Baxter on the Age Organization and Warfare

We will first consider the nature of Oromo warfare, since that has much relevance for Oromo history and for the place of the military in the Oromo democratic polity. Baxter has written one account that examines the role of age-sets in Oromo warfare. He says:

> The first duty of a newly named age-set is to terrorise the enemies of the Boran....I was told, for example that four age-sets were mobilized in 1946 to revenge the Oditu Kaallu of the Gona moiety who had been slain by the Guji. Legesse [1973:77-81] reports an eye witness account of that, from the Boran side, disastrous war, and also a brief account of a successful campaign in which about four hundred rifles and "innumerable spears" participated, against the Marrehan Somali. Both were national campaigns but men were mobilized in local age-set companies for the battles. But battles are nowadays infrequent. None have occurred in Kenya since the early nineteen twenties and, as Ethiopian central government became stronger and more efficient.[5]

After citing eye-witness accounts of two Borana national campaigns, one offensive and the other defensive, recorded by this writer, showing that they waged such wars organized in age-regiments, Baxter comes to the following conclusion:

> Boran age-sets are utilized for mobilization of personnel, for raiding and for war but they are not designed as a military organization. Dingiswayo and Shaka fashioned the organization of Zulu age-grades into military regiments of ruthless efficiency and discipline, but Boran age-sets...are not designed to wage wars; they merely provide convenient series of categories for the description of, and organization of warlike actions. There is no indication, for example, that the reorganization of the age-sets in the eighties had any consequences for military organization. *Indeed it is difficult to see how age-sets could be so utilized except in a centralized political system.* When Boran need to mobilize as a nation, a national assembly is called: this is a slow process and, through it may be both democratic and a means of ensuring consensus, it is not a quick way to get at an enemy. At such assemblies age-set officers are spokesmen who carry weight in debate, but *they are neither the disposers of, nor commanders of a determinate military force and there is no evidence that they were such in pre-colonial days.*[6]

There are several problems with this interpretation. It contradicts the evidence he cited earlier from my work, showing that the

Borana do indeed wage national military campaigns, that there is a definite military organization made up of different age-sets *(hariyya)*, tied to particular gada classes *(luba)*, and that the mobilization is done by a war chief *(Abba Dula)* who recruits the men from three or four gada classes and the age-sets within each class.

Baxter's impressions are based on cursory evidence obtained from one "deputy leader" and two "minor leaders" of age-sets. He admits that nearly all the real age-set leaders *(hayyu hariyya)* lived on the Ethiopian side of Borana and that he never interviewed any of them; that all important age-set transitions (rites of passage) occurred on the Ethiopian side and that he never observed them.[7]

The most problematic aspect of Baxter's ethnography is that the statements he made about Boran(a) warfare, at two stages of his career, are inconsistent. In his dissertation (1954), he described age-sets as a military organization and added that age-sets are involved in tactical raids, that two or three age-sets may be involved in the fight, that the war party is headed by an elected leader or *Abba Dula*, and that they go to war in proper *battle formation*.[8] All that is completely forgotten when he comes to re-write his material in his essay in *Age, Generation and Time* (1978) where he says age-sets have very little to do with warfare, except in a symbolic sense, and that the office of *Abba Dula* is an archaic title that has no relevance to their present organization.

Finally, his claim that the age-set leaders were not commanders of a determinate military force, even in pre-colonial times, is not based on an examination of any historic data. He presents no evidence that he looked at a single piece of archival documentation or obtained a single piece of eye-witness testimony from men who took part in wars, to determine if age-sets had military functions and what kind of war chiefs they had during the "pre-colonial" era. The period in question was well within the living memory of the oldest generation of Marsabit elders whom I interviewed in 1984 in Northern Kenya. The evidence is preserved in the form of 364 pages of oral testimony, transcribed from tape recordings of interviews. (See photograph "Marsabit Elders," pp. 90-91.) They testify, in no uncertain language, that British colonial rulers went to great lengths to destroy the Borana military organization as part of their pacification efforts. Having ignored that body evidence, Baxter is then in no position to confidently say what Boran(a) military organization was like in pre-colonial, or even in early colonial times, prior to pacification, or to attribute inherent weaknesses to it, contrary to the evidence available from both sides of the border.

### Historic Evidence of Oromo Warfare

The most important evidence on Oromo warfare comes from Bahrey, an Ethiopian monk who lived in Gamo, Southern Ethiopia, located west of Borana territory. He wrote a history of the Oromo people, in Ge'ez—the ancient language of the Ethiopian Christian Kingdom. The work was titled *Zenahu Lä Galla* and covers most of the 16th century (1522-1593). At that time, the Oromo population was a single nation that had not yet broken up into self-governing branches. Borana were still an integral part of that nation and ritually its most senior segment.

Bahrey's account is, in part, an eye-witness account, because he personally saw the great migration of the Oromo, going across the very land where he was living. His description contrasts sharply with the vague, deeply prejudiced, and frightened picture we get of Oromo warriors from writers who traveled with the Imperial Army, and saw the Oromo only from a distance. Despite the fact that Oromo warriors had destroyed his monastery, his aim was not to denigrate the Oromo, but to reveal the source of their strength, so that his king could do a better job of mobilizing the Christian Kingdom on the same scale that the Oromo had done.

Bahrey's entire chronicle is presented within the framework of the Gada System. In particular, the 16th century military campaign of the Oromo is told as the work of nine successive gada classes, organized as regiments, under the leadership of gada leaders, who came from one or the other of the great moieties of the Oromo nation. He tells how they occupied, with extraordinary speed, a huge section of what is today Ethiopia, over a period of less than eight decades, often defeating well-organized monarchic states.

There is also a body of evidence indicating that Oromo had an effective military organization, not only in the 16th century but also in the subsequent centuries, continuing up to the conquests Emperor Menelik in the late 1890s. Indeed, one of the finest historic documents we now have on Oromo warfare is an in-depth study of the confrontation between Menelik's legions and the mounted warriors of Arsiland, a confrontation that lasted for a decade. It is written by Dr. Abbas Haji, an Oromo ethno-historian with impressive credentials—trained at the University of Paris at the Sorbonne.[9]

## Ethnographic Evidence of Borana Military Organization

We have mentioned here only the *beginning and end of their pre-colonial recorded history.* More will be presented later. In spite of the historical documentation that is now available on Oromo warfare, however, we are still in the dark concerning the detailed organizational features of the gada- and age-regiments, their leadership, and their pattern of recruitment. For that we must now turn to ethnographic evidence on contemporary warfare among the Ethiopian Borana. This population was able to preserve its military institutions, because it was a frontier society on the extreme periphery of the expansive Christian Kingdom, where little control was exerted by the central government. In this remote area, Abyssinian colonists were in the habit of learning Borana language rather than the Borana learning the language of the conquerors. *The Borana were allowed to maintain a certain degree of autonomy, because they did not resist the Imperial conquest* and their moiety leaders (Qallu) were given a place in the new provincial government.

However, when the regime attempted to impose the *gabbar* system on them, that threatened to reduce them to the status of serfs, they moved across the border into Kenya in great numbers. In subsequent decades, they began *crossing the boundary in both directions, to escape from the depredations of one or the other colonial government—British or Ethiopian.* The colonial administration of the Northern Frontier District in Kenya sometimes welcomed the Borana into their territory, claiming that they were "refugees from Ethiopian injustice" and, at other times, they imposed severe restrictions on their southward migration, economic life, their hunting, and warfare.

## Warfare among the Ethiopian Borana

The information I gathered specifically on warfare in Ethiopia in 1963-64 (primary fieldwork), and in 1974 (urban survey); in Northern Kenya in 1984 (at the end of 3 years of ecological research on Boran and Gabra), and again in Ethiopia in 1995 (interviews with Galma Liban). This body of evidence shows that Borana warriors were organized as moieties, gada classes, and age-sets. It is a complex system that is not readily intelligible without some effort.

The leaders of the gada class were elected from both moieties. These two great sections tended to alternate in assuming the office of Abba Gada, through electoral contests. The top military leader *(Abba Dula)* came from the gada classes (generational cohorts). If the war chief is not an Abba Gada, he could be any member of the RABA-GADA grades, from either moiety. The decision to engage in war was made by Raba-Gada assemblies. The actual fighting force, however, was drawn from the age-sets *(hariyya)*. In warfare, the most relevant age-set is the group described as the *barbara* of the gada leaders. It consists of the oldest age group in a gada class, age 45-53 at the end of their term of office.

This core group—belonging to the same gada class and age-set— is the group that helps the gada leaders to mobilize the entire age-set, not merely the part of the age-set that belongs to their gada class. The concept of *barbara*, a critical linkages between gada classes and age-sets, is missing in the entire ethnographic literature on Borana, including Baxter's. It is barely mentioned by Bassi (2005:71).

Although age-sets are deeply involved in day-to-day socializing, singing, dancing, and going after beautiful mistresses—married women are allowed to keep lovers—our main concern here is with their involvement in warfare. In that regard, they play a most important role. Each age-set can mobilize one or more age-regiments *(ch'ibra)*, each headed by a regimental chief called *Abba Ch'ibra*. All regimental chiefs are under the authority of the *Abba Dula* or "war chief," who belongs to the oldest age-set *(barbara)* in the gada class. He may be the Abba Gada in power or an Abba Gada of the senior warriors or a renowned warrior from the luba.

Normally, nine age-sets may be involved in the *battle formation.* The ideal, however, is to avoid that number, if possible by exceeding it. The number nine is tainted because of the disasters that Abbayi Babbo (1677-1774) faced in battles with his numerous enemies: his fighters were all ordered in nine regiments.

If the war occurs in the *first half* of the gada period, the fighting force was recruited from three grades: GADA VI ("the rulers"), RABA V ("the warriors"), and CUSA IV ("the apprentice warriors"). If the war occurs in the *second half* of the Gada period, the Junior RABA (Va) and Senior Raba called DORI (Vb) consist of *two different lubas.* In such a case, the three grades that will be in the battle formation are one Gada grade (VI) and two Raba grades (Va & Vb).

Thus, during the second half of the gada period, which is when most offensive wars occur, GADA (VI), the class in power, has four age-sets it can mobilize: assuming that the war took place on the 6th year of the gada period the age brackets will be (45-51, 40-46, 32-38, 24-30). The Senior RABA (Vb) will have three age-sets (40-46, 32-38, 24-30) and the Junior RABA (Va) two age sets (32-38, 24-30).[10] This is the pattern that gave rise to the nine-unit organization of Oromo warfare. Historically, there were also supply carriers and other service providers who were volunteers from below and above those ranges. They did not constitute regiments. In recent minor wars, each warrior carried his own supply of food.

### *Dul Madha: the War of Madha Galma against Marrehan Somali*

Elders who were well informed about the 1950 War of Madha against the Marrehan Somali, indicate that the Abba Gada raised in excess of the full complement of regiments. Adding to what Madha Galma himself had reported, they said that the fighting force consisted of 400 men armed with rifles, several hundred men mounted on horseback, and the rest, an unspecified number, were foot soldiers armed with traditional weapons, mainly spears and shields. The cavalry and the seasoned warriors led the charge and the supply carriers were at the rear.

When returning from the war, the order was reversed. The cavalry and the seasoned warriors formed the rear guard, while the mixed group of young and old supply carriers that was driving the war booty on the hoof was at the head of the formation. They did not camp. Instead they drove the animals hard until they were beyond the reach of the enemy.

Asked if they used any investigative procedures during the campaign, they said they did but only during the offensive phase. Before launching the campaign, Madha sent scouts *(doya)* in two groups of seven *(torban lama)*. These trackers went ahead of the regiments to spy out the land. They looked for footprints and spoor that would indicate recent movements of people and livestock. Asked to be specific about this investigative procedure, the elders helped me to prepare sketches of footprints left by the sandals of Marrehan warriors in contrast to those of Arsi and Guji. Since the sole of their leather sandals were sown differently in each case, they could tell the ethnic identity of the enemy who was lurking around their territory by examining the footprints alone. The investigation of footprints is a skilled art. Scouts can determine the number of people, the direction of their movement, whether they were rushing, marching, or resting, whether they had livestock and pack animals, and so forth. In recent decades, the large number of men wearing commercial plastic sandals has tended to confuse this investigative procedure. However, the elders added that in the War of Madha there were enough warriors wearing traditional hand-sown leather sandals that facilitated the identification of the ethnic background of enemy warriors.

Another sign that the scouts looked for was ecological: When a fighting force was advancing, it destroyed some vegetation in order to feed the horses and pack animals. Evidence of this kind was minutely examined to determine whether the enemy regiments had recently camped in a region or how fast they were moving, and in what direction. Fast movers were said to leave deeper footprints at the heel or toe—when going downhill or uphill respectively—slow movers, on level ground, left flat footprints.

One of the strongest indicators of an approaching enemy is the ratio of men to livestock in the footprints. In normal herding, the ratio is in the order of one or two herders to about 50 head of livestock, in offensive warfare the ratio is reversed, and most of the spoor is that of horses or pack animals. When returning from a successful war, the proportions are again altered, depending on the number and types of animals captured. They lopped off branches of acacias and shrubs for the browsers, and cut grass for the cattle and horses. They did not let the animals graze or browse freely.

Above all, the scouts observe the movement of vultures in the sky and if, at any time, the vultures hover over one locality, it indicates that enemy warriors may have camped and may be slaughtering livestock to feed themselves. The number of vultures is thought to correspond to the number of livestock slaughtered, and thus an estimate of the magnitude of the danger that lies ahead.

Madha Galma had detailed information about Marrehan movements before starting his campaign. The scouts presented him with detailed accounts of their work. None of the evidence indicated that there were any large agglomerations of warriors on his planned war path. He went ahead only when he learned that there was no evidence of warriors on the move. The elders said that all the investigative procedures were employed before the attack, but that there was no need for them on the way back, aside from two groups of scouts who remained on high ground to observe any retaliatory activity. The Borana regiments were so heavily armed, that the attempt to retaliate would have been futile. The organization of the regiments was well controlled because the Abba Dula, Madha Galma, was a powerful man, able to mobilize, arm and discipline the warriors.

In other wars described by the elders, the warriors behaved more opportunistically to meet the contingencies that arose, including the failure to raise the requisite number of regiments and supplies, failure to raise the requisite number of horses for the cavalry, and crises brought about by an unexpectedly large counter-offensive.

The narrators—who gave the above account in 1974 and whose names have been withheld—made no mention of the actual engagement, the casualties, or the war captives. Asked specifically about these aspects, they said they preferred not to talk about them. They gave only such information as could be given without putting the war leaders in jeopardy, most of whom were then still alive.

### Defensive and Ritualized Wars vs Large Campaigns

Warfare is least organized when it is defensive. When there is an attack by enemy warriors upon Borana communities, the organization described above may fall far short of the ideal pattern. People may scramble to put together whatever fighting units they can mobilize and whatever weapons they can find. That, for instance, is what happened in the Guji attack on the Qallu's settlement in 1946 which resulted in the Qallu's death. It is only when they organized a counter-offensive that the regimental organization took shape.

It is important to remember that "wars" *(warana)* are not all violent encounters. Not all wars are well organized or have a number of regimental leaders. Some "wars" are nothing more than cattle raids. Other "wars," are so ritualized that they look more like war games or duels. They seem to be symbolic wars with honorable warrior nations that prognosticate the likelihood of victory or defeat in future encounters (See *Butta* ritual in *Gada* (1973):74-76). Still other wars, such as those waged against the Marrehan Somali or Laiki-piak Maasai were well organized, large scale, and violent and do not have any of the characteristics of a ritualized game or duel. In both these instances the Boran were resisting or retaliating against foreign invasions. The largest Borana wars of recent decades are still gada wars not fundamentally different from those described by Bahrey in his chronicle of the 16th century. It was an Abba Gada at a critical stage in his life-cycle career who launched the campaign, and he was assisted by regiments drawn from his gada class and two others. The main difference is in scale.

As indicated earlier, there is an old Borana constitutional formula that defines the nature of the relationship between gada classes and age-sets. The formula is *Wan gadaa mura, hariyyaa tolcha,** "What the gada class decides, the age-sets carry out." The statement expresses the law that the age-set system is a subordinate organization that operates under the authority of the Gada Assembly. Whatever its functions are, the age-set system cannot be understood without reference to the Gada System, as Baxter attempts to do.

Age-set leaders are only heads of individual regiments, and the military organization as a whole is headed by an Abba Dula or "war chief," drawn from the Raba or Gada grades, not from age-sets. Thus, one cannot, look at age-sets alone and determine whether or not their leaders were "military commanders" and, on that basis, decide if the system of age-sets was a "military organization."

### Oromo Warfare in Kenya: The Impact of Pax Britannica

All the above is a far cry from the situation that exists in Northern Kenya. The military organization described above is not in evidence among the Kenya Boran. Most "Boran warfare" in recent decades in Kenya is no more than cattle raids. The last major confrontations between Boran and Somali took place in 1963, when the Marsabit Boran supported the Kenyan independence movement and the Somali led the secessionist forces. That took place some ten years after Baxter's fieldwork, and was never picked up in any of his subsequent writings on Boran(a) warfare. It would have been an opportunity to document the character of Boran military organization. From a Kenyan perspective, the Boran were then engaged in a legitimate war, not an activity that borders on criminality.[11]

---

* Please note that this is venerable Oromo phraseology which, though precisely transcribed, as pronounced by the elders, sounds quite ungrammatical to modern Oromo speakers. The equivalent in contemporary Borana idiom is *Wan gada murte, hariyya (hi)ntolchiti.*

While British rule was still in force, the Boran and all their allies—the Gabra, Garri, Sakuyye and Ajuran—were subjected to military or civilian administrative regime that did not tolerate any form of warfare among the pastoral populations under its control. It is, therefore, legitimate for Baxter to see Oromo warfare as a thing of the past, but equally illegitimate for him to say that it is so because they had no military organization to begin with: the argument is fallacious since the change came about because of what British colonial rule did to suppress inter-tribal wars in the NFD.

Baxter reports half of the truth when he says that the Kenyan Boran did not wage war since the 1920s because of the efficacy of the *Ethiopian* administration.[12] The missing half of that statement is what happened to this population as a result of the much greater impact of *British* administration. Furthermore, the statement is factually incorrect, since Marsabit Boran fought the war against Somali secessionists in Kenya during the war of independence in 1962-63.

What the Boran experienced on the Kenyan side is an intense type of direct colonial rule by a settler society that did not only exploit and confine them economically, but also had a very destructive effect on their political-legal-military institutions. Gada law-making and law-enforcement functions were completely supplanted by colonial administrative law, army, and police. But it is mainly the military aspects that concern us here, including both warfare and hunting—two closely related phenomena in Boran(a) culture. In these areas, British impact was violent and relentless. Here is a very brief summary of the evidence without going into much detail, the kind of detail that will be presented elsewhere in a historic study titled, "Borana Under British and Ethiopian Empires."

From the time that Marsabit Boran arrived in Kenya, in large numbers, at the start of the 20th century, and three decades later, when the Borana were "pacified," British administration took many steps to destroy their military capabilities. By 1930, they had deprived the Boran cavalry of their horses,[13] and the warriors of the firearms which they took with them from Ethiopia to Kenya.

> All the tribes [of the NFD] were disarmed two years ago. A few rifles could not be found that had been registered: they are probably in Abyssinia. A list is attached. Any person carrying a rifle should be arrested on sight and action taken against him and the rifle confiscated.[14]

These were the words of a District Commissioner, named Sharpe, who introduced a method of *branding rifles* comparable to the method of branding cattle, both of which were pushed by the administration for the same reason: micro-management and control. The NFD administration did not only *confiscate their rifles*, it went so far as to *prohibit the use of spears*—the traditional weapons they needed so badly to protect themselves and their livestock from predators.[15]

The colonial rulers further introduced *"pass laws"* in the style of South African "influx control" to regulate the movement of the pastoral population across the Ethiopian border.[16] They also prohibited them from crossing the *tribal boundary lines* they introduced separating them from their neighbors within the NFD, and confiscated their livestock whenever they crossed those boundaries, thus effectively stopping all forms of indigenous warfare. These new regulations gave the administration an unexpectedly bountiful source of revenue—funds which, incidentally, were not controlled or audited by the Colonial Office in London. According to Marsabit elder, Hassan Diba, a Sakuyye, who was a cashier and accountant in the District Administration, there was much corruption linked to this confiscatory activity, a fact that is also recorded in the colonial archives.[17]

A further source of conflict between the administration and the Boran was the *hut and poll tax* that was imposed upon them.[18] When they showed no inclination to pay the tax, the administration imposed severe *retaliatory penalties*, for violations of all types of laws that were invented, including laws against "poaching" and crossing of tribal boundaries.[19]

Hunting, in Oromo tradition, was an adjunct to warfare, a test of manhood and the training ground for warriors. *Hunting big game* on horseback, with stabbing spears, was the way the Boran(a) warriors tested their valor at considerable risk to their lives. To the British, when the "great white hunter" hunted from a safe distance with powerful firearms and "bagged an elephant" it was a "sport,"[19] but when the Boran(a) hunted big game with spears it was "poaching," and a violation of British laws of "wildlife conservation." This Boran resented deeply as an unjust restriction on their rights.[20] It was a source of *conflict between the Boran and the government that festered for decades* until the independence of Kenya in 1963.

An earlier generation of Borana warriors had killed off and driven out a branch of the Laikipiak Maasai that had invaded their territory. Their victory over the Maasai was largely due to the efficacy of their cavalry and the speed with which they could attack, retreat, re-group and attack again. They repeated that process until the enemy was worn out and in disarray. (They hunted elephants the same way.) Using such methods, the Boran(a) cavalry was advancing steadily southward into the Kenyan heartland. To stop this advance, British Military administration resorted to all kinds of tactics including the *prohibition of horses* and *setting their villages on fire.*[21]

They also attempted to weaken the Boran(a) threat by *dismantling the "Pax Borana,"* a series of alliances which Boran(a) had established with neighboring societies—such as Gabra, Sakuyye, Garri and Adjuran, the last two being assimilated Somali clans.[22] They paid tribute to Borana ritual leaders and, in exchange, received protection and military support. *Naga Borana,* "the peace of Borana" that held them together was supplanted by Pax Britannica.[23]

An additional factor in the disintegration of the alliance was the fact that—when the *international boundary* was established by treaty—the main body of the Borana and their political-ritual centers remained in Ethiopia while *their allies became British subjects in Kenya* (Hamilton, 1974:353). The Borana who emigrated to Marsabit were refugees who succeeded in passing themselves off as "Hofte" Gabra in order to avoid expulsion. They were under the *reverse protection* offered by a powerful Gabra chief named Qalla Rasa. As such, they were not in a position to uphold the Pax Borana: they received protection, they did not give it.[24]

While all this was in progress, British colonial administration had introduced chieftaincies throughout the Northern Frontier District, a kind of colonial bulldozer institution that levelled all the people of the district. Chieftaincy is an entirely alien institution for the Boran(a), since the *chiefs were colonial agents and tax collectors, not local leaders.* Nevertheless, the chief was the only kind of political "representative" the administrators were willing to recognize. As a result, the *authority of Qallu and Gada institutions became practically irrelevant to the Marsabit Boran.*

It is not unfair to criticize Baxter for failing—in a lifetime of research and writing on Kenya Boran—to pay any attention to British colonial rule, whose declared purpose was to destroy those institutions and supplant them by its own chiefs, army and police force.

## Kenya Boran:
### Are They Representative of the Oromo?

Ethnographic and oral history data which I gathered among the Boran of Northern Kenya in the course of three years of field research in the 1970s and 1980s and archival data gathered in the Kenya National Archives (KNA) in Nairobi and the Public Records Office (PRO) in London over the same period of time reveal that the life, institutions, and culture of the Kenya Boran were deeply disturbed by the colonial experience.[25] As such their situation is not useful in trying to understand the nature of Oromo political life in pre-colonial times, nor is it representative of Oromo culture generally. *Marsabit Boran are a marginal refugee population that was moved en masse from one location to another by the British Colonial Administration* in order to keep them away from the Ethiopian borderlands and to separate them from their mounted and armed kinsmen in Ethiopia who continued to supply them with horses, rifles and ammunition.

Baxter states that "Kenya Boran often denigrated themselves to me as only being 'part-Boran' because of their separation from their ritual leaders and their remoteness from the oldest sacred sites at which generation-set rituals were performed."[26] We need to add only that this is not a 'self-denigrating statement' but a fair account of their situation. This is also corroborated by another statement Baxter makes elsewhere.

> I was *constantly instructed* that only there [in Ethiopian Borana] should I discover 'true' customs. Important elders whose herds graze in Marsabit and Moyale endeavor to visit there, and ambitious young men go there, partly to engage in warfare and big game hunting but also to learn custom. In this paper I cannot elaborate the intense moral solidarity of the Boran and their attachment to the Qaallu and the homelands but only assert that they are the center of the Boran moral, ritual, and legal universes. [27]

There is no question in the mind of the Kenya Boran as to who is the real bearer of their culture—they or their kinsmen in Ethiopia. The Boran of Marsabit are, in fact, estranged from their political, military, and legal institutions particularly the generational system *(Gada)*, the age-sets *(hariyya)*, and the national assembly *(Gumi)*. Aside from the fact that some of them return to the homelands in

Ethiopia to participate in rituals and receive the blessings of the Qallu, the institutions play no significant role in their daily lives. The only gada ritual they have preserved is Gada Mojji—the final stage of the Gada cycle. Their estrangement derives not only from the abandonment of most of the gada rites of passage and political ceremonies but also from the sheer *distance* between them and the centers of Qallu and Gada activities in Southern Ethiopia.

In addition to the physical distance there is also an *ecological barrier*. The lush pastures and complex perennial wells in their Ethiopian homeland are separated from the equally lush environment on Marsabit mountain by a huge waterless plain called Dida Galgalo. Cattle herders cross that barrier with some difficulty and some loss of livestock especially in times of drought.[28]

Yet another factor that contributes to their estrangement is the fact that active gada leaders in Dirre and Liban, Ethiopia, cannot go to Marsabit for any purpose whatsoever. They are prohibited by gada law from traveling beyond a defined perimeter within Dirre and Liban in Ethiopia. The *travel restriction on gada leaders* is based on the law known as *Seera Dawwe.*

By far the most important factor in the estrangement of the Kenya Boran from their institutions arises from the nature of the type of British colonial administration that was imposed upon them. Colonial officers from other parts of East Africa testify that British rule in Kenya—*a settler colony*—was probably an exceptionally repressive form of administration, compared with such territories as Uganda, Nigeria or Tanganyika (later Tanzania) where indirect rule was practiced. Thus, Sir Donald Cameron, governor of Tanganyika and an advocate of *indirect rule*, severely criticizes his Kenyan colleagues for trying to run the country by means of "alien agents" who did not command the loyalty of the population.[29] This then is the colonial environment in which the Boran of Kenya abandoned their political and military institutions.

To say that Boran(a) military organization is weak without any reference at all to colonial rule, stresses the presumed inherent weaknesses of the indigenous military system, not what happened to it after it fell under the overwhelming influence of British rule, in a frontier environment that was considered a threat to British ideas of peace and order. It was also an area that was, for several decades, contested by the British and Ethiopian empires. At times, the territory was subjected to a very ruthless form of military administration as were other "frontier" societies in other parts of the British empire, such as Kashmir in North India.[30] These factors obscure the character of the traditional institutions and make it difficult for us to understand of the pre-colonial systems by studying the Marsabit Boran alone.

## Methodological Questions

As we delve into these ethnographic and historic issues, we must stop to raise questions about the methodological strategies employed by Baxter and myself. There are three reasonable ways of learning what the indigenous African political institutions were like prior to colonization.

> **First, the researcher should examine historic sources in-cluding archival materials as well as oral histories covering the period prior to, during, or soon after colonization.**
>
> **Second, he (she) should look at a segment of the population where the colonial impact is weakest and use that as a guide for the study of pre-colonial conditions and institutions.**
>
> **Third, the researcher should use generative procedures aimed at experimentally replicating the quantitative and struc-tural aspects of demographic or economic transformation and on that basis making disciplined inferences about the anteced-ent conditions that brought forth the present state of affairs. By projecting the pattern into the future, it is also possible to esti-mate the direction and rate of change in the coming decades.**

Such procedures allow us to understand the history of precolonial Africa. An ethnographer who has followed none of these procedures does not have a strong position for judging the character of Oro-mo institutions prior to colonization or anticipating the patterns of change as they are unfolding today.

In the combined corpus by this writer, consisting of *Gada* (1973, 2007), this current work, *Oromo Democracy* (2000, 2006), and the paper titled "Borana under British and Ethiopian Empires," all three strategies have been employed. Generative procedures were utilized in Gada, chapter 7, titled "Simulating the Gada Process;" pre-colo-nial sources—oral histories and archival materials—are examined in the other two works. The fieldwork site, Ethiopian Borana, was selected from all Ethiopian Oromo lands, after one year of part-time preliminary field research, conducted to ensure that the site chosen was an area *least affected by external influences and most likely to have preserved the old institutions.*

## Criminalized behavior poses special difficulties for field workers

Of critical importance, from a methodological standpoint, is the difficulty that the fieldworker runs into when examining *criminalized domains* of traditional life that came under the control of colonial rulers or of independent African states. When that happens, it is most unlikely that the people will describe their *recent military or hunting activities* in detail to an outsider, since such information may be grounds for taking punitive action against them. It is worth noting, however, that Borana warriors give *individual narratives* of their deeds in the final retirement ceremony—decades after the fact.

The only descriptions of recent, major military campaigns I was able to obtain from Borana elders were either *defensive wars*, in which the Borana were repelling alien invasions, or offensive wars they waged *against societies with whom the Ethiopian state was at war.* Thus the war of Madha Galma against the Marrehan Somali, which I described as an example of a major campaign, was a counter-offensive that took place at a time when Ethiopia was at war with Somalia. Hence, it is a war that received the *implicit approval of the Ethiopian regime* and, thus, could be talked about with minimal danger of self-incrimination. But the danger is always there, as inter-state relations vacillate between war and peace: what is a heroic deed one decade may turn into a crime in another decade.[31]

Outside of these two types of situations, where warfare is more or less legitimate, we should not assume that the reports we get about contemporary warfare are likely to be truthful or complete. In particular, it is unwise to make highly evaluative statements about the viability, strength, and current status of a traditional military institution without regard to colonial regimes, since that is one aspect of traditional social organization that had to be violently suppressed by colonial authorities. *It is clear that colonial rulers could not tolerate armed and mounted African warriors who were not under the command of colonial police and armed forces.* Once the regime has taken a strong stand against it, indigenous warfare can continue only *contra legem*—as a covert or even criminal organization: it operates on a limited scale and is not openly talked about, least of all with anthropologists who might then proceed to lecture and write about it. It is only in the more distant historic context—25 to 50 years after the fact—that people can afford to give a fair account of their military and hunting activities and that is precisely the kind of "distance ethnography" which the here-and-now functionalist ethnographer treats with contempt.[32]

## Comparative historic evidence: Zulu and Oromo

Oromo warfare has been adequately described in past decades and centuries, especially as it relates to the great expansion of the Oromo nation. In my earlier study of the Gada System, I had suggested that the expansion of the Oromo was one of the great events in the annals of African history, comparable in its magnitude to the expansion of the Zulu nation of Southern Africa and the Fulani nation of West Africa.[33] These are three of the most expansive population movements by well-organized agro-pastoral societies that have been recorded by historians of Africa.

Baxter picks up this theme and says that the Boran age-sets of today, as he saw them in Northern Kenya, are a far cry from the powerful and ruthlessly efficient age-regiments of Shaka and Dingiswayo of the Zulu nation.[34] That is probably true but it is not a meaningful comparison. It is not valid to compare the Zulu army at its highest level of development, at the head of a powerful independent nation in the early 19th century, with Boran age-sets in their most weakened state, in a thoroughly exploited community in Kenya Colony, in the middle of the 20th century, after a half century of a most repressive variety of colonial rule, and an equally long period of harassment by well-armed Ethiopian shifta (bandits) who continued to raid Kenya Boran communities long after they had been disarmed and dismounted by their British rulers.

If we are to compare Oromo and Zulu warfare, we should assess their military capabilities when they were both at their zenith. At those stages in their history, they were both great self-governing African nations, far more integrated than they are today, able to defend themselves against all their enemies, armed only with spears and shields, using the efficacy of their gada or age-regiments as the military organization that hit their adversaries with great force, speed, and versatility. They used these institutions to expand their territory over huge regions of Africa. In Arsi, they resisted colonial domination for an extraordinary long period of time, when other African nations were collapsing before colonial armies after days or weeks of confrontation or without resistance of any kind. From that perspective, the Zulu-Oromo comparison is solid.[35]

## The Role of the Cavalry in Oromo Military Campaigns

One remarkable difference between the two warrior nations is that the Zulu had no horses, but Oromo had a powerful cavalry that stood at the head of their military campaigns—a force that had a devastating impact on their un-mounted adversaries, as happened in Northern Kenya and throughout much of Ethiopia. Oromo horsemanship is a highly prized aspect of their culture and it had a great deal to do with their military successes over the centuries.

In his *Social History of Ethiopia*, Richard Pankhurst discusses the role of the cavalry in 19th century Northern Ethiopia and then adds this insightful comment on the Oromo cavalry. Comparing different regions of Ethiopia he says "The largest number of horses… were to be found in the pastoral lands further south, and were a fine breed." He adds that the *Oromo cavalry at this time faced fire well, and even when forced to retreat, would often "suddenly wheel round and inclose the rash pursuer."* "Possession of a steed was a sign of distinction.…Horses were used solely for fighting, or tournaments, and were never ridden for any distance. Soldiers who could afford to ride, therefore, invariably traveled to and from war on mule back. A soldier's horse, mule and weapons, however acquired, were … considered as his personal property." [36]

We get yet another glimpse of Oromo warfare and the role of the cavalry in 19th century Shoa where the Oromo had occupied upland plateaus overlooking Ankober, the capital of the Shoan kingdom, which was later to become Emperor Menelik's first capital, before he moved to Addis Ababa, after the Battle of Adwa, in 1896. Atsmä Giorgis, a Christian Amhara historian, gives the following extraordinary picture of the situation.

The country they [the Abbicchu-Oromo] have occupied is a plain which is not hilly and which is suitable for horses and cattle. The Galla are also horsemen. But the [Amhara] people who lived in Manzeh and Tagulat were skilled in climbing cliffs, not in mounting horses. Thus they [the Galla] did not come up to the edge of the cliff. In order to shave their hair [i.e., a rite they perform on completion of the warrior grade], the Galla on their horses would watch from the summits just as a hawk would watch a rat from a tree. They were afraid of descending the slopes. They [the Galla] could not fight the people of Tagulat on foot. Mared-azmach Ammeha Iyasus made Ankwabar, below Moatit, his capital and began to fight the Abbecchu, the descendants of Dacch'a. The Galla could not descend to Ankwabar even if they were victorious. Should they descend, they would not return.[37]

In this passage, the pattern of the Oromo-Amhara confrontation in Shoa is very clear. *The Oromo cavalry was very strong as long as it remained in the lowland plains or upland plateaus,* the Amhara were also very strong as long as they remained in the mountain fastnesses. The statement goes a long way toward explaining an important feature of Oromo warfare and the types of environment where they were dominant. It also reveals how important Oromo cavalry was in warfare and what a terrible restriction it must have been when British colonial rulers deprived them of their horses.

*Oromo migration routes* can be followed through a maze of upland plateaus and lowland plains across the length and breadth of Ethiopian territory. Migrating across the country, they generally avoided very mountainous regions or intensively cultivated and terraced areas such as Konso or Gurage. When they got to such regions as Gurageland or the Ghibe region, the came face to face with an ecological wall: the *ensete culture.* The area was so intensively cultivated that there was no room for extensive livestock breeding or for the Oromo cavalry. When they did cross over into such dense regions as the Jam Jam rain forest and the Soddo-Gurage area, the Amabassel mountain range in Wollo, they abandoned or modified their way of life, their pastoral mode of production, and their cavalry and adopted the local mode of food production. (For a mobile warrior nation, sedentarization is tantamount to pacification.) Sometimes, as in the case of Gojjam, across the Blue Nile, the Oromo population was assimilated by the host communities. It is mainly in open country such as the Shoan plateau, the upper Awash river basin, and the Rift Valley grasslands, stretching from Shoa to the Kenya frontier, that they maintained their agro-pastoral way of life, their institutions, pattern of warfare and their traditions of horsemanship that heavily influenced highland Ethiopian culture.

Indeed, Ethiopian rulers probably took on one aspect of this grand *equestrian tradition* when the began giving themselves *noms de guerre* derived from the names of their horses. Thus King Sahle Sellassie is *"Abba Dina"*, Emperor Tewodros is *"Abba Tatek"* Emperor Menelik *"Abba Dagnew"* Emperor Haile Sellassie *"Abba Qagnew"* each horse name bearing the Oromo prefix *"Abba"* meaning "owner of." (Mahteme Sellassie, *Zəkrä Nägär,* p. 887.) (*See also* n. 69, p. 39, above, concerning the Oromo prefix *Abba.*)

### *Glimpses of Oromo military organization in history*

From the earliest stages of rapid Oromo expansion in the 16th century one finds evidence that Oromo warfare was well organized. Members of the Portuguese expedition to Abyssinia who came to the country toward the middle of that century (1541 to 1543) to defend the Christian kingdom against attacks by Muslims and "heathens," had every interest in presenting the adversaries of the Christian kingdom as "barbarian hordes." Nevertheless they present a remarkable picture of Oromo warfare as an orderly activity. One member of the expedition, Castanhoso, gives a long description of the cruelty of Oromo warriors and then adds:

> They were innumerable, and *did not come on without order like barbarians, but advanced collected in bodies, like squadrons.* When they saw us they halted, some waiting for the rest, and then marched in one mass and camped near us, at a distance where our shots could not do them harm.[38]

This is an image of military order presented by a man who had no interest in celebrating anything Oromo: He was supporting a king who was at war with them. Of course, he had no understanding of the gada regimental organization that caused the warriors to "advance collected in bodies, like squadrons." Nevertheless, his observation is a valuable piece of information about Oromo military organization when they were a dominant force in Ethiopia.

Bahrey, writing several decades later (1593), had a better understanding of the macro-level organization of Oromo warfare. He makes three statements that link warfare to the moiety and Gada organizations. First he says that the two great moieties of the Oromo, the BAREYTUMA and BORANA, originally, set out for war together, but later they separated.[39] Secondly, he says "As to the law concerning their circumcision, it is thus: When a luba is formed, all the Bareytuma and Borana give themselves a collective name, just as the king of Ethiopia's regiments called themselves by names like Sellus Hayle, ['trinity is my strength']...."[40] Later he adds that after the luba is formed and circumcised "they attack a country which none of their predecessors have attacked."[41] Indeed, the entire epic history is organized around the structure of the gada life cycle and describes the wars that Oromo warriors waged successively as each gada class came of age. From his statement that "when a luba is formed all the Borana and Bareytuma give themselves a collective name," which he then associates with Ethiopian armies and new conquests, we can see that the fighting force was headed by one luba drawn from both moieties.

*Ch'ifra strategy and battle array.* The most remarkable and truthful account of the *Oromo battle array* is to be found in the Chronicle of Emperor Susenyos (1600-1625) who, in his youth, had used Oromo warriors and military strategy to take the imperial throne in Gondar after growing up as a war captive among the Oromo. The chronicle describes Oromo warriors as being organized into three columns they call *"chi'fra"* [Oromo *ch'ibra*] consisting of the *luba* [married and circumcised], *qero* [bachelors], and *qondala* [youth]. Later in his career Susenyos employed the same "ch'ifra strategy" and battle array in his campaign against the Shoan army. The chronicle contrasts this type of battle array, taken over from Oromo warriors, with that of the 'Amhara' army of Zesellassie which is said to lack organization and went to war "like a crowd going to market."[42]

## Large Scale Introduction of Firearms (1890s)

Until the late 19th century in Ethiopia and Kenya, and until the early part of the 20th century in Southern Ethiopia, Oromo warriors and, in particular, Oromo cavalries demonstrated again and again that they were capable of showing the same kind of military efficacy and versatility as their ancestors in the 16th century. In the late 1890s, however, their fortunes were reversed. The situation of Oromo warfare was fundamentally altered during the scramble for Africa when their adversaries acquired vast numbers of firearms. In 1896, the Abyssinian army was made up of one quarter of a million men, of whom about one fifth were supplied with firearms.[43] In the following years, when the Shoan armies were conquering the South, the number of men bearing firearms probably escalated to 600,000.[44] That force was not merely powerful enough to destroy or subjugate many indigenous states in the Horn of Africa, it was also able to block the colonial encroachments upon the Christian Kingdom by British, Italian, and French forces coming from the north (Eritrea), from the south (Kenya), from the east (British, French, Italian Somalilands) and from the west (Anglo-Egyptian Sudan). In this process, Menelik did not only resist the scramble for Africa, he took part in it as a successful and credible adversary of the European colonizers.

Once the army was built up to such massive proportions in order to resist European colonial incursions, it could be used not merely to punish neighboring African peoples, who refused to submit to the authority of the Emperor, but it became a powerful instrument for a new wave of indigenous empire building.

Despite the great advantage that the Shoan army gained through the use of modern weapons, it still faced much resistance from Oromo and other Cushitic peoples. Its progress was sometimes blocked by highly organized indigenous states with an effective defense organization. As indicated earlier, Kafa and Arsi were the areas where the Abyssinian colonizers met with sustained and massive resistance. Kafa—a Cushitic kingdom adjoining the land of the Macch'a Oromo and the Ghibe Kingdoms—had an impressive defense system. The state was protected with moats, fortifications, guards, traps, and an elaborate road network and communication system. Outsiders could only enter or leave the state through gates they called *"kiella"* and by roads inside and outside the state that were maintained by their own work force and monitored by their own officers.[45]

More relevant is the Arsi-Oromo resistance in the 1890s. The Arsi were able to arrest the advance of Menelik's army by raising a huge cavalry and age-regiments and fighting a protracted defensive war. In all probability, Oromo warfare and military organization has never been put to a more severe test. That confrontation is an important event in the annals of African warfare and should have given students of Oromo society reason to pause, think, and rethink their persistent devaluation of Oromo military institutions. The Arsi were accomplished horsemen and warriors. They were much faster than the Imperial entourage which moved at a snail's pace. They kept the Emperor's army at bay for ten years and, on one occasion, captured the *negarit* (royal drums) from his camp and came very close to capturing Emperor Menelik himself, who escaped on horseback and fled all the way back to Shoa. This remarkable history has been richly documented in Dr. Abbas Haji's "The History of the Arssi 1880-1935" (1982) and *Les Oromo-Arssi* (1990). This body of data should permanently put to rest the false notion that the Oromo had no military organization, and if they did, it ceased to exist sometime after the 16th century.

## The Political and Military Functions of Gada

So much for Baxter on age-sets. He also has similar views about Gada. He says that the Gada institution, as he saw it, had no military functions at all, and that in Boran(a) it never had any military commanders in history. It is very rare indeed in African research to find a document like Bahrey's that tells us so much about how an African institution functioned militarily in the 16th century. It is unwise to ignore such a source and still go on to make authoritative statements about the history of Oromo military organization. Baxter briefly mentions Bahrey in one of his papers but makes no effort to follow up any parallels that may exist between Bahrey's data and Boran(a) warfare in the 20th century.[46]

Baxter's attempt to examine the political or military functions of Gada runs into similar problems as his analysis of the age-set system. Not only does he dissociate one institution from the other, he also lacks the basic information that is needed to understand the role of Raba-Gada Assemblies in Oromo warfare. He says:

> The gaada system appears to have worked as a means of grouping and classifying men for military purposes in Bahrey's time but quite clearly it very soon stopped doing so. At some time between the seventeenth century and the backward stretch of folk memory the

Boran adopted a quite different system of grouping men for military purposes. A generation-set title, for example is Father of the War, Aba Duula, but nowadays it is as archaic a survival as the title Queen's Champion (Cf. Legesse, 1973: 74). The gaada system became, increasingly, a mode of organizing ritual affairs and less and less concerned with secular affairs or with grouping men for workaday tasks (see Legesse [1973: 58-60, 76-81]).[47]

It is historically inaccurate to say that the Oromo and, more specifically, the Boran(a) stopped using Gada as a military organization at some unspecified time after the 16th century. We have evidence from Paul Goto, a Kenyan historian, and from Günther Schlee, a contemporary anthropologist who have recorded the war of the Borana against the Laikipiak Maasai in 1876.

> The Kibiya, as the Laikipiak Maasai were known to the Boran, were initially successful because Boran attention was focused on fighting the Somali in the east. When the situation became desperate, however, and the homelands of Dirre were threatened, the Boran responded to the Maasai and in one swift attack, made by mounted cavalry in two columns, Boran warriors descended upon their enemy from the escarpment. This was a major war for the Boran since it entailed the participation of the Borana gada and raba, the highest authorities of the Boran society. One column of warriors was led by Adi Doyo himself, Abba Gada [1897-1905], and the other by Dida Bitata, a former Abba Gada, 1873-1881, together with Guyo Ello, another famous warrior. The Laikipiak Maasai were...simply massacred for they were in no position to ward off their mounted adversaries who used horses to a devastating effect on them and later on the Samburu and Rendille.[48]

Schlee elaborates this history further and produces a date and place for the war. He states "These Laikipiak,...moved north, raiding cattle and driving large herds along, until they were beaten by the Warr Libin [Borana] cavalry near Buna. A British compiler of the accounts...gives 1876 as the probable date of the battle and Korondile as its place."[49]

Against the background of such evidence, the claim that Boran(a) had no military organization in precolonial times is entirely wrong. It is conjectural history, of the type roundly condemned in British political anthropology.

In sum, the available historic/ethnographic evidence suggests that (1) Gada was an effective military organization for a major part of Oromo history, not only the 16th century; (2) The level of military coordination between different segments of the Oromo nation declined over the centuries as the nation spread over a huge territory; (3) It became more and more difficult to use gada classes as regiments when they became less and less like age groups and developed an age-heterogeneous structure; (4) The society, particularly in Borana, then evolved a system of age-sets proper, which functioned as a military organization attached to the Gada System and operated under the leadership the Abba Dula, "war chief" who was often an Abba Gada. (5) The core of the fighting force was always the *barbara* group: men who belonged to the same age-set and gada class as the Gada leaders who launched the campaign. The two systems jointly, gada classes and age-sets, organized many national campaigns, such as the counter-offensive against the Laikipiak Maasai (1876) and the retaliatory campaign against the Marrehan Somali (1950).[50]

The War of Madha shows, in no uncertain terms, that the office of "Abba Dula" is not an archaic survival of some distant and fading institution. Indeed, it is quite remarkable that this war, which Baxter now acknowledges to be a "national campaign," took place two years prior to the time when he was conducting his fieldwork (1952). Madha Galma, the Abba Dula who led the campaign, was still in his fifties when I interviewed him in 1963 (photo p. 40). The office was, thus, an integral part of a living institution, and cannot be compared with the anachronistic office of the "The Queen's Champion" in British royal traditions.[51]

All that is not to deny the fact that traditional warfare was severely constrained after the Oromo were conquered by British and Ethiopian armies. Thereafter, the Oromo army's existence became apparent to outsiders only when its campaigns were directed at peoples with whom the state was at war. In such situations, the state may even mobilize the traditional army to support its own military and police activities, and the warriors will be freer to recount their exploits, in confidence, to ethnographers and historians. Baxter misreads and misinterprets my work when he cites it as evidence that the Gada System is not a military organization, that it never amounted to more than a "means of grouping and classifying men for military purposes," that it is, today, nothing more than "a mode of organizing for ritual affairs" and that the office of Abba Dula is a vestigial remnant of a defunct institution. Not only the war chiefs but the gada leaders as well are said to have no political responsibilities. He says that they "do not 'rule' or have 'power' of a directly political kind, nor do they, as sets, administer affairs nor settle disputes."[51] More pointedly, he adds they "do not control anyone."[52]

If Baxter has any data of his own that would lead him to such strange conclusions, he should present them. My evidence does not support the conclusion he draws from it. What it does show is that offices such as those of the elected political leader (Abba Gada) and the war chief (Abba Dula) are important for our understanding of the contemporary Borana of Ethiopia and of the history of the Oromo nation as a whole; that gada classes alone in earlier centuries and gada classes and age-sets jointly in later centuries formed the backbone of their military organization, and that the Gada System was the driving force behind the great expansion of the nation. In time, warfare became less pronounced and more likely to occur across rather than within national boundaries, and became intertwined with cross-border conflicts. As such, the pattern of warfare continued in most frontier communities until the 1930s and among the Ethiopian Borana until the 1960s, mainly because of the sustained southward thrust of their population. Much of the evidence gathered since then by this writer indicates that Borana institutions have continued their fundamental activities on the Ethiopian side of the border, partly because the Dergue—the communist military junta—recruited and re-armed the population to fight it own wars. These soldiers were never properly demobilized or disarmed after the junta was unseated by the liberation fronts in 1991. That created a new supply of modern firearms for the warriors, Kalashnikovs now taking the place of the antique weapons, remnants of the Italo-Ethiopian wars of 1935 and 1941.

The claim that gada leaders "do not control anyone," is a mistaken view since gada leaders do indeed have control of their people and resolve their conflicts. Gada service is mandatory in Borana, not only as part of the progression through the gada grades, but as a general national requirement imposed on all males. *Any Borana can be summoned to service at any time unless the Gada Assembly grants him release by declaring him to be "yuba"* (v.t., *yubomu).*[54] This concept is different from the Gada grade that bears the same name. The Yuba (VII-X) are not subject to recruitment if they are of the appropriate age and have rendered service with their luba when it was in power. If not, they too will be required to serve.

All clans have an obligation to furnish to the Gada Assembly with the labor force needed for warfare, government, and to relieve them of their normal pastoral chores. Should they fail to serve, the men selected for such tasks by their respective clans can be made to serve forcibly. The clans have *jallaba* who represent them in the Gada Assembly. They go to the village of the recalcitrant recruits and take away their livestock. The men follow.[55] In extreme cases, where the recruits have adamantly refused to serve, the messengers may even take their wives, children, and possessions away as added inducement. No Borana male is released from gada service unless the Gada Assembly declares him to be *yuba* or "semi-retired."[55] To say that gada leaders "do not control anyone" in the face of such evidence is not a matter of divergent interpretations of the ethnographic facts but a denial of the facts themselves.

In one case which I recorded in Borana, a man in Dirre, named Duba Guyyo, who belongs to the luba of Madha Galma and the Nonitu clan, was ordered to give service or to pay tribute *(kato)* to the Gada Assembly. The man refused. An order was then issued to Borana not to give him any assistance when he was in difficulty, not to bury him if he dies, not to let him marry, not to let anyone marry his daughters, and not to let him water his cattle in any *hara* (dam) or *ela* (well) in the land. He was effectively banished from Borana country. He went to live among the neighboring Oromo people, the Guji. When he returned to Borana many years later, he went back to the Gada Assembly, paid his *kato* and penalties, in the form of livestock, coffee, tobacco and cloth and was rehabilitated.[56]

There are many other situations where the Gada Assembly, through its various assistants and messengers (*makkala, wayyu*), and through the *jallaba*—serving as intermediaries between the Assembly and the clans—imposes significant obligations on the population. First, if a case of conflict is brought to the Gada Assembly for adjudication and a litigant fails to willingly submit to the sanctions they imposed, gada leaders can mete out punishment by sending messengers *(wayyu)* to the fathers of wells (*abba ela*) in Borana and barring him from getting access to the wells and dams. The offender is, thus, effectively banished from the country and is forced to pay his dues.[57] Secondly, they can force the clans to furnish warriors, materials and supplies for ceremonies, political events, or wars. The supplies may be given in the form livestock, honey, dairy products, or labor. Thirdly, they can obtain support for the normal pastoral chores of the Gada leaders and can mobilize people to offer supplies and labor for public works, such as the excavation, re-excavation, and maintenance of wells and dams. These can be major projects that take months to complete. I cite the following instance of such a project from my field research:

> The Abba Gada, Jaldessa Liban, who was in power during the years of my fieldwork, organized a project for the re-excavation of a well named after Morowwa Abbayye, his eighth ancestor *(abba luba)* in the Gada Chronology. He organized all the major lineages of his clan to contribute food and labor for the project. He personally contributed 20 head of cattle and his clan contributed 280 cattle. All the animals were slaughtered to feed the workers for a period of seven months. The well then became the property of the clan to which the Abba Gada belonged.[58]

It is clear that the Abba Gada was wearing *two hats* on this occasion: that of Gada leader and prominent clansman. It is nonsense to suggest, as Bassi does (2005, p. 172), that he was wearing only one hat in order to satisfy the a priori assumption that clans control everything, Gada controls nothing.

The final and most important point is that gada leaders can require the people to play their part in military campaigns, to mobilize at very short notice for offensive or retaliatory wars, and to supply the fighters with horses for the cavalry. In the past they also supplied livestock to be slaughtered to feed the fighters during long campaigns—a vital resource that serves as a mobile food supply. That gave the Oromo regiments a significant advantage over their Abyssinian adversaries, who had very poor logistical support and were required to "live off of the land" and to demand food and services from the host communities while the war was in progress, or to quarter themselves upon the conquered community for the long haul, after the war was over. In this regard, the Abyssinian army was more primitive than its Oromo counterpart and has, curiously, maintained some of these peculiarities into modern times.

## The Decline of Gada in Kenya,
### and the presumed residual functions

One of the best indicators of the decline of Gada among the Kenya
Boran is the fact that the Gada Chronology (Appendix I) covering
360 years of history, no longer plays any significant role in their
lives. It exists in severely abridged forms. Instead, the Boran have
created a chronology of British District Commissioners which they
use for their historic narrative with great flair and accuracy, complete with nicknames and character portraits. V.G. Glinday (1924-
25) is remembered honorably as *Farasade*, "the horseman" because
he administered the district on horseback, not from an office; *Bana
Shab*, H.B. Sharpe, is remembered for confiscating horses, rifles,
and entire herds as punishment for hunting, and for setting Borana
villages on fire to block their southward migration; H.G. Oldfield,
*Abba Hirriba*, "father of sleep" remembered for sleeping on the job;
*Bana Res*, Gerald Reese, (late 1930s) remembered fondly because
he respected their culture, spoke their language, was a rigorous but
just disciplinarian; Windy A. Wyld (1952-55) is *Bana Nyencho*,
"the lion," a South African who introduced "passes" for crossing
the border and branded Borana cattle to limit the number owned by
each family, remembered for his cruelty; and so on. The record of
the civilian district commissioners covering the second half of the
colonial era is turned into a framework for telling the folk history
of Marsabit. Boran culture of time and history thus survives with
a thick colonial patina encrusted upon it, but it survives. (Marsabit
Elders, 1984, p. 3, 15, 45, 56, 106, 216, 320)

Boran culture retreated on several other fronts in which the colonial regime had a heavy hand: The regime made laws, appointed
chiefs, controlled water resources, and limited access to the forest
and the crater lakes—the luxuriant environment that ultimately became a game reserve. In most of these areas, Gada lost some of its
key functions, resources and privileges. Boran culture also retreated
on several other fronts in which the force of the colonial regime
was pervasive, including legislative, political, economic and law
enforcement functions. In most of these domains, Gada lost some of
its key functions. But the most important reason why Gada became
an irrelevant institution in the daily lives of Kenya Boran is because
there were no Gada leaders in their territory. As indicated earlier, the

active gada councilors were prohibited from traveling beyond a defined perimeter within Dirre and Liban, on the Ethiopian side of the border. It is, thus, a mistake to think, as Baxter does, that "Any Boran may, and very many do, travel freely anywhere in Boranaland."[59]

Granted that what remains of Oromo political life in Northern Kenya is the culture and language of Gada and age-sets, but not the working institutions, my own inquiries in Kenya partially support this view: The Boran of Marsabit can talk about their institutions as if they were still governed by them but the institutions themselves do not exist. Their knowledge of the Gada System is very shallow, and they perform hardly any of the gada rituals or political ceremonies—Gada Mojji (the final rite of retirement) being the only significant exception.

Baxter gets completely sidetracked into a blind alley when he concludes his research by saying that the situation he observed in Kenya is similar to the conditions that exist among the Ethiopian Borana and that the differences between them "should not be exaggerated."[60] To come to that conclusion, he had to ignore the impact of the colonial era in Northern Kenya and dismiss a great deal of research on the Ethiopian Borana (and Guji) by four contemporary anthropologists—Haberland, Knutsson, Hinnant, and this writer and by the historic evidence on Oromo indicating the political, legislative, adjudicative, and military functions of Gada offered by the 16th century chronicler, Bahrey,[61] and by Domenico Pecci who wrote an article on Gada in Borana in 1941—a most important document which Baxter never saw until some years after his dissertation. Even today, Pecci's profile of Gada is more complete and more coherent than Baxter's.[62] All these writers have presented evidence concerning the political, judicial, legislative, military activities of the Oromo institutions, and more specifically of the Borana.

Among the authors cited here John Hinnant holds a peculiar position. He studied the Guji-Oromo in Southern Ethiopia, who, like the Borana, their neighbors, have preserved their political and ritual institutions. It seems that he fell under Baxter's influence before and after his field research and, thus, subscribes to the credo that the Gada institution has ritual but not political functions. He begins his analysis of the Gada System with such a generic statement. To his credit, however, he proceeds to tell us the following remarkable facts: that the Abba Gada "had some responsibility for warfare against other societies and the defense of his gosa [clan] territory,"[63] "he has the right to command the collection of vast quantities of food and the many cattle needed for the rank change [hand over of power from one gada class to another];" that he "proclaims new laws." He and his council settle disputes and "serve as the highest court of appeal..."[64] The councilors "evaluate the conduct of candidates [for gada office]."[65] they guide the activities of "hundreds or more of this group [who] act, the Guji say, as police." These latter officers "...are responsible for the physical safety of the abba gada and his belongings. They also perform any physical work needed by the *ya'a* [gada assembly]" while other officers called "cheddaba" also carry messages to other parts of the gosa territory."[66] "The abba gada has legal advisers called Hiyyu" and their station is distinguished from the ritual advisor called "faga."[67]

He then ends this discussion with the statement that Gada has ritual but not political functions. He might as well have ended his ethnographic analysis with an "Amen" because he is repeating Baxter's message to the faithful, whose truth endures whether the available evidence supports it or not.

Baxter himself has given us a precedent for this style of analysis. In his dissertation (1954), which was written soon after his field research, he makes the following statements:

> Haiyu [gada councilors] are learned and experienced in the laws and are appealed to in all cases when disputants are unable to come to an agreement among themselves, or one or the other refuses to accept the rulling [sic] made by the elders of his neighbourhood, or settles disputes between strangers....No Haiyu can impose any direct sanctions, but Boran consider it inconceivable that any disputant should reject the considered opinion of a Haiyu Gudda.[68]

In other words, they have the authority to settle disputes and they are obeyed. It is clear that mediators need wisdom, not power, to resolve conflict. He is thus disregarding his own evidence when he later says "sets as sets do not settle disputes."[69] Mediation is a variety of judicial activity that has far greater significance in traditional Africa than does adjudication. Oromo resort to litigation, adjudication and sanctions only as last resort, to be used when all efforts at mediation have failed, and then only by highest authorities—Gada Assembly or National Assembly—two political bodies that exist only in Ethiopia, i.e., outside of Baxter's purview.

## The Impact of Gada in History: the military factor

Baxter concludes his assessment of Gada and age-sets by saying that neither the generational organization nor the age set system are, or have been in recent centuries, efficient political or military organizations. If that is so, then, there are some key historic questions he must answer: How did the Oromo expand over a distance of 1200 miles (2600 kilometers) along a north-south axis—going through nearly all of Ethiopia and Kenya in less than a century? Was the Oromo expansion a formless flood of people and livestock, as some would have us believe, or was it an organized campaign, as the Bahrey and Susenyos chronicles testify? How did the Boran(a) drive the Laikipiak Maasai out of their territory, and the Rendille-Samburu off much of Marsabit mountain and establish Pax Borana bringing several tribes under their protection?

The kingdoms of central and southern Ethiopia which the Oromo assimilated and those of Northern Ethiopia, which they infiltrated or dominated,[70] are not weak states since some of them were able to block European colonial incursions for many decades. The army of Emperor Menelik, against which the Arsi fought for so long was, in all probability, the largest military force ever assembled by an indigenous African state during the colonial era, albeit with substantial assistance from the European colonial powers who armed it to advance their own economic and political interests.[71] A force that can block such military might is not a formless body of warriors or a meager arrangement of "local age set companies" or a mere social taxonomic device by which people are classified to engage in wartime rituals and "warlike actions."

It is the Gada institution that was at the core of the great Oromo expansion of the sixteenth century that transformed the face of the Horn of Africa. It allowed the Oromo to occupy a vast territory stretching from Malindi in South-Eastern Kenya to Tigrai in the far north of Ethiopia, crossing nearly all of Ethiopia and Kenya. Gada was the force behind the great movement of peoples that resulted in the total absorption of the populations of several kingdoms including Dawwaro, Fatagar, Bali, Ifat, and Damot and in the penetration of virtually all the Christian kingdoms of Northwest Ethiopia including Gojjam, Gonder, Shoa, and Tigrai, each one a kingdom of substantial magnitude.

## War and Peace in Democratic Societies

Part of the weakness of Oromo warfare, according to Baxter, is that it is governed by democratic assemblies and that it is, therefore, not very efficient.[72] The comment refers to the fact that the ultimate right to declare war rests not with the military leaders but with the Gada Assembly and often with the Abba Gada acting in consultation with his assembly. Furthermore, there is a customary expectation that every Oromo battle should have its own *Abba Dula* or "war chief" and that the gada leaders should not lead in warfare after they have given up office, except, perhaps, in a supportive capacity or in joining defense forces when the nation is threatened. At the end of his military career in the Raba and Gada grades, the distinguished war leader is given accolades and returned to his pastoral life. That is the situation that Madha Galma was in when I met him in 1962, 12 years after his Marrehan campaign, and 2 years after completing his term in office as Abba Gada.

The fact that the right to make war ultimately rests with the Gada Assembly effectively separates the actual warrior organization *(Hariyya)*, from the decision-making organization *(Gada)*. The danger in this arrangement, is that when there is a sudden threat from outside, the military leaders and the gada councilors may continue their protracted debates while the enemy advances. That weakness must be viewed along with a corresponding source of strength, that when the army does rise, it is a "people's army" and its commitment to the common cause is great in comparison with armies forcibly recruited by autocratic regimes. They fight under the pressure of the rewards and punishments instituted by the leader, and are likely to disintegrate when the war chief falls in battle.

That, for instance, is what happened when Emperor Yohannes was shot and beheaded by the Sudanese Mahdists at the Battle of Metemma, on March 12, 1889. His biographer, Zewde Gabre-Sellassie, says "News of the death [of the Emperor] spread very rapidly and the Ethiopian offensive collapsed. The expected victory turned into a rout."[73] In this instance, it is clear that the hierarchically ordered military organization with an emperor at its pinnacle is "centralized government and warfare" par excellence, but it is a fragile structure. Centralization too has its own infirmities. Granted that the Oromo approach to war produces a paradoxical situation and it is not the quickest way of responding to military threat, as Baxter rightly points out. That is, in fact, a paradox that democratic societies everywhere must face and is not a peculiar "failing" of the Oromo institutions. Indeed the view that this is a "weakness" reveals a certain measure of insensitivity to some of the deepest concerns of democratic societies and how vigilantly they must protect themselves from their own armies.

All democracies must devise institutional mechanisms that can ensure that military power does not become entrenched and invade the rest of their political life. Despotism is often a by-product of an efficient war machine, that turns into a tool for gaining unfair advantage over political adversaries. What distinguishes Zulu militarism from Oromo warfare is that the former became despotic and the latter remained subordinated to a democratic government, in most parts of the Oromo nation, for a major part of their history.

Thus, when Baxter speaks admiringly of the Zulu and disparagingly of the Oromo he reveals a weakness that shows up in all his writings: He has never taken the issue of *human liberty* into consideration and examined how it is handled by traditional institutions. He does not seem to realize that when the right to declare war is handed over to the warriors, for greater "efficiency," wars become more frequent, the society as a whole is militarized, and the leaders assume despotic powers. That is what happened during the reign of Shaka, when most young-adult males were housed in "barracks," thoroughly trained in the martial arts and kept in a perpetual state of readiness. War became an annual event in their lives.[74]

On the other hand, peace is a pervasive and sustained concern in Oromo life. The long blessings that are given daily by Oromo elders are prayers for peace. The theme of peace is everywhere. Baxter refers to this as a "river of blessings," a felicitous phrase which is appropriate when it refers to the Oromo's deep concern with and prayers for peace.[75] My own experience supports the evidence he has presented but we differ in our understanding of the wider context in which the "river of blessings" flows. Peace to Baxter signals the absence of war. In my view, war and peace are two sides of the same coin. If one walks into an Oromo community in peacetime, it is difficult to imagine the traditions of warfare that dominated their turbulent history. However, their military tradition does not spill over into their daily lives. Observers who visit Oromo communities expecting to see a nation of warriors decked out in military regalia, parading about on horseback, rattling their sabers or firing rifles in the air are disappointed. In Oromo life, war is war, and peace is immensely tranquil.

Along with the *"river of blessings"* there exists also the *passion of war chants,* which Baxter dismisses as "bravado." I have seen the RABA (V) warriors singing such chants in their ceremonies—their bodies shaking with emotion. I have seen GADA MOJJI (XI) giving martial recitations—a moving account of a lifetime of hunting and warfare. I have observed that ceremony in both Ethiopia and Marsabit, Kenya, where the ceremony is performed in the same style as in homelands. The event takes place at the end of the gada life cycle in huge complex of ceremonial huts that are filled and surrounded by curious crowds. There is more passion in these situations than I have ever seen in Borana life—a life that is generally orderly and disciplined. Baxter sweeps all this evidence under the rug when he presents the Gada Mojji as an entirely peaceful lot.

Even in these emotional moments, however, the warriors are expected to be restrained and truthful. The type of behavior that Baxter dismisses as "bravado" is totally prohibited. If they overstate their achievements, their age mates will expose them without mercy. The entire performance is a controlled burn, not a conflagration. Borana have thus managed to balance these two aspects of their lives. Outside of wars and raids against other societies, Borana generally abhor random violence. As I have indicated elsewhere, homicide within Borana society is virtually unknown.

Baxter has never seen the retiring elders giving a recitation of their lifetime of military and hunting achievements. It is, therefore, a bit of an understatement for him to say "I have not witnessed the rituals of gadamojji."[76] It is not only the Gada Mojji rituals that he as failed to observe. In fact, he has seen none of the nine transition rituals and political ceremonies of the gada life cycle in which the martial traditions and war pledges *(murti)* alternate again and again with the meditative prayers for peace and fertility.[77]

Of the Oromo culture of war and peace, he has seen one side and not the other. It is an error for him to assume that only the side that he saw exists and that other researchers must have imagined what he did not see. Nothing demonstrates this dialectic of war and peace better then the Gada Mojji grade itself, the terminal stage of the Gada life cycle. The men spend eight years in a sacred, peaceful state, their lives hemmed in by taboos, serving as intermediaries between man and God, and blessing every household they visit.

They end the grade with a passionate, but restrained, account of their wartime and hunting achievements. Thus, the formal life cycle ends not with prayers and blessings but with martial recitations and a "farewell to arms." *War and peace are two faces of the same society: the peace ritual and the warriors drumbeat alternate in people's lives even if Pax Britannica, or any other peace, has been imposed from above.*

## The Transformation of the Oromo Political System

Admittedly, the traditional Oromo polity has not survived unaltered and their traditional warfare today is only a reduced version of what it was in history. Some of the changes Oromo institutions underwent are the result of internal demographic changes. The Gada institution changed because one cannot treat genealogical generations as age groups. When the Oromo tried to do that, younger and younger boys were born into the gada classes. That is an inherent aspect of the Gada System that caused a significant part of the population to be retired at an early age.[78]

However, the functional effect of this structural weakness was limited, because it was matched by internal adaptive transformations, including the emergence of age-sets as the subsidiary military organization and the extension of the "franchise" to the *prematurely retired gada classes* who were represented in the Gada assemblies by the Garba Council. This was a strange council that consists *exclusively* of men who were retired at an early age i.e., Yuba or Jarsa.[79] The evidence showing that they were being *re-activated to serve in the Gada Assembly* indicates that the institution was changing throughout its recent history. Writers who dwell on the internally generated decline of the Gada System, often citing my research as evidence, do so by methodically ignoring all such adaptive features. These features too are an integral part of Oromo history. [80] Here too, the ethnographers are telling half of the story, the half that fits their skewed perspective.

## Vanishing Africa: a Fragment of Doomsday Ethnography

Finally, we come to a disturbing aspect of African Studies that is devoted to predicting the demise of African institutions, or at least those institutions considered to be particularly weak. The impact of Western civilization is presumed to be so great that African socio-political systems are expected to vanish and give way to Western or Westernized institutions. What is the basis for this prediction?

How much of it is scientific, and how much is sheer guesswork or wishful thinking? What happens to African societies and their political institutions when they confront the colonial order? The institutions of the conquerors are, of course, imposed but it does not at all follow that the institutions of the conquered thereby vanish.

Baxter's final verdict on Gada comes in the form of an assessment of the historical weakness of Oromo institutions and the belief that Gada, and all institutions like it, are destined to disappear:

> East African age-set and generation-set systems...seem doomed to extinction or at best to be preserved, like the elephant and other survivals of less polluted times, in a reserve for tourists to wonder at uncomprehendingly.[81]

> I anticipate revolutionary social and political change in Kenya and Ethiopia will swamp gada before it seizes up of itself.[82]

This is conjectural history: we do not know whether these institutions will vanish or not. The Gada System and its cultural foundations have been around for at least five centuries, and some aspects of that culture—particularly the astronomic calendar—may be of far greater antiquity, possibly going back to 300 B.C., as indicated by recent archaeo-astronomic findings.[83] What possible justification do we have for predicting that all this will suddenly vanish under the impact of "revolutionary change?" In the case of Kenya, one cannot even be sure what the "revolution" is that is supposed to bring about the demise of Gada.[84]

In the Ethiopian case, recent developments suggest that it is not Gada but the Marxist-Leninist revolution of Ethiopia—along with other endangered species of communism—that became extinct. Decorated officers of the Dergue, the communist military junta, beg in the streets of Addis Ababa, their medals still pinned to their tattered uniforms, on display "for tourists to wonder at uncomprehendingly." They are the pathetic vestiges of a dead world.

In retrospect it seems that the predictions about the impending demise of traditional institutions confronted by the overwhelming influence of revolutionary forces have not come to pass in Borana Ethiopia, and Baxter's prophesy has proved to be peculiarly ill-timed and baseless.

## Methodological Implications of the Debate: Lessons Learned

Readers may very well ask, "How can two highly trained professional anthropologists who have spent years studying and writing about the same African society come to conclusions that are so totally at odds with each other?" It is clear that ideological factors may cause the researcher to focus on some types of evidence, but not others. Granted that divergent ideologies will cause one to accumulate some but not other types of information, or to overvalue some aspects of society and devalue other aspects. In that case the ideology should be made *manifest*. In particular British Political Anthropologists should forthrightly put their ideological cards on the table and acknowledge all their conservative philosophical predecessors, from Hobbes to Burke to Lugard to Maines to Evans-Pritchard and stop claiming that their brand of anthropology is an empirical science without philosophical roots or assumptions.

Going beyond political *philosophy*, the critical question of *methodology* must also be raised. Here are five propositions that define the range of legitimate observation and the kind of inferences that can be made based on each type of observation. Let us assume that our purpose is to study the distribution of that magnificent animal, the Greater Kudu, in Boranaland.

> **(1) If we say there are Kudus in Borana country, all we need to do is find enough of them to prove the case (*positive hypothesis*). (2) If we say that there are no Kudus in Borana country, we have to scour the whole country to prove the case *(negative hypothesis)*. (3) If the appearance of Kudus is infrequent or periodic, then we have to stretch our times of observation to cover the situations when they do appear *(time-dependent occurrence)*. (4) If they turn up in some places, not others, we have to select our fieldwork sites to include places they do frequent *(space-dependent distribution)*. (5) If Kudus have learned to hide from predators, because they are hunted, the observer must use stealth to get to the evidence *(covert phenomena)*.**

If we do not fulfill these five necessary conditions for legitimate field observation, it is a flagrant violation of the scientific method to claim that Kudus do not exist in Borana country as demonstrated by the fact that "we did not see them."

For institutions that are based on time, such as the Gada institution, the timing of field research is critical. The movements of gada leaders are restricted by laws that prescribe when and where they can move. If the anthropologist chooses the time and place of his fieldwork without taking such factors into consideration, the field data are necessarily defective. To say, as Baxter does, that his "...fieldwork did not coincide with the peak period of gada activities," is not an acceptable excuse.[85]

He also says that the Gada institution has no political or military functions, because he has never seen a political or military meeting or activity of Gada "sets" or age-sets at any time during the period of his fieldwork in Northern Kenya.[86] From such observations he concludes that gada roles in Boran(a) Kenya *and* Ethiopia are imaginary, and the institution is nothing but a dramatized philosophy, or a phantom of the mind.[87] That is not a legitimate inference. The fact that he has never seen such meetings or activities has little evidentiary value, because he was in Boran(a) at the *wrong time* and in the *wrong place:* wrong time because he was never in the field when the critical political, electoral, legislative, judicial, and ritual events were in progress; wrong place, because it is in Ethiopian Borana, not in Northern Kenya, that the Gada, Qallu and Gumi institutions as well as age-regiments are *living institutions*, with well known leaders, political centers, shrines, transition rites, and ceremonies.

When the ethnographer sets out to study traditional institutions which turn out to be weak or radically altered in his chosen fieldwork site, one realistic option available to him is to examine their transformation over time and in response to all the forces impinging upon them, not to go on studying "traditional institutions" as if they were a mirage, with elaborate devices offered to explain how the mirage is reflected in their speech and conduct. Alternatively, he can also change his fieldwork site and study traditional institutions where they are alive. *That is the Malinowskian imperative Baxter has ignored, at considerable cost to the validity of his research enterprise.*

Furthermore, it has become clear how treacherous it is to study aspects of traditional culture that have been delegitimized or criminalized by colonial governments. In this regard we have learned that traditional warfare can be documented only in some highly restricted situations that are ignored, tolerated, or encouraged by the state. Thanks to Pax Britannica, African warriors have been rendered obsolete in colonial Kenya, and it is thus not a useful area to study the character of traditional warfare, though much can be learned about what became of them under the draconian regime and the government of hired chiefs instituted by British rule in Kenya.

It is not only warfare that is delegitimized by colonial governments. All manner of conduct including hunting, customary laws concerning crime and punishment, rites of passage that involve hazing, mutilation or infanticide and many other such practices may be prohibited and violators punished. *People who face deep censure for innocently doing what they have always done develop cultural, linguistic and behavioral defenses to fend off the condemnation,* i.e., secrecy or feigned ignorance on particular topics, ambiguity or oblique speech habits, and avoidance of inquisitive strangers when they tread on the tabooed subject. When that happens, the gathering of data is no longer straightforward. Unless the necessary methodological maneuvers have been undertaken the ethnographer cannot legitimately claim that the practices in question do not exist because he or she has not seen them.

In conclusion, it should be added that the devaluation of African societies, of their histories and institutions, may not have great significance for some liberal Western scholars who view themselves as supporters of African political and mental liberation, but, nonetheless, consider deficit ethnography, doomsday ethnography to be harmless aberrations or merely curious varieties of social science. It is important for African scholars to reassess the methodological and ideological bases of such devaluation, because it has implications for the viability and legitimacy of African political institutions.

## NOTES

1. *Age, Generation and Time: Some Features of East African Age Organization,* ed. Paul Baxter and Uri Almagor (London: C. Hurst, 1978). It is especially in the introduction and the chapter by Baxter titled "Boran age-sets and Generation-sets: Gada a Puzzle or a Maze?" that Baxter develops the above arguments.

2. P.T.W. Baxter, "The Social Organisation of the Galla of Northern Kenya," (D. Phil. diss., University of Oxford, 1954); "The Social Organisation of the Boran of Northern Kenya," (London, 1954) [summary of the dissertation]; "Absence Makes the Heart Grow Fonder," in *The Allocation of Responsibility*, ed. Max Gluckman

(Manchester, 1972); "Boran Age-sets and Warfare," (1979); "Ethiopia's Unacknowledged Problem: the Oromo," *African Affairs,* 77, No. 308 (1978): 283-296.

3. Part of the reason for this mis-representation is the fact that the Gada Mojji rites are the only important rituals of the gada cycle which are held in Kenya. This writer and father Paolo Tablino —the author of *I Gabbra del Kenia* (Bologna: Tipografia Novastampa di Verona, 1980)—observed the rite in Marsabit in 1979. Father Tablino had my book, *Gada* (1973), in hand and was checking the details of the ritual against the written record. Baxter, and Plowman before him, describe the final ceremony as the center piece of the institution. That is because they were looking at the institution from a marginal area where the heart of the institution is missing, but the Gada Mojji ritual had survived.

4. This refers to Baxter's dissertation and the summary of it.

5. Baxter, "Boran Age-sets and Warfare," 87, emphasis added.

6. *Ibid.*, 93, emphasis added.

7. *Ibid.*, 87.

8. Baxter, "Social Organization," 418-419. He does not tell us if he has gathered new evidence that caused him to change his understanding of the institution or that he is even aware of the conflicting evidence in his ethnography.

9. Abbas Haji, "Les Oromo-Arssi: continuité et évolution des institutions d'une societé éthiopienne," (Thèse de doctorat de l'Université de Paris I, Pantheon-Sorbonne, 1990).

10. The retired gada classes may also participate in wars, particularly those members who were retired at an early age.

11. There is no question of criminal action against people who fought against Somali secessionists. Indeed some Kenyan Boran heroes who supported Kenya at this critical moment of its history have had streets in Nairobi named after them.

12. Baxter "Boran Age-sets and Warfare," 88.

13. Boru Elle in Legesse, "Marsabit Elders," 259.

14. Asmarom Legesse "Marsabit Elders," 232-33, 269. See also Kenya National Archives, or KNA, for short, PC/NFD2/2/1, Marsabit Handing Over Report, Sharpe to Bailword, 1930, 11-12.

15. KNA, DC/MBT 7/1/1 Campbell to DC, MBT, 19 May 1927 and Dub Gindole in "Marsabit Elders," 60.

16. Adi Ukha in "Marsabit Elders," 76-77. Throughout Kenya there was a three-tier system of Apartheid—for Africans, Asians and Whites—similar to the South African system.

17. Hassan Diba in "Marsabit Elders," 18-19; See also evidence indicating that the enforcement of the "hut and poll tax" was rejected by Boran and abused by colonial officers: PRO, CO 533/466/5 & 6, A. Chisholm to C.E.R Brocklebank, M.P., Colonial Office, Sept. 26, 1936.

18. KNA, PC NFD 4/1/2, 1928, Handing over report from Butler to Hemsted; KNA, PC NFD 4/1/2 H.B. Sharpe, Marsabit District Political Records.

19. The archival records and oral testimony indicate that Lord Delamere, the founder of Kenya Colony, was one of the most profligate hunters in the early history of Marsabit Mountain.

20. Their resentment arises from the fact that senior colonial officials were hunting on a grand scale in Marsabit. See H.B. Sharpe's description their hunting sprees on the mountain in KNA, PC NFD 4/1/2, H.B. Sharpe, "Marsabit Political Records 1926-28," p. 2.

21. Dub Gindole in "Marsabit Elders," 1984, p. 48; Major Miles' Report on Borana, undated ca. 1927 titled "Notes on the Province of Borana, Southern Ethiopia," chapter 5 of KNA, PC NFD 4/1/2.

22. Günther Schlee, *Identities on the Move* (Manchester: Manchester University Press, 1989), 44 ff.

23. Schlee also suggests that there may have been internal processes that contributed to the collapse of the alliance, "The Oromo Expansion and its Impact in Northern Kenya", *Proceedings of the Eighth International Conference of Ethiopian Studies,* vol II, ed. Taddesse Beyene (Addis Ababa: University of Addis Ababa, 1984) 712, 716.

24. David Napier Hamilton, *Ethiopia's Frontiers: the Boundary Agreements and their Demarcation,* 1896-1956 (Ph.D. diss. Oxford University, 1974) p. 374; On Qalla Rasa and the protection he gave the "Hofte" (Borana) emigrants to Marsabit see Daudi Dhaddaccha Dambi, in "Marsabit Elders," 5-13.

25. See Asmarom Legesse, "Borana under British and Ethiopian Empires," in *The Oromo Republic: Decline under Imperial Rule* (forthcoming); Asmarom Legesse, *A Pastoral Ecosystem: Field Studies of the Borana and Gabra of Northern Kenya,* (forthcoming); and Asmarom Legesse "Adaptation, Drought and Development: Boran and Gabra Pastoralists of Northern Kenya," in *African Food*

*Systems in Crisis,* part 1, ed. Rebecca Huss-Ashmore (New York: Gordon and Beach Science Publishers, 1989); Asmarom Legesse, *Kenya Boran: Flexibility and Change in a Pastoral Society* (New Hampshire: American Universities Field Staff, 1975). The latter is a very slight pamphlet addressed to a wide, non-scientific audience intended to accompany a popular film on the Boran(a) and Gabra. It should not be treated as part of my scholarly work on the Boran(a).

26. Baxter, "Boran Age-sets and Generation-sets," 162.

27. P.T.W. Baxter, "Acceptance and Rejection of Islam among the Boran of the Northern Frontier District of Kenya," *Special Studies,* 1962 (Univ. Nairobi xeroxed text, Africana collection), 238.

28. Asmarom Legesse, "Adaptation, Drought and Development: Boran and Gabra Pastoralists of Northern Kenya," 269.

29. Margery Perham, *East African Journey: Kenya, Tanganyika 1929-30* (London: Faber and Faber, 1976), 43. Compared with the language and attitudes of settler-colonists of Kenya, such as Lord Delamere, who think of Kenya as *"White Man's Country,"* Lord Lugard's writing is much less destructive. F.D. Lugard, *The Rise of our East African Empire,* v. 2 (London: Frank Cass, 1968), 649-651.

30. Examples of this type of frontier society are Jammu and Kashmir in North-West India—a relatively "unruly" area contested by three states: India, Pakistan, and China.

31. My interviews on this war were constrained, because I feared that it might put my informant, Madha Galma, at risk. I am now freer to probe more deeply, and to give a more data on the war, because Madha is no longer alive.

32. See, in particular, "Boran Age-sets and Generation-sets," 180.

33. Asmarom Legesse, *Gada,* 7-8.

34. Baxter, "Boran Age-sets and Warfare," 93.

35. *Ibid.,* 88; For the Zulu military system at its peak during the reign of Shaka, see E.J. Krige, "The Military Organization of the Zulu," in Krige, *Social System of the Zulus* (London: Longmans, 1936), 261-279 and James Stuart, *History of the Zulu Rebellion* (London: Macmillan, 1913).

36. Richard Pankhurst, *A Social History of Ethiopia* (Institute of Ethiopian Studies, Addis Ababa University, 1990), 152.

37. *Atsmä Giorgis and His Work: History of the Galla and the Kingdom of Shäwa,* ed. Bairu Tafla (Wiesbaden GMBH, Stuttgart: Franz Steiner, 1987), 308-309.

38 R. S. Whiteway, *The Portuguese Expedition to Abyssinia in 1541-1543* (Hakluyt Society, 1902, Lichtenstein: Krauss Reprint, 1967), 229.

39. Bahrey, "History," 112.

40. *Ibid.*, 115.

41. *Ibid.*, 122.

42. Pereira, *Chronica de Susenyos,* 22-24, 79; Getachew Haile, *Yä Abba Bahrəy Dərsätoch* [The Works of Abba Bahrey,] 129, 135, 137. Getachew states that the *Oromo had an amazing military strategy which Susenyos employed to regain the throne.* How Susenyos employed this strategy in his battle with the Shoan army is illustrated in the following passage from Getachew's Amharic translation:

> ንጉስ ስልጣን ሰገድ [ሱሰንዮስ] ዘሰላሴን ለሙሙጋት ወሰነ።
> ዘሰላሴ በታላቅ ትዕቢትና ብተነፉ ልብ፡ ማነው በፊቴ የሚቆም፡
> ማንስ ይደፍረኛል እያለ ሙጣ። ንጉስ ስልጣን ሰገድ ደግሞ
> ከነበረበት ተነስቶ፡ ጦፍራውን (የርብርቦሽ ሱፉልን) እንደ
> ጋላ አሳሙረ። የዘሰላሴ አማራ ስራዊት ደግሞ በዝያን ጊዜ
> ጦፍራ (የርብርቦሽ) አሰላለፍ አያውቁም። እንደ ገበያተኛ
> እርስምስምሶች ነበሩ። (p. 137),

43. Richard Pankhurst, *An Introduction to the History of the Ethiopian Army* (Addis Ababa: n.p., 1959), 135.

44. Harold Marcus, *The Life and Times of Menilek II, 1844-1914* (Oxford: Clarendon Press, 1975), 218.

45. F. J. Bieber, *Kaffa: Ein Altkuschitiches Völkstum in Inner-Africa* (Anthropos-Bibleotek, vols. 1 and 2, 1923).

46. See the chapter below on Oromo moieties that examines the parallels between Bahrey's account of gada wars and the contemporary Gada chronology, within which the history of wars is narrated.

47. Baxter, "Boran Age-sets and Warfare," 84.

48. Paul Goto, "The Boran of Northern Kenya: Origins, Migration and Settlements in the 19th Century," B.A. thesis, Nairobi: University of Nairobi, 1972, 63.

49. Schlee, "The Oromo Expansion," 716; If the date offered by Schlee is correct, it implies that Dida Bittata was the Abba Gada in power, not a retired leader, and Adi Doyyo was in the warrior grade. That conforms perfectly with Borana military organization.

50. Ambitious men in the senior warrior grade are entitled to initiate military campaigns, but it is the exceptional warrior who succeeds in doing so.

51. Baxter, "Boran Age-sets and Generation-sets," 152 & 153-56.

52. *Ibid.*, 153.

53. The relationship of the Dergue to Borana was not always hostile. On one occasion when the Gumi decided to take the electoral responsibility away from the Warra Qallu, the regime saw it as a "progressive" move and officially witnessed their action.

54. In addition to the normal meaning of *yuba* or "semi-retired" the verb form *"yubomu"* is used to describe the release of an individual from gada service. It does not simply mean entering the *yuba* grades.

55. See the law of recruitment in Asmarom Legesse, *Gada*, 97, and the sections on the recruitment of *jallaba, makkala,* and *torbi.*

56. Arero Rammata, in A. Legesse, "Borana Field Notes," 1963, 86.

57. *Ibid.*, 87.

58. Asmarom Legesse, *Gada*, 86-87.

59. Baxter, "Boran Age-sets and Generation-sets," 163.

60. *Ibid.*, 162-163.

61. Bahrey, "History," (1593); Haberland, *Galla Süd Äthiopiens* (1963); and Knutsson, *Authority and Change* (1963).

62. Domenico Pecci, "Note sul sistema delle Gada e delle classi di età presso le popolazioni Borana," *Rassegna di studi etiopici,* 1 (1941): 305-21.

63. J. Hinnant, "The Gada System of the Guji of Southern Ethiopia," (Ph.D. diss., Chicago: Univ. Chicago, 1977), 183 (emphasis added).

64. *Ibid.*, 183 ff..

65. *Ibid.*, 189.

66. *Ibid.*, 189.

67. *Ibid.*, 189.

68. Baxter, "Social Organization," 39.

69. Baxter, "Boran Age-sets and Generation-sets," 153-56.

70. During the "era of the princes," Oromo kings and queens played a major role in national political life, particularly in the Gondarine court. See Belletech Dheressa's "Oromo Women in History," in *The Oromo Republic,* (forthcoming).

71. This is the aspect of the colonial relationship which Bonnie Holcomb and Sisay Ibsa have labeled "dependent colonialism" in their book *The Invention of Ethiopia: the Making of a Dependent Colonial State in Northeast Africa* (Trenton, N.J.: Red Sea Press, 1990). The study reveals how colonial powers found it to their advantage to arm the Shoan colonial enterprise.

72. Baxter, "Boran Age-sets and Warfare," 93.

73. Zewde Gabre-Sellassie, *Yohannes IV of Ethiopia: A Political Biography* (Oxford: Clarendon, 1975), 249.

74. Krige, *Social System of the Zulus,* 261-279.

75. *A River of Blessings: Essays in Honor of Paul Baxter,* ed. D. Brokensha (Syracuse, N.Y.: Syracuse University, *circa* 1994)

76. Baxter, "Boran Age-sets and Generation-sets," 175.

77. His account of the Gada Mojji rites is based entirely on second hand data, not participant observation. What he describes as the children's naming ritual is a private event, a ceremony performed for the children of the retired, not a gada rite of passage.

78. Asmarom Legesse, *Gada,* chap. 4.

79. Cf. Bassi (2005: 64). His statement that Hayyu Garba "can belong to any generational class (*luba*)" is factually incorrect. They can only belong to the Yuba and Jarsa classes including also members of the Gada Mojji *luba* who have not achieved the Gada Mojji status. These three categories are "retired" in the sense that their role in government, adjudication, warfare is greatly reduced or non existent. Within these three groups, the Yuba are described as semi-retired because they participate every eight years in Gumi Gayo. Otherwise they have no standing office or assembly.

80. *Ibid.,* 160-162, 163-178..

81. Baxter and Almagor, *Age, Generation, and Time,* 20.

82. Baxter, "Age-sets and Generation-sets," 177.

83. B.M. Lynch and L.M. Robbins, "Namoratunga: the First Archaeo-astronomical Evidence in Sub-Saharan Africa," *Science,* 200 (1978): 766-78. Laurance R. Doyle, "The Borana Calendar Reinterpreted," *Current Anthropology,* (June, 1986): 287.

84. It is not revolution but the colonial impact that has greatly weakened the political institutions of the Boran of Kenya.

85. Baxter, "Boran Age-sets and Generation-sets," 155. The concurrence of the Gada transition rites and my fieldwork (1962-63) was also coincidental. Once I realized that they were due to occur

during my fieldwork period, I made sure that I was at the ritual and ceremonial site. On the other hand, most of my subsequent visits to Borana and Marsabit were timed to coincide with the most intensive political and ritual activities.

86. As he puts it in one of his many statements "I can recollect no instance during my time in Kenya that members of a [gada-] set met as a set." Baxter, "Boran Age-sets and Generation-sets," 154.

87. *Ibid.*, pp. 175, 179.

---

*Marsabit Elders* (1984)   (From left to right)

(1) Dokko Garse, Konso elder who emigrated in his youth from Ethiopia, (2) Daudi Daddacch Dambi, 95, convener of the group of elders, emigrated from Ethiopia in his youth with the second wave of Borana migration, fathered a son who subsequently became governor of Eastern Province, (3) Kide Okkotu, a merchant who was some 30 years younger than the elders, but just as competent, seated behind, (4) Dub Gindole, (with white turban facing camera) a renowned hunter whose leg was smashed by a bull elephant. (5) Adi Ukha, a merchant knowledgeable about taxation and trade.

(6) Chief Jilo Toukena, 73, for 33+ years chief of the Marsabit Boran, removed from office on the occasion of the total solar eclipse of June 30, 1973; [the duration of his chieftaincy was then wrongly    reported as 20+ years in "The Day the Sun Died."  By his own later account (1984) he was appointed by Gerald Reece, DC, in the late 30's.]

(7) Hassan Diba, a wealthy elder who served with the British forces in Burma (1943), later became an accountant with the district administration, had first-hand knowledge of colonial policy and British officialdom in the NFD.

Important informants not shown in the picture: Ali Doti Qalla Rasa, grandson of Qalla Rasa, the famous Gabra-Boran chief during the early colonial era, well informed about colonial history.  Boru Elle, a Boran elder most knowledgeable on warfare, age-regiments, horsemanship and the Oromo cavalry.

*Chapter 3*

# THE OROMO POLITY
## The Key Institutions

D
emocracy is not a purely Western phenomenon. It was not invented at a certain time, in some definite ancestral European cradleland, and thence disseminated to other parts of the globe. Such dissemination is, of course, taking place today, but that was not the case prior to the end of the colonial era. The colonialists had no interest in disseminating democracy, or in recognizing its existence among the peoples they conquered.

The Oromo are one of the many peoples in Africa who invented their own variety of democracy. The institutions of the Oromo nation, as a whole, will be presented in those areas where the historic data permit such an analysis. That is possible at present with regard to the Gada System. In other respects, especially concerning the Qallu institution and the moiety system on which it rests, the written

---

← *Women building a ritual pavilion* where the initiation of their DABBALLE (I) sons will take place, after completing the first eight years of the Gada life cycle. Until they are named in this rite, the sons are in a genderless sacred state as are their grandfathers in the final stage of the gada life cycle (GADA MOJJI XI). The women's hairstyle *(ch'ibra)* indicates the stage of the life cycle their husbands have reached. The mothers of dabballe are greatly honored; their blessings are sought by women. *Dabballe dhali!* "May you give birth to a dabballe" is a common greeting, and blessing, for Borana women.

historic evidence is so fragmentary that we must rely more heavily on oral historic sources and on ethnographic data from the most conservative Oromo populations.

For our current analysis of the Oromo polity, the ethnography of the southern Borana branch of the Ethiopian Oromo must be the principal source of evidence, for several reasons: (1) because the Gada System, the Qallu institution, and the moiety system which it represents, are fully operational there; (2) the Qallu are still honored every eight years in the Muda ritual, an event in which the Borana and many other Oromo peoples participate; (3) the Qallu institution is politically linked to the Gada System and thus reveals how the two institutions interact in the political, not merely the ritual, arena; (4) both institutions have survived the colonial experience under Abyssinian and Italian rule in Southern Ethiopia, whereas in other parts of the Oromo country, such as Central Ethiopia or Northern Kenya, the people had their institutions largely replaced by colonial institutions. The Ethiopian Borana too were technically colonized by Emperor Menelik. However, as indicated earlier, their remoteness from the Ethiopian center of power and their location in a frontier region they freely crossed back and forth, to escape from excessive pressures from one or the other government, were factors that helped to preserve their institutions.

### The Oromo nation: conservative and innovative elements

Subjectively, the Ethiopian Borana view themselves as the custodians of Oromo heritage and are least likely to trade their identity for some other identity. Other Oromo populations recognize that fact and have historically gone on pilgrimages to Borana to find their roots and rekindle their distinctive identity as a nation.

The Arsi (and Orma) too performed a similar role as guardians of the second Oromo cradleland for those Oromo who are mainly of BARETTUMA descent. Throughout most of the post-migration history of the Oromo, therefore, there were two sets of cradlelands and two centers of Muda ritual—one for the BARETTUMA-dominant groups and the other for the BORANA-dominant groups, located north-east and south-west of the Gennale River respectively. (See map of Oromo Cradlelands, p. 184, below.)

That situation was, however, thrown off balance because of several events that took place in the BARETTUMA cradlelands. To begin with, the Orma abandoned the cradlelands prior to the start of the great migration. This branch of the BARETTUMA-dominant groups emigrated because of drought and famine, not as part of the cyclical wars that dominated the great migration, in 1522 and later. Thereafter—from the time of the great migration in the 16th century until the colonial conquest in the 1890s—the Arsi alone remained tied to the BARETTUMA cradlelands, until they too lost their political and ritual institutions under the double impact of a ruthless branch of the Imperial Army, led by Ras Darghe, and their acceptance of Islam as their religion and their shield.

By contrast, BORANA-dominant groups, such as Macch'a and Tulama, left the cradlelands, but remained closer to their roots, and were tied to them through pilgrimages to Walabu, the land of the "Abba Muda."

To this day, the heirs of two ancient moieties exhibit social characteristics that are quite different: the BORANA-dominant groups being more conservative in their migration and adherence to traditions, whereas the BARETTUMA-dominant groups behaving more like pioneers and explorers who have taken the Oromo nation to its furthest reaches: the extreme outliers being those of the Rayya-Azebo in the far north in Ethiopia and the Tanaland Orma in the far south, in Kenya. In the process, the *BARETTUMA-dominant groups broke off from the Muda networks* that, for so long, had held the Oromo nation together. Most of them—Wollo, Yejju, Barentu, Arsi and Orma—also *accepted Islam*. On the BORANA side, only the Waso and Isiolo Boran and the Ghibe Kingdoms are predominantly Muslim today, the rest are either adherents of the ancient monotheistic religion or mainly Christians with many layers of the traditional religion attached to their Christian worship.

In most parts of Oromo country, the traditional institutions underwent different levels of transformation ranging from alteration of the institutions in an authoritarian direction, to the near total destruction of the macro-political institutions and their replacement by colonial instruments of direct rule in Kenya. In some areas, such as the Ghibe region, Oromo abandoned their democratic organization and adopted monarchic political systems. This, however, was only a partial transformation, because they continued to uphold their democratic cultural values and civic organizations, long after Gada had been supplanted by kings.[1] In the central and western regions of Oromoland, the authoritarian political organizations that emerged in the late 19th century, developed around dominant military figures such as Jote Tullu and Bakare Godana and their descendants. These new forms of centralized government were based on war chiefs who tended to grab more power than was allowed by custom and law; and new types of leaders, called *abba lafa,* "owners of land," who used the accumulation of property to build up their power. An external factor was also the feudal-military institutions of the Abyssinian colonizers that were methodically planted in the newly conquered territories. Imperial rule sometimes reinforced the authoritarian tendencies of the office of Abba Dula, but most often created new forms of subordination, with *balabbats* serving as intermediaries.

As we indicated in the previous chapter, the political organization of Kenya Boran is not a useful source of evidence for the study of the pre-colonial Oromo institutions. Under a ruthless form of efficient colonial rule in Marsabit and under colonial and Islamic influences in the Waso and Isiolo regions, Boran lost their macro political institutions.

There are Boran communities in the far north of Kenya, close to the Ethiopia border, around Moyale and Sololo, which have direct ties to the Gada and Qallu institutions of the Ethiopian Borana and have, therefore, retained a much greater knowledge of their institutions than their kinsmen in other parts of Kenya. That is where the anthropologist, Marco Bassi, conducted some of his field research on Boran(a)—a body of primary, firsthand research that became the basis of his book titled *I Borana: Una societa assembleare dell'Etiopia.*[2] His work on the clan assemblies is far richer than the work of any of the other researchers who have dealt with traditional Oromo political life. However, his comments on Gada are irrelevant since they are not based on primary participatory-observational evidence. He never visited the ruling Gada Assembly, and thus gives erroneous information on the political role of the Garba councilors in the Assembly, the role and location of Olla Batu (the satellite village of Garba hayyus) in the seat of luba government.

The great majority of the Kenyan Oromo are fundamentally estranged from the core institutions—Gumi, Gada and Qallu. In the rest of this chapter, when we speak of "Borana" political institutions we do not refer to the Kenyan but the Ethiopian Borana. Any mention of the Kenya Boran will be so specified.

The key questions we consider in this chapter are these: (1) How did Oromo institutions function in the most conservative and least affected branches of the nation? (2) What were the pre-colonial institutions and their functions? (3) What kinds of relationships existed between institutions?

## THE STRUCTURE OF THE OROMO POLITY

In its historic form, the Oromo polity was organized as three principal institutions.[3] These are the generational organization (Gada), the dual organization (Qallu), and the National Assembly (Gumi).

Of the three institutions, the most important, in the political sphere, is the National Assembly. It is known as *Gumi Gayo* in Borana and *Ch'affe* among other Oromo groups. Gumi means "the multitude" because it is a very large assembly made up of many councilors *(hayyu)* and assemblies *(ya'a)* drawn from different sections of the Gada institution. Clans take part in the *pre-Gumi meetings*, or when *clan caucuses* are held while the Gumi is in session and their recommendation are presented by their Gada representatives. (Bassi, *Decisions in the Shade,* 2005, 103-07, 258 and A. Legesse, *Gada*, 1973, 94-95). In theory, all Borana adult males have a right to participate *(direct democracy)*, in fact, they can only get access to the Gumi deliberations through their representatives in the Gada Assemblies *(representative democracy)* (*Gada*, 1973, p. 93)

Although this great assembly is the macro institution that defines the essence of Oromo democracy, lesser versions of it survive in the Oromo nation at the local level in the form of the village meetings *(cora olla)* or the clan meetings *(cora gosa)*. This bedrock of Oromo democratic culture has continued to thrive, at its lowest levels, long after all the larger institutions were weakened by colonialism. Village- or clan-level democracy survives today in many parts of Oromo country, in Ethiopia and Kenya, regardless of the type of superstructure that was imposed upon the society.

Perhaps one of the finest descriptions of Oromo democracy, prior to Menelik's conquest, is the work of the French savant, Antoine d'Abbadie, who lived in the 1870s in Gudru, a self-governing region of Macch'a he describes as a "republic." He had *firsthand knowledge* of this society through his friend "Xumi Maca," an Irressa or ritual leader, an active participant in political debate, and a gifted orator. D'Abbadie described "the separation of powers" *(distinction des pouvoirs)* in the republic, by identifying four different types of institutional leaders.[4]

> *Abba Saa,* chief of public finances
> *Irressa,* "grand pontiff," or ritual leader
> *Abba Bokku,* president of parliament
> *Moti,* "king" or "chief executive" or war chief

He describes the Abba Bokku as the peacetime leader, with legislative and judicial authority. This officer conducts his parliamentary business under the shade of great trees that are highly respected. He carries on his belt the *bokku,* a wooden scepter that d'Abbadie compares with the mace of the English parliament. It serves as the symbol of his authority. The parliamentary assembly continues its debates until it reaches consensus. Any member can veto a proposed decision by uttering the word "I stop! [the discussion]" and the meeting will be postponed. When the discussion is coming to an end, the Abba Bokku asks each clan, *by order of their birth,* if they agree to pass the law. If they all approve, the meeting ends. The assembly meets again the next day, to sacralize the law by sacrificing a bull, and dipping the bokku in the blood of the sacrificial animal.[5] Because d'Abbadie attended the meetings of the assembly, his findings are the result of participant observation and cannot be easily dismissed, as some contemporary writers have done. However, when he comes to describe the office of *Moti* ("king") the data are not as compelling. It turns out that the Moti is neither "chief executive" nor "king." He has nothing to do in peace time, but assumes the role of war chief in times of war. Custom requires him to lead the warriors, but forbids his personal engagement in combat. Hence, the office would be better described as that of a "war chief."

Antoine d'Abbadie concludes his discussion of the "separation of powers" by identifying the three on-going supreme functions of Abba Saa, (chief of public finances) Irressa (ritual leader), Abba

Bokku (president). These have continuing authority, whereas the Moti (war chief) has authority only in times of war. After retirement, they continue to enjoy a privileged position in society.[6]

Does d'Abbadie identify one of these as the supreme authority of Gudru? He certainly does not. He describes three peacetime supreme authorities and one wartime leader. He leaves us with the clear impression that he is dealing with four separate powers or, in our idiom, a multi-headed democratic political system.

D'Abbadie presented his lecture titled "Sur les Oromo: grande nation africaine," to the French National Assembly on April 5, 1880—a mark of the respect he accorded to Oromo democracy.

Approximately two decades later, the Ethiopian historian Atsmä Giorgis wrote his *History of the Galla* [Oromo], a work that is a compilation of older documents. However, some parts of his work, such as the chapter on "History and Law," are very impressive and seem to be original information based on first-hand knowledge of the Macch'a and Tulama.[7] In that chapter Atsmä reports his informants as saying that their ancestral "Chaffe" was a place where all the people "met to administer justice, to hear the historical and judicial report of the expiring eight years, to criticize some of the existing laws and legislate new ones, and to proclaim the future law and procedures...."[8]

He then goes on to explain that *this ancestral Ch'affe broke up into regional assemblies during the great migration.* "After they left Borana, the Chaffe of the whole Awash was at Malka Bollo. The Ayyu [Hayyu] who used to administer justice was also from the Galan." Later on when they "quarreled among themselves, when the area became too small for them, and when they separated their Met'echa [*meddhiccha* "ritual wrist band taken from the skin of sacrificial animals"], they also separated their Ch'affe. Thus, Awash Malka Bollo became the Chaffe of the Teloma [Tulama] and the Ayyu [Hayyu] remained within Galan. The Mec'a had their [Ch'affe] at Tule."[9]

On the subject of the National Assembly, what d'Abbadie records in the 1870s on the Gudru Republic, and Atsmä records at the end of the 19th century from his sources in Macch'a-Tulama are similar to what exists today in Borana.[10] They stress the separation of powers and the political, adjudicative and legislative functions that they performed, as an assembly.

The national assembly as it exists to day among the Borana of southern Ethiopia is profiled here. The profile covers the range of its activities and its place relative to the other institutions.

> The NATIONAL ASSEMBLY, (Gumi) is made up of all the Gada assemblies of the Oromo, who meet, once every eight years, to review the laws, to proclaim new laws, to evaluate the men in power, and to resolve major conflicts that could not be resolved at lower levels of their judicial organization.
>
> The present and former Abba Gada are the leaders in the main session of the Gumi.[11] This great gathering in Borana is comparable to the great assemblies recorded in other parts of Oromo country such as the "Ch'affe" of the central Oromo.[12]
>
> The Gumi stands in a superordinate position vis-a-vis the other institutions. It is the institution that gives structural substance to the notion that power rests ultimately with the people—a right they exercise by direct participation or by delegating power to five groups of Gada leaders, active and semi-retired.[12]

All the sectoral assemblies of the clans, moieties and age-sets are allowed to attend the general assembly and bring their proposals to the *pre-Gumi meetings*. However, only the gada assemblies— active and semi-retired—take part in the Gumi proper as the main participants who have a say in legislative debates. Others may have sporadic inputs in the meeting but they have no institutionalized position in legislative debates.* One prospective gada class (V), one active gada class (VI) and four semi-retired gada classes (VII-X) participate fully in the discussions through their respective leaders. They are all in the second half of the gada cycle and are presented by triangles on the graphic (p. 123). Key positions are reserved for the Abba gada in power and for all the living semi-retired Abba Gadas in the Yuba grades. Normally, the Abba Gada in power serves as the presiding councilor i.e. as Abba Sera, "father of law."

---

* In *Decisions in the Shade,* (p. 264) Bassi misrepresents the structure of the Gumi by giving the five Qallu councils a prominent place in the convention. He presents no primary observational, participatory or eye-witness testimony in support of this contention. His claim that *clan caucuses* play a role in the deliberations, however, is largely correct,

The second element of the polity is the Qallu institution. In the historic literature it is referred to as "Abba Muda" by writers who do not realize that the Qallu and the Abba Muda are one and the same. Properly speaking "Muda" is the ceremony, Qallu or "Abba Muda" is the ritual leader, and neither is a place name. In contemporary Borana the place of the ritual is at the Oda shrine. In previous centuries, the usual site was at Walabu in Borana territory, for the BORANA-dominant groups, and at one of the shrines such as Mormor in Arsi territory, for the BARETTUMA-dominant groups.

Moiety organization is part of the classical political system as it was recorded in the late 16th century and has come down to the present in various modified forms. The office of the Qallu or Qalliccha exists across most of the Oromo nation, sometimes taking on the character of a "spirit possession" cult. In Macch'a the office is still referred to as "Qallu," but it is seen as an institution that gained prominence only after the decline of Gada.[13] Separate and apart from the Qallu institution also exist the clan councils representing the lower order juridical organizations within the kinship system.

It is only in Borana, Southern Ethiopia, that the Qallu institution continues to operate today as a parallel organization counterpoised against the Gada System. In this region, where some measure of indirect rule had been put in place by Emperor Menelik, the Qallu lineages assumed administrative responsibilities as the chief balabbats. But recent data indicate that the institution ran into major problems in 1980, during the period of the Dergue when they lost their electoral authority, not because of the Dergue's actions, but by a decision of the Gumi.[14] We can profile the institution as follows:

> **The QALLU are the ritual leaders of the Oromo, representing the two great societal halves of the nation, whose shrines were historically associated with the cradlelands of the BARETTUMA and BORANA Oromo. They are honored, every eight years, by pilgrims who come from the Oromo lands and the allied nations, to take part in the Muda, "the anointing." The Qallu are showered with gifts and, in return, they give their blessings. They mediate cases of conflict and oversee the election of Gada leaders but they and their kin are barred from holding such office. Dedicated as they are to peace-making they may not bear arms, shed blood, or inflict punishment, tasks which are left to the Warra Bokku.**

Historically, the position of the Qallu is so critical that pilgrims came to the great Qallus of the cradlelands from many parts of the Oromo nation and they continued to do so even when the other Oromo institutions were in decline. The ritual leaders were referred to as *Abba Muda* or "fathers of anointment," and the pilgrims were called *"jila."* Today the Borana perform this great ritual, every eight years, for themselves and for other Oromo who come to their land as pilgrims. However, in Borana, the term *'jila'* means ritual, not pilgrims, although the phrase *warr jila* "people of rituals" serves as a colloquial label for people taking part in rituals, including Muda.

All electoral and many ritual activities are governed by the moiety assemblies *(ya'a Qallu)*. In Borana today, there are two main Qallus at the head of the Sabbo and Gona moieties, just as there were two Qallus or "Abba Mudas" at the head of the BARETTUMA and BORANA moieties of the Oromo nation in earlier centuries.

**The great significance of the MUDA RITUAL derives from the fact that it was and is the confluence of the ritual/ceremonial cycles of the Gada and Qallu institutions. It represents the encounter between the two co-ordinate institutions of the Oromo. As such, Muda is laden with meaning and stands on par, in its symbolic and integrative significance, with the gada power transfer ceremony *(balli or jarra)* and the meetings of the national assembly *(Gumi or Ch'affe).***

Oromo ideas about the *separation* of their coordinate institutions are reflected in the conduct and relationships between their leaders. *The heads of the Gada and Qallu institutions were required to avoid each other for the entire term of office of the Gada leaders.* The pattern of avoidance between the elected political leaders (Gada) and the hereditary ritual leaders (Qallu) is one of the most interesting features of the separation of powers in Oromo democracy.

Besides the Muda ritual, there are two political events in which both types of leaders take part: *lallaba*, where the newly elected Gada leaders are proclaimed before the nation, and the National Assembly where the laws are recited, revised and ratified. In both instances, the Qallu say nothing and do nothing: they are there as observers, not participants. In the third event, Muda, the leaders of the two institutions face each other and address each other. The Abba Gada pays homage to the senior Qallu and receives his blessings.

This is the only event when the ritual seniority of the Qallu over the Abba Gada is made manifest. The political seniority of the Abba Gada over the Qallu is evident in every gada ritual and political ceremony. Nevertheless, the momentary humbling of the Abba Gada before the Qallu in the ritual of anointment has deep significance for the Oromo nation. It is a powerful symbol that stands in the way of monolithic ideas about authority that surface from time to time on the political landscape, as ambitious war chiefs threaten to grab more power than is their due. It is like requiring a "warrior-king" to kiss the feet of the "high priest," once every eight years, to remind the nation and the war chiefs that ritual authority is in its place, as a supernatural symbol of order, in case secular authority fails.

The third institution is the generational system or Gada. This is an old element of the Oromo polity whose cultural significance to all Oromo can be summed up as follows.

**GADA is the heart of the political-military organization. So deep is the people's valuation this institution that it stands at the core of the Oromo cultural identity. Gada serves as the Oromo national emblem even in areas where the institution has lost its functions under the weight of colonial rule, cultural assimilation, religious proselitization, and communist revolution. Any institution that can withstand such onslaught does, I believe, have some staying power.**

However, it would be a mistake to try to understand Oromo political life by reference to Gada alone. Both the Gada and Qallu institutions are important. One cannot be understood without reference to the other. Credit is due to Karl Eric Knutsson for having brought the Qallu institution to the forefront of Oromo studies, forcing all other students of Oromo culture to look at the interdependence of the Gada and Qallu institutions rather than studying each without regard to the other.

By combining Knutsson's contribution on the Qallu institution as presented in his *Authority and Change: A Study of the Kallu Institution among the Macha Galla of Ethiopia,* with the study of the Gada and Qallu institutions presented by this writer in connection with electoral politics in *Gada* (1973) as well as the observational study of the solar eclipse titled "The Day the Sun Died," we get a clearer picture of the Qallu institution in relation to Gada.

Here is a definition of the Gada system and the Gada Assembly that is more complete than the profile given earlier.

The **GADA SYSTEM** is a system of generation segments or gada classes that succeed each other every eight years in assuming political, military, judicial, legislative and ritual responsibilities. Each active gada class—beyond the first three grades—has its own internal leadership *(Adula)* and its own assembly *(ya'a)*, but the leaders of the class become the leaders of the nation when their class comes to power in the middle of the life cycle—a stage of life called *"gada"* among the Borana or *"luba"* among the central Oromo. The class in power is headed by the *Abba Gada* in Borana, *Abba Bokku* elsewhere.

The **GADA ASSEMBLY** is made up of two different councils, called "the senior council" *(ya'a arbora)* and two "lateral councils" *(ya'a kontoma)*. The lateral councils are off to the side under the leadership of the two deputy Abba Gadas. They have their own assemblies representing the two sub-moieties of Gona. They live apart from the main assembly in their own communities. It is a type of "shadow government" that serves as a back up system in case disaster strikes. Junior councils *(hayyu garba)*, who are recruited exclusively from the semi-retired *(yuba)* and fully-retired *(jarsa)* grades, are attached to all three councils (one ya'a arbora and two ya'a kontoma). Those attached to the ya'a arbora live in a satellite village called Olla Batu. The deputy Abba Gadas *(abba gada kontoma)* along with the Abba Gada *fit'e* ("apex") make up the **GADA TRIUMVIRATE** *(Gada Saden)*. All three are members of the six-man senior Gada Council *(Adula)* that comes together in a single Gada Assembly in the final stages of the Gada period.

**GADA LEADERS** are collectively referred to as the "Warra Arbora" or "Warra Bokku" and counterpoised against the "Warra Qallu," the ritual leaders. "Warra Bokku" means "the people of the scepter" because all the councilors possess a specially carved baton, held on ceremonial occasions. That is also why, among the central Oromo, the position of top leader is referred to as "Abba Bokku."

There is a fourth institution, the age organization *(hariyya)*, which is not universally present in Oromo society, but appears to have evolved in Borana after the great migration. There are strong indications that the Gada System was originally an age organization, and that, as the population expanded greatly in the early 16th century, the rules of the Gada System were imposed upon it, probably for the purpose of limiting the massive population growth the nation was experiencing. These rules then caused the institution to become unstable, and to transform itself from an age-homogeneous into an age-heterogeneous organization. A simpler organization, called "hariyya," was then introduced to serve as a *subsidiary institution* that supplements the social, maturational, and military functions of Gada. This is a thesis that was presented and documented in depth in *Gada* (1973), by this writer, using methodologically complex procedures. Outside of Borana, the word "hiriyya" is recognized as a term that means "age mate," or "companion" but not as a term that refers to a formal organization of age groups.[15]

Whatever the genesis of the Gada and Hariyya systems may have been, the facts, as we now observe them, are these: Both institutions co-exist today among the Ethiopian Borana: they have *different functions* and are *highly interdependent.*

Students of Oromo history need to pay special attention to the age-set system. Its historic significance, however, is primarily inferential, in the sense that it helps us to learn about the antecedent conditions that gave rise to it. The expanding age-span of the *luba* is a problem that existed everywhere in Oromo country, as a function of the nearly universal 40-year generational rule. It is, thus, an important aspect of the historical background.

On the whole, gada classes and age-sets combined are doing today the work that gada classes alone performed in previous centuries. Hence, we can use the ethnography of recent Borana warfare to gain insight into the history of Oromo warfare in past centuries. Many aspects of Oromo warfare, including *investigative procedures, scouts, regimental leadership and organization, the subordination of warriors to the Gada Assembly, and gada leaders serving as war chiefs* are fully illustrated by the study of contemporary gada classes and age-sets.

Here is a comprehensive profile of age-sets.

> The AGE-SET SYSTEM *(hariyya)* is a supportive orga-
> nization under the authority of the Raba-Gada assemblies: it
> is organized strictly on the basis of age and has, structurally,
> nothing to do with genealogical generations. The part of an
> age-set *(hariyya)* that is re-organized for warfare becomes an
> age-regiment *(ch'ibra)*. There are two, three, or four age-sets
> of fighting age in each gada class (IV-VI). Each is capable of
> producing one or more age regiments. Age-sets have their own
> groups of councilors *(hayyu)* who lead them in times of peace
> and regimental leaders *(abba ch'ibra)* who lead them in times
> of war. They are under the authority of the war chief *(abba
> dula)* who is, often, an Abba Gada-in-council who has called
> the nation to arms.

The domain of age-sets includes ritual and social activities, in
addition to their military duties. The critical word for "age-regiment"
*(ch'ibra)* refers to the age-set re-organized for warfare. The Amharic
word *ch'ifra* and the Oromo word *ch'ibra* for "regiment" are cognates. *The Susenyos chronicle (Pereira, p. 79) indicates clearly that
the word, the concept, and the associated battle array were taken
over from the Oromo by the army of Emperor Susenyos.*

The age-set system developed mainly among the Borana and
probably came into being in recent centuries, after the Gada System
underwent demographic and structural changes that made it less useful as an organization dedicated to warfare. Hence, gada classes and
age-sets jointly began to serve as an effective military organization,
and Gada progressively became more political and less military in its
functions, although it retained the core unit, *barbara,* and the top role
of *Abba Dula*, as critical elements of the military organization.[16]

## SYSTEMIC ANALYSIS OF THE OROMO POLITY

So far, the institutions were presented one at a time, although some
incidental information was also offered about linkages between
them. Muda, for instance, has such a role linking Gada and Qallu
institutions. It also dramatizes role reversal between Gada and Qallu
and keeps these leaders, and the nation, conscious of the fact that
*authority is divided and separated, by design.* Below is a continua-
tion of the macro-level analysis that goes deeper into the structure

of the political system. We approach the institutions here from a primarily relational perspective. How do the institutions work as components of a single sociopolitical system? What elements of coordination or sub-ordination are in evidence? This is the aspect of the political system that is virtually missing in the historic and current literature on Oromo institutions. In the ethnographies of Haberland, Baxter and Bassi, they are *simplistically described seriatim*, one institution at a time, and they are left hanging like so many beads on a string. The frailty of the resulting structure is a product of poor ethnography, not a feature of the political system under investigation.

Three of the four institutions under discussion—Gada, Hariyya, and moieties—are made up of *cross-cutting ascriptive groups that work in tandem as elements of the same political system*. In Western Cultures, "ascriptive" usually means "un-free," because one becomes a member of ascriptive groups by birth not by choice, in contrast to voluntary associations where the individual chooses to become a member.

Borana ascriptive groups work as *alternative organizations*. People are free to try to achieve their political purposes through one or the other institution. That gives the people choice of political affiliation and action. In other words, one is born into these groups but one is free to activate one's affiliations with one or another group in order to achieve one's political goals. The institutions are partly specialized in function and partly they have overlapping responsibilities. Two of the institutions, Gada and Moieties-clans, are tied to each other as interacting and/or mutually regulating bodies.

It is worth noting that the diagram below, Fig. 3.1, is a simplified representation of the institutions. Within the Gada institution there is an organization of individual gada classes and their leaders. Within the moiety also, there is an organization of clans and lineages and their respective leaders. Similarly the age-set system consists of eleven age cohorts ranging in age from 0 to 88. How many age-sets have surviving members, at any one time, is entirely a function of demography.

Because our focus is largely on the macro-level institutions, we have not paid much attention to the lower order organization of the gada classes, age-sets, clans and lineages.

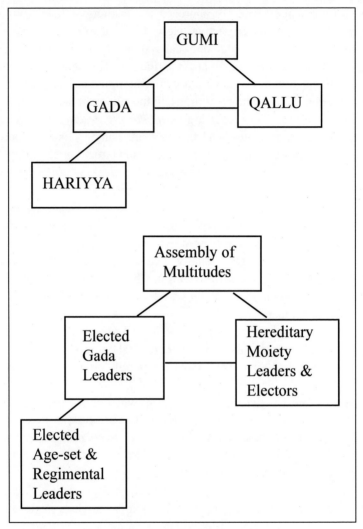

Fig. 3.1, The Structure of the Oromo Polity

This chart represents the macro-level organization of the Oromo polity, showing the relative position of the four institutions. In this presentation, Gada and Qallu stand side by side as coordinate institutions and are both subordinated to the authority of Gumi, the national assembly. The age-set system is subordinated to Gada and performs its most important military functions under the authority of the Raba-Gada Assemblies.

## Special Functions of the Institutions

There is a fairly clear set of functions assigned to the national assembly and the age-set system. However, the relationship between the co-ordinate institutions—Gada and Qallu—is more complex and more ambiguous. Sometimes, these institutions are in an adversarial relationship with each other, at other times, they are territorially and functionally segregated from each other, and perform complementary functions that are quite distinct.

Gada and Qallu are the only institutions that form the ongoing core of the political system. They are continually engaged in daily activities. The National Assembly meets only once every eight years and the age-sets are mobilized only in times of war. We are, of course, ignoring the continuous social function of age-sets and focusing, at this time, only on their military activities.

Leaders of the two coordinate institutions differ in terms of their recruitment, succession to office, nature of their authority, and their term of office. The first type of office is *elected*, has authority over *all Borana* for a period of *eight years*; the second type is *hereditary*, has authority over *half of Borana*, but stays in office *for life*. In all three respects the two institutions complement each other.

When they are engaged in *adversarial* relationships, their functions tend to overlap, and they operate in one and the same political arena as opposed entities in demanding the peoples loyalties. When they are *complementary*, they are physically apart and they avoid each other and offer similar conflict adjudication or mediation services to the people. The two modalities, i.e. generational and kinship loyalties, are never mutually exclusive, since one or the other is always available as on option. Members of gada classes or clans, respectively, seek their services, leaning toward one or the other, according to the abilities and reputation of the leaders. Any attempt to give a simplistic and univocal analysis of these institutions is be misleading. It is a *complex, multivocal, ambiguous,* and *dynamic* relationship.

The adversarial aspect of their relationship can be easily provoked by simply posing the following question to any Borana: "Who is more senior or more powerful—the Abba Gada or the Qallu?" This is a surefire question that will generate heated debates. How they answer the question will reveal which of the optional political affiliations they have chosen to activate. Some will say that the Abba Gada is senior because he is the ruler of all the people, whereas the Qallu has authority over only one half of the people. Others will say the Qallus are senior because no gada officer can come to power without their blessing. In more exaggerated debates, people will also say that the Abba Gada is the true leader of Borana and the Qallus are only his *"makkala"* or ritual assistants. They add that, in the past, the Qallus were just like the other assistants in the service of the Gada Assembly. Those who make this statement may or may not believe what they say, but they say it, anyway, when they are trying to cut the Warra Qallu down to size.

Other contrasting viewpoints have to do with the symbolically powerful *sacred* and *mysterious* characteristics of the Qallu, versus the relatively pragmatic, *secular* and *transparent* characteristics of gada leadership. Both perspectives are justified by Borana custom and myth. In recent decades, gada leaders enjoyed greater legitimacy than the hereditary Qallu because the Qallu were said to have been vulnerable to corruption and to have done some illegitimate power-grabbing during and since the era of Emperor Menelik.

It is futile to try to "resolve" this ambiguity or reconcile the divergent views in order to arrive at "the truth." As Donald Levine so powerfully demonstrated in *Wax and Gold: Tradition and Innovation in Ethiopian Culture,* ambiguity has its proper place in political life. However, ambiguity takes a very different form in Oromo democracy. It takes the form of a *penumbra of meanings* that surrounds the coordinate institutions.

---

There is sustained debate concerning the *seniority, authority, antiquity,* and *legitimacy* of the Gada and Qallu institutions and all four issues are discussed heartily in Borana assemblies and around the family hearth.[17]

---

In practice, this ambiguity means that the people have freedom of choice, i.e., they can appeal a case of conflict to the Qallu Council or the Gada Council. The Qallus have authority to *mediate* cases of conflict in moieties or between clans. The Abba Gadas have authority to *mediate* or *adjudicate* conflict within or between gada classes. There is a certain measure of functional redundancy in this allocation of responsibilities. As a result, there is ample opportunity for jurisdictional crises. Of two parties in conflict one side might want to take its case to the Qallu Council and the other might want to take it to the Gada Council for mediation. That often produces a deadlock and the case must then be taken to the National Assembly. Whether or not the assembly considers it to be worthy of its attention is, of course, another matter. One basis for choosing the Gada council over the Qallu council is in situations where conflict cannot be resolved through mediation alone, since the Gada Assembly has the power to enforce its decisions, but the Qallu council does not.

### Areas where the functions are distinct

When the issues are framed in terms of war and peace, however, the division of labor sheds all its ambiguity. Raba-Gada assemblies alone can decide whether the nation is going to be at war or at peace. They and they alone have the authority of organizing, leading, or overseeing warfare. They alone have the authority to summon fighters from the clans via their respective clan representatives—the *jallaba*—to commandeer horses for the cavalry, and, thus, to put the nation on the war path. *The Qallu are wholly excluded from the entire domain that involves the legitimate use of force.* This division of labor is acknowledged by both the Warra Qallu and the Warra Bokku alike.

Gada leaders alone are empowered to adjudicate cases of conflict and to enforce their decision through the use of sanctions. They can punish offenders using a variety of techniques that stop just short of capital punishment. *In collaboration with the clans, as distinguished from the Warra Qallu,* they can punish the offenders by depriving them of access to water resources, banishing them from the land or excluding them from all life crisis services. They can even curse the offenders, and when they do the victims often die, *somehow,* and the "somehow" is left dangling for good and sufficient reasons, since capital punishment is formally in the hands of national courts of law. That is an issue about which there is considerable tension between national and traditional governments.

In short, whatever organized monopoly of violence there is in Oromo life—for use in conducting wars or maintaining societal discipline—it is in the hands of the Gada Assembly or the assembly of gada assemblies called the Gumi. It is fitting, therefore, that the age-sets (convertible into age-regiments) are accountable to the Gada leaders and have virtually nothing to do with the Warra Qallu, except in the sense that they may be called upon to guard the defenseless Qallu's community from raiders.[18] The sedentary Qallu community sits, like a fatted calf, well fed and ready for slaughter. It will indeed be slaughtered, as in the Guji-Borana war of 1946, unless Warra Bokku and age-sets are on the lookout for its safety.

During his term of office, the Abba Gada-in-council is also charged with the responsibility of overseeing all political and ritual life-cycle events. When the Qallu lineages take part in these rites of passage and political transition ceremonies, they do so as participants not as leaders, as clients not ritual or ceremonial experts. Like all other members of their society, they too must go through all the life crises. However, the Qallu himself is not required to go through the normal rites of passage since every stage of his life, from birth, through marriage and death, is unique.

### Competing claims on loyalty, as people vote with their feet

One of the most interesting types of pressure the institutions exert on each other is mediated by public sentiment and the character of the leaders. People are free to seek political support from members of their moiety and/or clan or they can try to mobilize support among their own gada class. In this situation, people are operating in two optional arenas and are, thus, able to "vote with their feet."

The net effect of this freedom of choice is the differential and variable empowerment of the officers who head one or the other institution. The empowerment of the officers is a function of the political loyalty and popular support they command, expressed in the frequency and significance of the cases bought before them—a service which is often rewarded with gifts. The more *unjust, incompetent, or litigious* the leaders are, the less likely that the cases of conflict will come before them. Character plays a role in this informal aspect of the system of mutual regulation, and it becomes apparent in the life and work of all the living Abba Gadas or the two Qallus who were, in recent decades, in positions of political, military, judicial, legislative *or* ritual leadership.

I was in Borana in the 1960-68 gada period when Jaldessa Liban was in office and continued to visit for some decades thereafter. I, therefore, became personally acquainted with Jaldessa and with four other Abba Gadas, the two Qallu houses, and one prominent age-set leader. As a result, I became conscious of how the character of each Abba Gada or Qallu influenced their conduct in office and the nature of the office itself.

## *Authority and character: personal encounters with leaders*

Of the active and retired Abba Gadas that I have known, some like Madha Galma (1952-60) or Jaldessa Liban (1960-68) were fairly effective leaders. Jaldessa was a gentle man, loved by his people. His great feat was in mobilizing his luba and his clan to rebuild El Morowwa, the well of his ancestors that had caved in. He was, however, severely criticized for the egregious delays in the performance of the ritual-ceremonial cycle. Madha (1952-60), on the other hand, was a celebrated warrior who had no verbal skills to speak of. What he lacked in eloquence he made up for by his courage and his physical presence—which was always impressive and somewhat intimidating. He shunned the lavish praise that people heaped upon him for his military accomplishments.

Other Abba Gadas, like Guyyo Boru (1944-52) and Gobba Bule (1968-76), were well known and highly respected mediators and adjudicators in their society and they continued, informally to serve their luba long after handing over power to their successors. Gobba Bule was a powerful, if somewhat impulsive, speaker. Guyyo Boru was the great peace maker: his home was a veritable magnet; his wisdom, humility, and extensive knowledge were such that he commanded the deepest respect of his people. He had a gentle, avuncular face, a soothing voice and an uncanny ability to pacify the most contentious litigants who came before him. His reputation probably created changes in public opinion that helped to bring about the shift in power away from the litigious Warra Qallu (moiety leaders) to the more astute Warra Bokku (gada leaders).[19]

Of the two Qallu houses, the house of the senior Qallu of Oditu were much more conservative and commanded greater respect. The Karrayyu on the other hand allowed various forms of laxity in their community, such as the introduction of alcoholic beverages. As a result, the level of drunkenness in the community was such that it drew the ire of many Borana. As will be described later, my main encounter with them was on the occasion of the solar eclipse of 1973, when the office was shaken down to its roots, but survived.

I was better acquainted with the senior Qallu house of Oditu because their residence, in Liban, was not far from the seat of the luba government (Olla Arbora) where I was living for several months. The Qallu was a gentle child in his early teens named Kura Tutto.

He was under the guardianship of his middle-aged half brother, Boru Tutto. The Qallu lineage was effectively split along a functional line of fission: one side retaining ritual authority, the other taking the office of balabbat and in the service of the provincial government. Boru effectively managed the Qallu's affairs, and his younger brother Jatani was a junior balabbat.

The Qallu lineage had split a generation earlier and the two branches held the position of Qallu and senior balabbat respectively. Although this was seemingly an orderly division of labor, the Warra Qallu were beset by litigation among themselves. Instead of being exemplary peacemakers, as the culture demands, they were running frequently to the government courts to settle their own disputes concerning succession and division of labor between the political (balabbat) and ritual (Qallu) lineages. The Warra Qallu are thought of as the peaceful and peace-making arm of Borana government, who, sadly, could not keep peace in their own ranks.[20]

The great constitutional changes that deprived the Warra Qallu of their electoral authority were brought about by the Gumi of Gada Jilo Aga (1976-84)—an Abba Gada from the powerful Digalu clan. I knew him as young man in the junior warrior grade: he had the makings of a adequate leader, but not much more. At that stage I had no way of anticipating what he was later to accomplish. Now, with the benefit of hindsight, I realize that it is the fact that he was wearing historic mantle of a renowned lawmaker—Dawwe Gobbo (1706-14), his 8th cyclical gada ancestor—that drove him to persuade the Gumi to make a fundamental change in the Oromo constitution.

The above account of the Gada institution is, therefore, a composite profile that takes into consideration the character and conduct of many recent and historic leaders that is quite different from the normative descriptions offered by writers who never saw or knew a single Abba Gada and never set foot in the Gada Assembly.

### *Uprooting of leaders: secular and ritual methods*

For a variety of reasons—of which character, ethics, and competence are the most important—leaders may either exceed or fall short of their mandate in the way they exercise their authority. When that happens, Oromo society has methods of controlling the damage.

Over and above the laudable and the not-so-laudable character traits which the Warra Qallu and Warra Bokku exhibit, and the formal and informal reciprocal influences that constrain their behavior, there is also the superordinate authority exercised by the National Assembly over all institutions. Compared with the Gada and Qallu assemblies, the Gumi has functions which are sharply defined. There is no ambiguity here—no need for it, since there is no coordinate institution with which it must share power.

A most important political function of the Gumi is the authority to review the activities of the gada class in power and to decide whether the leaders are fit to complete their term of office, and continue to lead the gada class (and the nation) for the rest of its active career. Their work can be evaluated on rational-legal grounds.

There is nothing hypothetical about the power of the national assembly in this regard. They have the right to impeach gada leaders and have done so on several occasions in the last three centuries (1700-present). In other words, this is not a dormant provision in the Oromo constitution, that causes leaders to behave themselves, merely because a constitutional threat is hanging over their heads. On the other hand, Borana does not have a rational-legal method of ridding themselves of the hereditary, sacred figure of the Qallu. Appropriately, however, Oromo have a divine procedure for accomplishing the same purpose.

I have described this procedure in a paper published in 1979 and titled "La mort du soleil: signes naturels, tabous et authorité politique," (The death of the sun: natural signs, taboos and political authority) in G. Francillon and P. Menget, editors, *Soleil est mort, L'ecplise totale de soleil du 30 Juin 1973,* (Nanterre, 1979). It is a report of participant-observations of the total solar eclipse sighted in Marsabit, Kenya, in 1973. For many years prior to this event, I had been told that when and if "the sun died," the Borana may remove from office any elected, appointed, or hereditary leader—including the Qallu. When the eclipse is sighted, the Qallu may, for instance, be held responsible for the ominous event and the misfortunes that ensue from it. Of course, the same technique may also be employed to remove any kind of political or ritual leader, when the rational-legal method of impeachment has failed, or is deemed to be less likely to succeed. [21]

In the first week of July, 1973, a week after the sighting of the total solar eclipse, the chief of the Marsabit Borana—Chief Jilo Toukena (photo, p. 91)—was removed from an office he had held for more than three decades, since colonial times. Similarly, the position of the Qallu of the Sabbo moiety was severely shaken, but he survived the crisis, mainly because the full eclipse was not actually sighted in Southern Ethiopia (Yavello) where the Qallu of the Sabbo has his permanent residence. Significantly, no questions were raised concerning the Qallu of the Gona moiety who lives about the same distance away from the path of totality, i.e., the band of territory in which the total solar eclipse was visible. Both Qallus villages saw the same kind of partial eclipse—a non-event. Yet one Qallu community was in turmoil over the *news* of the eclipse from Marsabit, while the other Qallu was unaffected. In other words, the treatment was administered selectively on the basis of the people's diagnosis of the current deficits in leadership. Hence, the procedure had a rational basis, despite the mystical context in which it occurred.

Of the two coordinate institutions presented here, Gada is more important in the political sphere. The rest of this chapter will, therefore, be devoted to that institution and the next chapter will present the Qallus and their moieties viewed from a historic perspective.

## Gada: the Generational Organization

Throughout recorded history, "gada classes," known as *luba*, succeeded each other every eight years in governing, waging wars, conquering new territories, assimilating aliens, and, in the process, they helped to make the Oromo nation what it is—one of the very largest in the African continent. *Oromo people created Gada, and Gada created the Oromo nation.*

Before going any further with the description of the Gada System, however, it is necessary to deal with a terminological confusion in the literature. Anthropologists refer to gada classes as "generation-sets." We will not use the term "set" in describing gada classes because the word "set" is a diminutive term inappropriate for the scale of the phenomena under discussion. In common English speech, the word "set" is used to describe such things as a bunch of similar tools in a tool kit, a clutch of eggs in a birds nest, a tea set, a chess set etc., all minute collections of items. An organization that served as the main engine driving the great migration of the Oromo nation, a political military system that took control of an area the size of Germany in eight decades and, in the process, changed the face of the Horn of Africa, cannot be described as consisting of "sets." It is an egregious misuse of the English language. Academic ethics requires that we adjust our language to the magnitude of the phenomena we observe. Otherwise our characterizations look like caricatures—where misrepresentations of scale are welcome humorous devices or oblique words of ridicule. In the present study, therefore, the *luba* is a "gada class," not a "generation set." With that understanding we can proceed with the analysis.[22]

Five successive gada classes make up a generation that occupies a complete hemicycle of 40 years. We can define the gada class or luba as a segment of a generation that assumes power for a period of eight years, whereas the gada period or simply gada is the years when the members of the class stay in power as the rulers. Stated differently, luba is a group of people and gada is the term of office of the leader of that group, and by extension it is the name of the era during which the leader and his luba were in power.

At any one time, there are ten or eleven active gada classes in Borana. The eleventh class may be viewed as being marginal or entirely outside of the gada life cycle, because the members are in fact in a liminal state of ritual sanctity. Compared with other parts of Oromo country, the number of gada classes *in* the Gada Cycle seems to have been a variable factor. Some regions had as few as five and the largest number recorded, such as the Borana system, is eleven. This variation is not critical. The important fact is that the luba is strictly defined as an 8-year segment of a genealogical generation of 40 years. If an individual belongs to a particular luba, all his sons, regardless of age, belong to the luba that follows his own by forty years or five gada grades. The Tulama-Oromo refer to this law as *afurtama abbakotti*, or "The forty years of my father." This is the law that seems to have been observed everywhere in Oromo land.

This rule, which was very rigid, caused many structural problems that Oromo society had to grapple with throughout its history. I have analyzed this problem in depth elsewhere (*Gada*, 1973, ch. 3-6). Simply stated, the problem is that under the influence of this law, the gada class gradually evolves from an age-homogeneous to an age-heterogeneous group.[23] The aim of this book is not to analyze the underlying structural transformation but to focus on the political consequences of the arrangement of the population into segments of generations that cross-cut the age-sets. The segment of a generation, called luba or "gada class," enjoys a great deal of autonomy: it has an internal government.

### Ebba and mura: the power of blessing and decision making

Some provisions have been made to ensure that the electors do not usurp power themselves. The electors can never assume a position of authority in warfare or lawmaking. They and their kinsmen are forever barred from membership in the gada councils which they help to recruit. They are said to have *ebba* "blessing" or ritual power, but not *mura* "cutting" or decision-making power.

Why should the word "to cut" (*muru*, vt. *murti,* n.) have any connection with the concept of "decision-making?" I believe that it derives from the nature of Oromo deliberative assemblies. All democracies face the crisis of protracted discussions that can be endless, unless there is a procedure for bringing each debate to a conclusion acceptable to all, or nearly all, the participants. In these meetings the Abba Gada exercises his power in two remarkable ways. First, he can wind up the meeting when he feels that he can formulate a viewpoint that is shared by most. It requires considerable wisdom to sense when that moment has arrived. He presents his summation by declaring, "Would there be anything but peace, if we came to such and such a conclusion?" If the response is, "Peace! Peace! Peace!" and if that is the overwhelming voice of the assembly, the conclusion is adopted. The leader is then said to have "cut" *(murte)* the discussion.

If, on the other hand, the discussion is still overheated, if people are not listening attentively to what others are saying, or what the Abba Sera, in his capacity of mediator, is proposing, he may suspend the discussions in another way. At the moment when the debate has become irrational, hostile, and unproductive, he may stop the meeting to give the participants a protracted blessing. Roughly speaking, the more badly nerves are frayed, the longer the blessing. I saw this happen on one occasion when young men had spoken in a deeply offensive manner to members of the senior Gada Council. The Abba Gada was presiding, seated under the shade of a large podocarpus tree. They were trying to decide what kind of penalties should be imposed on the offenders. The meeting was continuing well into the second day, when the insulted councilors lost their temper, and began shouting at the top of their voices, while the offending clan responded in kind. The meeting was virtually out of control when the Abba Gada made a surprise announcement. He told the assemblymen to turn toward the east. All the participants who were seated in a semi-circular arrangement around the Abba Gada stood up and turned toward *"il boru,"* the place "where the sun rises," the place of origin of the Borana, the cradleland. In that position the Abba Gada gave them a blessing that lasted some 15 minutes, or so it seemed, I did not time it. It was a type of slow call-and-response cycle of blessings, that stilled much of the anger. When the meeting resumed, tempers had greatly subsided.

It is important to realize that, in this instance, the two concepts of *ebba* and *mura* were wonderfully intertwined. The presiding officer momentarily suspended the meeting by "blessing" (ebba) the participants. In other words, he arrested a political meeting by means of a purely ritual act—an act that was, nevertheless, highly effective, and allowed the assembly to bring its affairs to a close.

All democratic societies must find ways of controlling tempers, keeping adversaries engaged in rational dialogue, and bringing their debates to a reasonable conclusion. It is no surprise, therefore, that, in such societies, the word "to cut" is associated with the concept of "ending discussion" and, thus, "making a decision." After thinking for so long about the language of democracy in Oromo culture, it was no surprise for me to learn that the English word "to decide" also has a similar etymology. It derives from the Latin *caedere* "to cut."

The differentiation of the concepts of *mura* and *ebba* does not result in a sharp division of labor between the political and ritual domains. In limited areas, namely in intra-moiety matters, especially concerning elections, the Qallu too has some power to resolve conflict through mediation. Conversely, the Abba Gada also acts as peacemaker in the angry exchanges that take place in assemblies.

On one critical ritual occasion, when Abba Gada and Qallu are in one and the same ritual arena, the Abba Gada submits to the authority of the Qallu. Conversely, in political life-cycle events, where the Abba Gada presides and the Qallus participate but do not lead: they submit to the secular authority of the Abba Gada and the ritual authority of the Bokku—the ritual leader of the gada class.

Some scholars, such as Baxter (cited) and Bassi (2005: 255) have chosen to paint Borana political life with a broad brush and suggest that nearly everything they do within the framework of gada classes or age-sets is ritual, not political, in character. They do so by greatly inflating the *ebba* (blessing) factor and diminishing or ignoring the concept of *mura* (decision-making) or entirely failing to acknowledge the distinction. It would, therefore, be very useful to cite a most revealing conversation with Galma Liban that sheds some light on this matter. I asked Galma to clarify the language used in the Gumi. I said that in all the rituals I attended in Borana, the plea, "Jila beka! Jila beka!" was made to reprimand people who do not behave themselves appropriately. [It means "Know the rituals!" or "Respect the rituals!"] I mentioned that fact and asked Galma if there was a similar language that was employed in the Gumi. Galma shot back with the answer "Gumi is not jila!" or "the National Assembly is not a ritual!" I was taken aback by the force of his response. I thought all such public events had a ritual or celebratory aspect and that they were all called *"jila,"* but I was mistaken. Galma went on to say, emphatically, that events such as the *Gumi* (the National Assembly meeting) or *lallaba* (the induction of the newly elected Gada leaders) or *balli* (the gada power handover ceremony) are not *jila* or "rituals." He illustrated the distinction by saying, "In all rituals, people speak in *afan seeda* "the language of ritual," i.e., a ritual argot or dialect in which all references to violence (fire, flood, knife, spear, death etc.) are replaced by oblique argot terms. That is how you can tell what ritual is. "And again," he said, "people carry their spears and firearms when they go to the Gumi and the lallaba. They do not carry weapons when they go to rituals such as *Muda* [the anointment of the Qallu] or *dannisa* [fatherhood ritual]. Instead, they carry ritual objects," i.e. branches and wreaths of sacred trees.[24]

Galma added: *Gumi fula jila miti, fula waranaati,* "the National Assembly is not a place of ritual, it is a place of war." I asked him to explain what he meant and he said that it is the Warra Bokku, not the Warra Qallu who make decisions about the law, and that they sometimes resort to a war of words. More importantly, they punish offenders and use force, if they must. Hence, they bear arms. That is why Gumi is said to be the place of war, not of rituals. In these revealing statements, the elder has drawn a clear distinction between ritual activity, the domain of the Warra Qallu, and political-legal-military-activities, the domain of the Warra Bokku. He also specifies the nature of the language, conduct, and gear of the participants in the two situations. Most importantly, he indicates that the Qallu are the men of peace and blessings par excellence. As such, they are prohibited from bearing arms, shedding blood, making laws, and imposing penalties. They are excluded from the highest decision-making body, the Gumi, which they attend as honored guests, but not as active participants.

When Baxter describes the gada life cycle as a "River of Blessings" made up of endless rituals, it is a mis-understanding of the wide range of activities encompassed by Gada. Ritual leaders, are excluded from all these activities, except dispute settlement, where their role is still that of peace makers, a task that is consistent with their non-violent ritual leadership.

> **It is now clear that warfare, lawmaking, decision making, adjudication, punishment of offenders, the election contest, the proclamation of leaders, the transfer of Gada authority, and the Gumi National Assembly are not part of the domain Borana culture defines as *jila*, "ritual," even if they occur at definite turning points in the life cycle and appear to us as rites of passage.**

This clarification will be reflected in all my descriptions of the Gada Cycle henceforth: I shall use four different terms for the transitional events in the Gada life cycle: rites of passage *(jila)*, political transition ceremonies *(lallaba, balli...)*, meetings *(cora)*, and conventions *(Gumi)*. Only the first of these is ritual in character.

## The Gada Life Cycle

During its life cycle, every luba or gada class passes through a series of functionally differentiated stages. Most stages are demarcated by *rites of passage* or *political transition ceremonies*. At each stage, it assumes different responsibilities vis-à-vis the rest of the society. The organization of the Gada class and its activities change from one stage to the next. It is most complex in the middle of the life cycle, GADA (VI) and it is severely reduced in the Yuba grades of semi-retirement. It is stripped of all complexity at the beginning and end of the cycle, DABBALLE (I) and GADA MOJJI (XI) grades, the liminal stages. Beyond that, in the Jarsa stage (XII+), men have no political or ritual Gada life cycle roles.

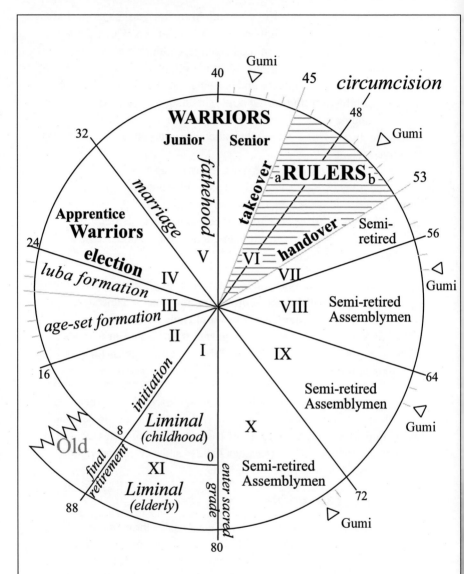

Fig 3.2a The Gada Cycle (English vesion)

I-XI  Grades        I & XI sacred grades        0-88 Maximum age

Two types of life crises: *rites of passage* & **political transitions**

△  **Gumi Gayo: Assembly of Multidues**

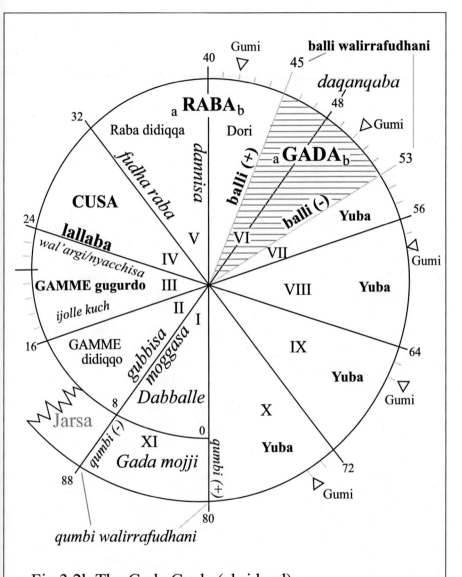

Fig 3.2b The Gada Cycle (abridged)

I-XI  Grades    I & XI sacred grades    0-88 Maximum age

Life crises: *rites of passage* & **political transitions**

△  **Gumi Gayo: Assembly of Multidues at Gayo**

## Gada Grades: the Stages of Development

Gada has eleven different stages of development. These stages have been described in far greater detail in my earlier study of the Gada System.[25] Here I give only a highly abridged sketch. At each stage, the member has a different hairstyle or headgear that lets others know where he is on the life cycle: people adjust their conduct toward him accordingly. That very approach is at the root of their very successful method of political socialization. So conceived, political socialization is a social *process*, not a ritual *event*.

The Borana have no generic name for "grade." In our terminology, the stages in the life course of a luba are referred to as "generation grades," or "gada grades," or simply "grades." These grades are associated with the following statuses, roles, activities and transitions:

(1) The earliest grade (DABBALLE I) is a stage of childhood that is ritually protected. The children are often raised by surrogate parents, so as to give their young parents (Vb,VIa) an opportunity to fulfill their military obligations and to protect the children from violence, raids and counter-raids. They are liminal figures who have neither gender, nor name, and serve as intermediaries between man and God. Imbued with these sacred qualities, they and their mothers are honored daily by the society.[26] The grade ends with their naming ritual.

(2) Older children, in the second grade (Jr. GAMME II), are given the responsibility of looking after livestock, but have no role whatever in political life. They do not have any formal leadership. They often go on *fora:* they take the family herds away from the parental settlements, nomadize extensively, and lead a life of adventure.

(3) During the years of late adolescence and early adulthood, in the third grade (Sr. GAMME III), the boys are initiated into age-sets *(Ijolle Cuch)* and gada classes *(Nyacchisa-Wal'argi)*. Their father's luba and the Qallu assemblies elect their six leaders *(Hayyu Adula)*. For the rest of its active career, the luba is governed by that council.

(4) At the next stage (CUSA IV) all members of the luba become apprentice warriors, and if they are old enough they begin to take part in raids and major military campaigns. They now follow their seniors in campaigns organized by the latter. The grade ends with the marriage ritual of the oldest members, the *barbara* cohort.

(5) The next stage is that of junior warriorhood (RABA V). The men marry but they are not allowed to have children. If children are born, they are generally given up for adoption outside of Borana society. In the past they were abandoned to die *(gata)*. At this

stage, family life is severely curtailed, because they devote a great deal of their time to hunting and warfare. Upon completion of the first part of the fifth grade (Va), on the fortieth year of the gada cycle, they perform the fatherhood ritual and start raising sons. From then on, for another 8 years, their sons enter the DABBALLE (I) grade: these are the children that are often given to surrogate parents (Wata) for eight years, so that the fathers can continue their careers as warriors unencumbered by the restrictions of child-raising and without exposing children to the danger of raids and counter-raids. The fathers are now in the senior warrior grade, RABA DORI (Vb), which continues for another 5 years. Throughout the Raba grade the leaders live in a village, *Olla Arbora,* that serves as the seat of government for their luba.

From now on, the position of father and son are linked. The rites of passage and political transition ceremonies of the generations in the same *gogessa* are simultaneous or occur in quick succession.

(6) They then enter the sixth grade, GADA (VI), and assume power as leaders of the entire society in the *balli* (power takeover) ceremony. Their community, Olla Arbora, now becomes the seat of the Gada Assembly in power and the political center of Borana. Disputes that cannot be settled in clan or luba councils are brought to the ruling Gada Assembly.

Mid-way through their term, on the 4th (or 5th) year, they are circumcised. That occurs at the same time as the naming ceremony of their sons at the end of the DABBALLE (I) grade. Although circumcision has great significance in their individual lives, as a class, they are now simply 'marking time,' linking up with the rest of the system.

One of their major obligations is to organize and lead the National Assembly meeting, held on the 5th or 6th year of their term of office. On the occasion of this convention (marked with triangles on the Gada Cycle), all the Gada councils and assemblies of Borana come together. This is a grand assembly and carries the highest authority in the land.

The luba remains in power for eight years and it hands over power to the next luba at a designated place, called Nura, and a designated time, the month of *gurrandhala.* Time-reckoning experts play a significant role in determining the time of the handing over of power.[27] The ceremony by which power is transferred from one luba to the next is called *balli* or *balli-wal-irra-fudhu,* "the transfer of Ostrich feathers." It is the same ceremony mentioned earlier, but the handing over of power is now done by the outgoing class.

The following four grades (VII, VIII, IX, X) consist of four distinct gada classes, although they are collectively known as *yuba.* In these grades—which last 3, 8, 8 and 8 years respectively—the luba is said to be in the *"yuba"* or *"yuboma"* state, i.e., the state of *partial retirement.* The luba continues its activities informally as a self-governing body, but it has a greatly restricted set of responsibilities in the larger political arena. They no longer have a seat of luba government (ya'a).[28] The luba now takes a central role in the national convention (Gumi). This happens once every eight years, during the 27 years of partial retirement. The Gada leaders who oversee the meetings are called *Abbotin Gada* "the Gada fathers," or *liccho dullatti* "the old whips," in contrast to the Abba Gada *fit'e* ("apical") who is in power (GADA VI) and serves as the *convener* and the *main presiding officer.*

At this convention, representatives of the entire second half the gada cycle (Vb- X) come together to review the laws and make new laws, to judge the adequacy of the group in power (GADA VI), to assess their successes and failures, and if they are found wanting, to remove them from office and replace them with others. Hence, the society delegates limited kinds of power to the luba leaders, for a limited period of time, and they can be uprooted midway through their term of office if they are unfit. This is the Oromo version of "government by the people."

The active *(Raba-Gada)* and semi-retired *(Yuba)* grades have oversight responsibilities throughout the Gumi convention. As such the Gumi can be seen as an assembly of Gada Assemblies. But, as Marco Bassi (2005:171 ff) has amply demonstrated, it is also an assembly of all Borana clans, who hold caucuses while the convention is in progress and submit their recommendations to the Gumi through their representatives in the Gada Assemblies (*hayyus* and *jallabas*).

One important feature of the life cycle is the temporal displacement of the ruling grade, which two key authors, Pecci and Bassi, have completely misunderstood (see note 48, p. 243, below). It may be useful to visualize the life cycle as a historic clock divided into ten eight-year "sections," and the position of the power grade, which is the 6th "section," as having been ***displaced clockwise***—I repeat, "displaced clockwise,"—by five years, altering the size of the adjoining "sections," but leaving the rest of the clock intact. In other words, this alteration lengthens the 5th "section" by 5 years and shortens the 7th "section" by 5 years. That arrangement leaves the 6th and most important section intact. It is 8 years long, but it is not the same 8 years as the other sections.[29]

On the eightieth year of the gada cycle, when the luba completes the four grades of partial retirement (YUBA VII-X), the members enter the final grade (GADA MOJJI XI). This is a sacred grade. At this stage, the members of the gada class enjoy great respect as ritual intermediaries between man and God, but they are deprived of nearly all secular, political, judicial, and military authority. Their entry into the sacred grade happens at the same time as the fatherhood ceremony of their sons at the end of RABA grade (Va).

They end their active gada careers with the final retirement ritual. This takes place at the end of the sacred grade (XI), on the 88th year of the gada cycle. This event is structurally linked to the circumcision of their sons, the luba in power (VI), and the naming ceremony of their grandsons, the dabballe (I). Please note that all three events are on the same axis on the Gada Cycle, refer to the same *gogessa* (patriclass), and take place at about the same time.

On that grand, memorable event, the retiring elders come together for one final rite of passage called *qumbi-wal-irra-fudhu* or "the handing over of incense." The peer group gathers in and around the massive U-shaped complex of ritual pavilions *(galma)*, constructed for each one of the retiring elders. Inside the pavilions, surrounded by their age mates, the old men give an emotional account of all their accomplishments, as warriors and hunters, to their sons, and to Borana. Those who are able to give a ringing recitation of impressive accomplishments and do so eloquently are praised by the listeners. They must be truthful, however, for they are exposed mercilessly by their peers, if they mention any feats they did not perform.

This rite is the formal end of the gada life cycle. Beyond that, the elders have no authority—political, military, judicial, ritual or otherwise.[30] They are called *jarsa*, "old." In contrast to gerontocracies, "old" means out of power, for old age per se confers no power whatsoever. If the men were retired prematurely, they are called *il-man jarsa*, "the children of the aged." In recent decades the numbers of these retired classes increased—for complex demographic and structural reasons we cannot go into here.[31] As a result of many adaptive changes that took place in recent decades, the retired and semi-retired classes have been reinstated in the political order. Their representatives make up a junior council *(Hayyu Garba)*. They serve as assistants to the Adula in the Gada Assembly and live in a village, Olla Batu, adjoining the Olla Arbora, the seat of luba government.

We can sum up the meaning of the life cycle as follows:

> **The GADA LIFE CYCLE ensures that all generations take turns in getting ritual protection in childhood and in assuming authority and/or responsibility to perform domestic labor, take part in wars, govern their people, make laws, mediate or adjudicate conflicts and, during their partial retirement, sit in judgment of the ruling gada class, give legislative leadership to their people and end the life cycle in a sacred state and a day of reckoning. All these activities are performed and statuses are achieved successively during the life cycle. As such, Gada is an effective method of distributing authority and responsibility across the entire life course. It is the tool the people use to realize their commitment to inter-generational equity and the separation of powers on a grand sequential scale.**

The Gada System is not a gerontocracy or "government by elders" because it is people in the middle of the life course (age 45-53) who hold the greatest authority, not those in later stages. The rulers are in their prime—although their elders *and their juniors* (the warriors) are a countervailing political force. In other words, Gada is an elaborate, well-constructed system for distributing power among all the generation segments of the society. All generation classes enjoy different kinds of power at different stages of the life course. It is a type of "separation of powers" that the West has not even dreamt about except perhaps in a fictitious, utopian world.

Western democracies are very unjust in the manner they distribute power across generations and age groups: those who are in the prime of life hog most of the authority, power and wealth, whereas the young and the elderly are politically, economically, and psychologically marginalized.

What was offered above is a profile of Gada—one of the key political institutions of the Oromo. It is important to realize, however, that the institution was greatly simplified in order to view it on a macro level in relation to the other institutions. For a more complete account of the gada life cycle, of the transition rites and ceremonies, and a detailed case study of the election contests, see *Gada: Three Approaches to the Study of African Society*, 1973, or the forthcoming second revised edition, 2007, which incorporates much information gathered by this writer and others authors, in several fields of knowledge, including astronomy, archaeology, and mathematics.

# NOTES

1. Herbert S. Lewis, "Aspects of Oromo Political Culture," *Journal of Oromo Studies,* 1(1994): 53-58.

2. (Milano: Franco Angeli, 1996).

3. We do not consider the age-set system here because it occurs only in Borana and is a recent innovation. However, the *barbara* sub-set of the luba, remains the core of the fighting force, regardless of the age-structure of the luba.

4. Antoine d'Abbadie, "Sur les Oromo: Grande nation africaine," *Societé Scientifique de Bruxelles,* 4(1880): 176.

5. *Ibid.,* 174. Note how *order of birth* serves as a *queuing device.*

6. *Ibid.,* 180.

7. Bairu Tafla, *Atsmä Giorgis and his Work,* pp. 119-135. Bahrey, in C.F. Beckingham and G.W.B. Huntingford, *Some Records of Ethiopia, 1593-1646* (Nendeln, Lichtenstein: Krauss Reprint, 1967)

8. *Ibid.,* 133. Atsmä's statement is right in substance, but not on the timing of the event, since it occurs in the middle of the term.

9. *Ibid.,* 133

10. *Ibid.,* 56-59 for a date of Atsmä's work.

11. In the Gumi of 1966 *seven sessions were led by Abba Gadas,* including the Abba Gada in power: only one was handed over to an elder on the last day and his role was to recite the laws and guide the discussion. *Baxter's claim that all leadership of the Gumi was handed over to an elder who had no position in Gada assemblies is a complete misreading of the facts* as reported in *Gada,* 1973, p. 94. At the time I had indicated that he was a gada councilor but that I had not found out in which his gada assembly was. His name in fact appears in the record of Gada Councilors (*Gada,* p. 321) as Jaldessa Liban, *hayyu garba,* son of Liban jaldessa, Abba Gada (1891-99), hardly a faceless citizen picked up from the multitude, as Baxter would have it.

12. Abbas Haji has established that the *Ch'affe* of the Arsi is the national body that encompasses the Gada as well as the kinship organizations, whereas the *Qitt'e* is made up mainly of clan representatives. See his essay "Egalitarianism, Justice and Democracy in an Oromo Polity," in *The Oromo Republic* (forthcoming).

13. Karl Erik Knutsson, *Authority and Change,* pp. 184 ff.

14. Cf. Bairu Tafla, *Atsmä Giorgis and his Work,* pp. 56-59.

15. Lambert Bartels, *Oromo Religion,* (Berlin: Dietrich Reimer Verlag, 1990), chap. 26.

16. Among Kenya Boran, the institution exists only as age-sets *(hariyya)* not as age-regiments *(ch'ibra).* The *chi' bra* at war is known only to first generation immigrants from Ethiopia, such as Daudi Dhaddach Dambi.

17. Asmarom Legesse, *Gada,* 96.

18. The senior Qallu of Oditu lives very close to the Borana-Guji border and is, therefore, perpetually in danger of Guji raids. As the population shifted southward, which went on for a century, the shrines were left behind. Since it is an Oromo people who have moved into the abandoned territory, they share the general Oromo respect for pilgrims and they honor Borana's right of access to the shrines, on ritual occasions.

19. The age-set I knew best was Wakhor Liban and its leaders, the *hayyu hariyya,* among whom Arero Khottola was the most outstanding. He was an impressive figure and maintained close ties with the Abba Gada and the Warra Qallu of Oditu. Most of the information on the laws governing age-sets was obtained from him, from my mentor Arero Rammata and from several eye-witnesses who took part in wars, such as the Oditu war with Guji and "War of Madha" against the Marrehan Somali.

20. The main reason for the contentiousness of the Qallu lineage had to do with the fact that their lineage became the node where the *clash between national and local institutions* was most acutely felt.

21. My essay, "The Day the Sun Died," is part of the specialized body of literature which may have historic significance, but it is not part of this book that focuses on viability of institutions in the contemporary world.

22 . Mainland Europeans use the word *"class"* in these contexts, e.g., *classi di eta,* Ital., *alterklassen,* Ger. English writers also used to write about *age classes* not age-sets in earlier decades. Somewhere along the line, they switched to "age-sets" and "generation-sets," a reflection of the language of devaluation that prevails in British writing.

23. *Gada,* 1973., p. 130 ff., 153 ff.

24. Please note that what is cited here is a small fragment of Galma's tape recorded hour-long interview on the issue of *ebba* and *mura.*

25. Asmarom Legesse, *Gada,* chap. 3.

26. Initially, I had explained that the reason the warriors gave up their dabballe children to Wata surrogate parents was to allow them to fulfill their military obligations. In his critique of *Gada (*1973), Hallpike (1976:49) asked, why do they not leave the children with their mothers and go off to war?—a legitimate question. Further inquiries made in response to Hallpike's comment suggest that the main reason may have been to protect the children from harm. Wata villages are not a legitimate target for raids among Borana, Arsi, Guji. Hence they are a safe haven for their children.

27. In Borana, the Bokku is a ritual officiant of the gada class and is quite distinct from the Abba Gada, the head of the gada class.

28. Marco Bassi's (2005:65) raises a question about my use of the phrase "partial retirement" to the Yuba grades. The rationale for this language is based on three facts: the Yuba have no *ya'a* (assembly), their

oversight responsibilities in Gumi occur only once every eight years, and they have a much reduced role in the ongoing, daily, activities of the Gada institution. From RABA-GADA (V-VI) to YUBA (VII-IX), there is a huge reduction in political, legal, military, ritual and ceremonial activity. The label, I believe, is thus fully justified. Bassi is of course wedded to the "gerontocracy" thesis borrowed from Baxter, and thus wants to elevate the Yuba to a supreme status they do not possess, on the presumption that they alone are "old enough" to assume such responsibilities. If old age were the criterion for "full political maturity," it is the *jarsa* "old" who should be in charge of the system, but they are not. It is, I believe, up to Borana, not Bassi, to decide who is "old enough" to assume responsibility. The Amhara rulers too declared Gada to be *yegobez gizat* or "government by young men." If the practice appears not very legitimate to Marco Bassi or to the Amhara rulers, it is *their* problem, not a Borana problem.

29. Unable to understand this irregularity in the structure of the gada cycle, some writers conclude that the gada grade itself is abridged to 4 years. Domenico Pecci, for instance, makes that error. See his chart opposite p. 318. That, in my view, never happens.

30. It is important to remember that "retirement" is achieved progressively in three stages known as *Yuba* (partial retirement) *Gada Mojji* (the sacred liminal grade) and *Jarsa* (the stage of final retirement)."

31. Asmarom Legesse, *Gada*, (1973), 160 ff.

---

### *Arero Rammata, a man of knowledge*

Arero was my mentor in 1962-63 and served as the advisor to successive Gada and Gumi Assemblies (1952-68). He had the entire Gada Chronology—three hundred and sixty years of history—the Oromo astronomic calendar, as well as the ritual-political order of the Gada System stored in his prolific and very precise mind. He had remarkable mastery, not only of the facts of history, but also of the rules that govern the calendric, ritual-political, and historic cycles. A Mathematician (see M. Ascher) has used his knowledge to examine the nature of mathematical concepts and techniques of reckoning in non-Western societies. Archaeo-astronomers (see B.M. Lynch and L. Doyle) have used his account to examine the astronomic bases of the Borana calendar, testifying that it is based on a clear understanding of lunar motion. They have used his knowledge to make sense of the nonsense surrounding the interpretation of Namoratunga, the archaeological remains of the Ancient Cushites in Northern Kenya, dated ca. 300 BC, indicating also that the calendar was in operation as early as the third century in the pre-Christian era. The results are remarkable. Through him, Borana have found a place of honor in the annals of Anthropology, Mathematics, Astronomy, and Archaeology. His biographical profile has been placed in the *Encyclopedia Aethiopica*.

*Chapter 4*

# OROMO DUAL ORGANIZATION
## and the Qallu Institution

In the preceding chapter, evidence was offered concerning the institutional foundations of Oromo democracy, focusing mainly on the human life cycle and how it served as the structural basis for the polity. We now leave the temporal field and examine aspects of their political life that are built on the kinship system. The two dimensions are cross-cutting: they are comparable to the "vertical" and "horizontal," or the *time* and *space* dimensions, that lie at the root of all human social systems. However, Borana society is a mobile society which does not rely much on territory as an organizational base. That has caused some grief to territorially-minded colonizers of Africa, the anthropologists who sought to be of service to them, and the political philosophers on whom they relied for conceptual frameworks. Borana society uses the "horizontal" plan of kinship as a substitute for the role played by territory in more sedentary societies. That, however, is true only at the top levels of the kinship system. At the level of the clans and lineages, the society is well grounded. For the moment, our focus is on the top layer of the kinship order i.e. the dual organization and the Qallu institution that is built on it.

## The Ancient Moieties: BARETTUMA and BORANA

No aspect of Oromo social organization has been as badly neglected or misunderstood as the Oromo moieties. Gada is often documented in the historical literature, whereas, the concept of moiety is scantily recorded, partly because it is an unfamiliar concept for historians and an entirely alien concept for highland Abyssinians. If moieties ever appear in Ethiopic literature they appear as the names of two Oromo "tribes," or *nägäd* in Ge'ez and Amharic.

Oromo society is divided into two halves that are major components of the kinship system. We refer to them as moieties—an anthropological term that derives from the French word *moietie*, which means "half." The concept can be defined as follows:

*Moieties are two halves of a society that are linked to each other and interdependent in their structure and/or activities.*

This is a minimal definition. It tells us what the common denominator is in all moieties. Exogamy or preferential marriage across moieties are examples of structural linkage that give rise to vast numbers of affinal bonds between the moieties. Indeed members of the two moieties address is other as "in-laws." Hence, one's in-laws in Borana number in the tens of thousands souls. Political competition for office, power sharing, mutual regulation, and ritualized patterns of behavior are examples of activity-based interdependence. Comparative data from around the world, recorded in the Human Relations Area Files, indicate that the equality of moieties or the give-and-take relationship between them may be framed in demographic, territorial, political, ritual or kinship-and-marriage terms.

At different stages of history, the full range of types of linkages, except the territorial base, were exhibited in Oromo society, although exogamous marriage, which is the most rigorous form, appears to have declined over the centuries and to have given way to preferential marriage, i.e., people choosing to marry across moieties without having any obligation to do so.

Two other prominent features are in evidence across the broad. (1) *cross-distribution:* nowhere are the moieties territorially segregated from each other; (2) *avoidance of endogamy:* nowhere have the moieties developed into endogamous groups, much less castes.

Throughout most of the 16th century, there was one dual organization that encompassed the entire Oromo nation. The two halves of the nation were then called BARETTUMA and BORANA. Today, the most detailed accounts of a moiety organization that is fully operational in the political, social, ritual, and kinship-and-marriage spheres is the system of the contemporary Borana, where the senior moiety is called "Gona" and the junior moiety is called "Sabbo."

Macch'a has a new kind of dual organization: Gabaro and Borana. According to most authorities, the dual organization contains an element of social class stratification that makes it different from the Borana and Orma systems. Whether Gabaro are ethnogenetically linked to BARETTUMA, possibly because the assimilated aliens evolved around a dwindling core of ancient BARETTUMA clans, will be tested when and if the necessary clan-lineage data become available.[1]

In the eastern part of the nation, particularly Harar, a variant of the term "Barettuma" is used: the people call themselves "Barentuma" which is close to Bahrey's Bareytuma. They call their ancestor "Barento"—a term derived from the alternative name of the people, Barentu, an abridged form of Barentuma.[2]

Most of the BARETTUMA-dominant branches of the Oromo of Ethiopia—Yejju, Wollo, Barentu, Arsi—have converted to Islam. As a result, they appear to have lost the exogamous features. This is due, in part, to the fact that Islam favors maximal endogamy (i.e. first cousin marriage) whereas Oromo favor maximal exogamy (i.e. marriage outside of one half of the society). In this regard, Islamic and Oromo customs are at the opposite ends of the human continuum. Thus, among the Orma in Kenya, who converted to Islam in the 1920s, we can see how exogamy is today giving way to lesser forms preferential marriage, including marriage within the clan, a practice that was historically considered nearly incestuous (Ensminger, 1997).

## Political and Historic Significance of Moieties

Oromo dual organization is not only critical for our understanding of social structure, it also contributes to our understanding of the great migration, the associated military campaigns, and the structure of territorial groups that came into being after the migration. If we ignore moieties in writing Oromo history, we will have knocked out a significant part of our resource base.

### Balancing mechanism

What is the political significance of moieties, or more broadly dual organization today? It is a structural feature that divides the political community into permanently opposed groups. It is the prototypical basis for balanced opposition and power-sharing. Among the southern Borana of today, gada assemblies contain representatives of both moieties. The top leadership of each gada class, the Adula Council, consists of three members of the senior moiety and three members of the junior moiety. In any one gada period, the Abba Gada may come from one or the other moiety, depending on the vagaries of the electoral contests. Whichever moiety he comes from, the Abba Gada is the head of the entire society, i.e. of both moieties.

Not only the governing council *(Adula)* but also every local community *(olla)* has a group of elders drawn from both moieties. The clans, on the other hand, have an entirely different balancing mechanism, one based not on moieties, but on the Warra Bokku/ Warra Qallu division, or the Oromo/Gabra division. In such divisions, however, there is no uniform requirement that there be the same number of representatives of each section. It is not quantitative but qualitative balancing: i.e., based on different status, stage of type of assimilation or type of service offered viz. ritual, political or military. Nevertheless, the principle remains the same: the authority of one section is balanced by the other section.

### Moiety leaders as electors and mediators

In much of the literature on Oromo culture, the moieties and their leaders—the Warra Qallu—are described as having "only ritual functions." That view fails to take into account the *political uses of ritual* and how they use it to resolve conflict, achieve peace, or in the case of *Naga Borana* (Pax Borana) to offer protection under a shared ritual umbrella. More specifically, the main political responsibility of the moiety leaders was, until the Gumi of 1980, to serve as electors for their moieties. The electors as a group are referred to as the *ya'a Qallu,* or "the Qallu assembly."

Their most difficult task was to reconcile the interests of luba and clan delegations who come to them to recommend different candidates. These delegations should be labeled *clan-luba delegations* because they speak for the clan and the luba—two cross-cutting groups that are the interface between the two institutions (moiety and Gada). Each moiety conducts its electoral work autonomously. However, in special circumstances, one moiety can intervene in the internal electoral affairs of the other. If the electors of one moiety fail to perform their duties, if conflicts arise that cannot be resolved within the moiety, if they are unresponsive to the wishes of the luba or clan, and if there is mounting criticism suggesting that very un-popular candidates are about to bribe their way into office, there will be a stalemate between the electors and their critics. An appeal will then be made to the other moiety, asking them step in to mediate the crisis. All that was vividly and empirically revealed in the elections of 1963 and the contentious case of Adi Dida (Photo, p. 194).

All the electors belong to the Qallu lineages of one or the other moiety. The segment of Borana society that has ritual and electoral responsibilities are called "Warra Qallu," a term that literally means "the family or descent group of the Qallu" but, in fact, encompasses an entire major lineage or clan that is excluded from membership in the military and political institutions. The span of exclusion dif-fers in the two moieties. In the case of the Gona, it is the entire clan (Oditu) that is thought to belong to the Qallu's descent group and, therefore, barred from ever holding Gada office. In the case of the Sabbo, it is only the Warra Qallu major lineage of the Karrayyu clan that is so excluded. The rest of the clan is very much involved in Gada government. In fact, those Karrayyu who are not members of the Qallu lineage hold a very important place in the top leadership of the gada assemblies, below the apical Abba Gada *(fit'e)*.

### Moieties and their Qallu councils in electoral politics

The election of gada leaders can be very intense and protracted. It has been recorded in some detail in my first publication on the sub-ject.[2] That study describes the full range of activities the electors are engaged in, while hosting the clan-luba delegations that come to them to present their candidates. On the occasion of the election contest, the Qallu lineage and its council were extremely busy. For several months, while they were listening to the candidates' self-adu-lating speeches, Borana was in a state of great tension. There was a high level of public awareness and open discussions of the strengths or weaknesses of the candidates and their ancestors. Most, but not all, of the discussions were conducted in full view of the public. However, the sporadic secrecy that engulfed the deliberations of the Warra Qallu is a source of discomfort for most of the Warra Bokku.

Most Borana men and women I interviewed felt they had a right to comment on the electoral process, and they did so amply whenever the opportunity offered itself. Concerned individuals travelled great distances, to come to the Qallu's council and to present their opinions. The Qallu's lineage was eager to complete the debates as quickly as they could, since the process was a heavy burden on their resources. That was true in spite of the fact that delegations brought gifts for the Warra Qallu. As in all other councils and assemblies, the council of electors and the representatives of the clan-lubas who come to the electors to seek political office did not use a voting procedure to decide who the best candidates were. Decisions were made quite effectively by consensus alone.

It is true, however, that sometimes disagreements reach crisis proportions and the meetings are deadlocked. The requirement that the discussion be continued until unanimity is achieved may lead one to believe that the councilors have vast amounts of time available to them. They do not. There is a time limit that is economic rather than legal in character. The customary expectation that the Qallu and his lineage should host the luba and clan delegations, while they are pleading for their candidates, is a drain on their resources. It imposes severe constraints on the electors and on the duration of the meetings. The economic balancing mechanism that is at work here is quite different from the other balancing mechanisms presented in the earlier analyses. Beyond that, they also have very effective consensus-building strategies that keep lengthy meetings in check.

### The role of moiety and clan councils in conflict resolution

The moiety leaders also have the responsibility of *mediating* conflicts within the moiety that cannot be resolved by the constituent clans, lineages, or local groups. If the lower councils are unable to resolve their internal conflicts, they can appeal a case to the Qallu councils for mediation. Any problems that are not resolved at this level can always be taken to the Gumi—the octennial pan-Borana convention—where final judgment is made and, if need be, sanctions imposed. Beyond the Gumi, there are no higher bodies that can intervene.

Marco Bassi's pioneering work, in *Decisions in the Shade* (2005), on the *political, judicial, lineage assistance (busa-gonofa), pastoral resource management* roles of clan councils takes the analysis of Oromo institutions to new frontiers. Unlike the Qallu councils, the clan council have the authority to impose sanctions. Indeed, some of the Gada Assembly's power is contingent on collaboration between the national and clan institutions, through the intervention of the *jallaba*, who represent clans in the Gada Assemblies.

### Seniority and equality: complementary concepts

In the moiety organization of the Oromo, one half is said to be senior and the other junior. *The junior moiety is always honored by being listed first in the kinship narrative: i.e., it is always Sabbo/Gona, never Gona/Sabbo.* In itself, seniority does not become the basis of social stratification. It is very easy to fall into the trap of seeing these as "social classes" and describing the senior and junior moieties as "aristocrats" and "commoners." Such an interpretation is far removed from the central ethical premises of the Oromo nation. There is no way that the halves could be interpreted as social classes because they enjoyed equal power in the ruling Gada Council, even if one always preceded the other in rituals. One is said to be senior to the other in the same sense that brothers are said to be senior and junior.

Seniority *(angaftitti)* is considered to be a fact of life. Borana say that all social groups and all individuals within them succeed each other in accordance with the principles of seniority. The fact that generations succeed each other and are thus ordered sequentially is a perfectly natural fact. However, the recognition of that fact does not constitute an abandonment of the Oromo egalitarian ethic, anymore than a queue represents the abandonment of the egalitarian values. Queuing is an essential sociological device for arranging people sequentially when limited access to resources makes such an arrangement necessary. In the life of the herder, the prototypical situation that requires queuing, and thus seniority, is the well. When they come to water their animals at any one of the great wells *(tula)* or any of the lesser wells *(ela)* of Borana, all the herds and their owners are arranged in sequence and the resulting arrangement is remarkably orderly. In this system, no one is deprived of water because they stand at the end of the queue. If the queue completely fills up the 24 hour cycle, as it sometimes does during the height of the dry season, all members of the community, high or low, senior or junior, will be asked to send their surplus livestock away from the wells to the river basins.

There lies the true meaning of equality and seniority and why, in the Borana case, they are complementary not contradictory concepts. In spite of these fundamental realities, some writers have sought to find elements of aristocracy, hierarchy or social class in Oromo ideas of seniority.

### One moiety is said to be older than the other

It is in this sense that the two halves of Oromo society are said to be "senior" and "junior." Their position is described by using a pair of terms whose primary meaning refers to older and younger brothers i.e. *angafa* (first born) and *mandha* (junior brothers).[3] Legend has it that one moiety was "born" before the other. That is the main reason why it holds a higher position. As such, it simply represents the "order of birth" of the moieties. It is possible that one moiety did indeed precede the other in terms of *historical social formation*. Of critical importance is the fact that the three Sabbo clans are collectively known as "Galalcha Saden." That suggests that seniority here refers to an ancient historic process of moiety formation. That is an older version of what is happening in Macch'a today, where the senior section (Borana) came into being before the junior (Gabaro) because the latter evolved into its position as a component of the dual organization during the great migration, whereas the Borana was part of the ancestral system of moieties. Today, it is assumed that the Gabaro are entirely made up of "conquered populations." In my view, that assumption should be re-examined with the aid of genealogical records, to determine whether or not Gabaro society today contains genealogical elements whose genesis antedate the great migration. It is also clear that the Borana of Macch'a too assimilate aliens into their own lineages and clans, not merely into the Gabaro part of their society. Hence the identification of Borana as autochthonous and Gabaro as assimilated aliens may be a simplification of a more complex process.

### Absorption of aliens:  total, partial, individual, or corporate

Whatever the situation may be in Macch'a, it is clear that, among the Borana in the homelands, both moieties assimilated populations who came under their cultural umbrella, but the assimilation strategies they employed were quite different: one moiety allowed aliens to merge with existing clans, and the other allowed them to retain their identity and form new Borana clans bearing names that recall their origin. As a result, one moiety appears to be more highly segmented and to contain more assimilated aliens than the other. Thus, the Gona moiety contains marginal clans that are called "Guji" and "Arusi-Gosa" suggesting that these groups were absorbed from the adjoining Oromo populations called Guji and Arsi. By contrast, the

Sabbo moiety has no such clans because the aliens were absorbed completely, as individuals, into existing clans, and, in the process, they lost their original identity, and acquired a new identity. As a result, the Gona moiety appears to be growing more rapidly, not because its population is increasing faster, but because its clans and lineages are segmenting more rapidly by a process of internal fission, and because they are assimilating aliens as corporate groups. The half that segments more rapidly and resorts to corporate assimilation of aliens is the one that is thought of as the "big" moiety. It is worth noting, however, that in Borana it is the senior moiety that behaves this way and is thought to be bigger, which is the converse of what happens in Macch'a dual organization.

### The problem of the few and the many

Another aspect of the dual organization that has caused difficulties for students of Oromo society and history is the problem of "the few and the many." There is a common formula that suggests that one moiety is much larger than the other. Thus, the Macch'a Oromo say *Borana sagal, Gabaro sagaltama* "the Borana are nine and the Gabaro are ninety." (The Tulama version is *Sagaltama Gabra, Saglan Borana.)* This idiom has led writers on Macch'a to conclude that one moiety is many times larger than the other. Bartels, for instance, says that "the Gabaro outnumbered the Borana many times over."[4]

The southern Borana also describe their own moieties in the same kind of language. They say *Sabbo saden, Gona Gumi,* "the Sabbo are three, and the Gona are a multitude." The Sabbo are said to be three because they consist of three large clans which do not break up over time, but absorb aliens individually or corporately into their ranks: Internally, these clans are, in fact, highly segmented, but the fission never occurs at the clan level. The Gona are said to be "a multitude" for two very different reasons. First, the clans divide into new clans as they grow larger—there are now fourteen clans in all and some of them are of very recent vintage—and second, the assimilated clans or lineages are allowed to retain their names, even when these names indicate their foreign origin, as in the case of the Guji and Arusi clans. These assimilated clans, however, are not second class citizens. They are now Borana, full-fledged, though they tend to straddle the border between Borana and their neighbors, as the Ariaal do in Samburu.

The same idiom of "the few and the many" is, thus, at work in Borana (south) and Macch'a. Yet we have hard survey evidence showing that among the Borana the two moieties, Sabbo/Gona, are numerically balanced. This evidence shows that one cannot infer demographic reality from an idiomatic expression. It is a mistake to give the metaphor of "the few and the many" a literal meaning, or to assume that there is any kind of demographic imbalance between the two parts of society thus described. There is a rich lore of *dynamic asymmetry* that exists side by side with the culture of *balanced opposition*. We need to know which of these polarities they are invoking when making generic statements about the moieties.

When they say in Macch'a that "the Borana are nine and the Gabaro are ninety," it may not mean that one moiety is ten times the size of the other. It may simply mean that the methods of the expansion, segmentation or assimilation are different in the two cases. If one branch (Gabaro) allows the clans to segment more rapidly than the other; if the Gabaro resort more often to corporate adoption of aliens, and the Borana resort more often to individual adoption, one branch will then give the impression that it is growing, and the other will appear to be more stable. The asymmetric proliferation implied in this language may refer to the process of clan/lineage segmentation, and to corporate or individual assimilation rather than to population growth or population size per se.

Whatever the situation might be in Macch'a, the evidence for Borana (south) is not subject to debate, because it is based on a meticulously conducted survey, that yielded a representative sample of the population in which every household head was identified by moiety, clan, and lineage. The sample consisted of 560 randomly selected households.[5] The information was gathered in villages and marketplaces, over a period of two years, across the whole of Borana country. The result showed that one moiety (Gona) was 49 percent and the other (Sabbo) 51 percent of the population. The difference was smaller than the margin of error of the sample survey. Statistically, therefore, they are identical in size.

A similar sample survey must be taken in Macch'a to resolve the question of the numeric balance or imbalance of Borana and Gabaro definitively. Otherwise, how we read the moiety idiom of "the few and the many" can lead to potentially erroneous social, historic, or demographic inferences.

Granted that Macch'a is one part of the Oromo nation that was remarkable in the rapidity of its evolution in an authoritarian and stratified direction, and in the abandonment of all or most of the institutional regulators that are part of the older structure of Oromo democracy. Hence, we do not know the extent to which the Borana/Gabaro dual organization serves as a political balancing mechanism. It would be difficult, but not impossible, for it to perform that political function unless some demographic balance existed. Nor can we determine with any degree of certainty whether the formula of "the few and the many" is a metaphor of incorporation-segmentation or if it represents a real demographic imbalance. This is an empirical question for which an empirical answer must be sought. It is quite possible that a demographic imbalance between Borana and Gabaro did indeed develop as a result of very rapid mass incorporation of aliens into one but not the other part of Macch'a society, a process that would not allow the pattern of enfranchisement to catch up with the assimilation of aliens. Hence, the Borana/Gabaro situation may be a relatively early stage in the development of genuine moieties or a tangential path that leads to stratification. The available evidence is not good enough to help us settle the matter one way or the other.

Some Macch'a informants who were interviewed by Lambert Bartels are adamant about the *political equality of Borana and Gabaro* even if they do not view them as being ritual equals or numerically balanced with each other.[6] It is worth remembering that political equality can be achieved in spite of ritual, economic and demographic inequality. These characteristics are shared with many other democracies, ancient as well as modern.

## The Names of the Ancient Moieties and their Derivatives

As indicated earlier, we know, from the work of Bahrey, that the two halves of Oromo society were called BAREYTUMA (or BARTUMA) and BORAN(A)" in the 16th century. The same nomenclature continued in the 17th century as evidenced in the chronicle of Emperor Susenyos. The name "Boran(a)" has survived as the name of the senior segment of the population in much of the western half of the Oromo nation, particularly among the Macch'a and Tulama. This category is then counterpoised against the Gabaro category which is presumed to be comprised of the descendants of assimilated aliens. This, it seems, is how a dual organization, if not a full blown system of moieties, has been re-established in the evolving institutions of Macch'a.

The term "Barettuma" (or its derivatives) is associated with of the eastern half of the nation: from Orma in the far south (Kenya), through Arsi in the homelands, Barentuma in Harar, Karrayyu in the upper Awash valley, all the way to Wollo and Rayya-Azebo in the far north. As indicated earlier, some variant of it, i.e., Barentu, exists today among the eastern Oromo of Harar, but it survives not as the name of a moiety but as a collective designation of the population as a whole. Concerning this branch, a critical question that remains un-answered is this: is Barentu also the name of the descendants of the ancient BARETTUMA moiety? If so, then what is the name of the other moiety or, as in Macch'a, what is the name of all the peoples whom the Barentuma absorbed during the great migration or in sub-sequent centuries? Is there a Gabaro division? Has any aspect of the moiety organization endured among the contemporary Barentuma? On these matters we are, at present, in the dark.

There is, however, evidence coming from the Kenyan ethnog-raphy of the Orma. According to the findings of Hilarie Kelly and Günther Schlee, the Orma are of BARETTUMA origin and that the name "Barettuma" has been preserved as the name of one of their moieties, whereas the other moiety, which is of BORANA descent, is named "Irdida," and shares several clans with Borana of Southern Ethiopia.[7] This is one more piece of evidence that can uncover the parent system at the root of the ancient moiety organization.

The phonological properties of the old moiety terms also require some clarification. It is clear that the senior moiety in the 16th cen-tury was called "BORAN(A)" and there is no debate about that. But what was the name of the other moiety? The authors who have writ-ten about this ancient moiety and its derivatives render it in a be-wildering variety of forms: Bareytuma, Barentu, Barento, Bartuma, Barttuma, Barentuma, Barentoma etc. Why is it that "Barettum(a)" is subjected to this kind of ambiguity and proliferation? Is it in any way connected with the inherent asymmetries of the moieties and with the fact that one moiety is more conservative and the other, more unstable and more dynamic?

For a moment, let us go back to the phonological problem and try to clarify the precise name of the junior moiety. In the original

Geez text, Bahrey renders the name of the junior moiety as "Bäräy-tuma," and "Bärtuma," the internal 'a' vowels consistently rendered as "ä" which is not a phoneme in Oromo, and is thus a meaningless alteration. Only one of these renditions, Bäräytuma, comes close to the name that has been preserved in the most conservative branches of Oromo, i.e., Orma and Borana. It is likely that Bahrey had difficulty dealing with the phonemic features that do not exist in his language. That happened with regard to the long vowel "ee" in Bareettuma which he renders as "äy." Since long vowels are not phonemic in Amharic or Ge'ez and there is no way of representing the feature in the alphabet, he is being quite precise rendering it with the addition of a semi-vowel "y" to reflect the long vowel. Again, Bahrey's record proves to be correct even when his resources are deficient.

After contemplating Bahrey's text for a long time, trying to fathom the meaning of the very complex and highly parsimonious story he tells, I found—lodged in my subconscious memory and buried in my field notes—a word almost identical to Bahrey's "Bäräytuma" that was still in use in the sacred oral texts of Borana rituals. They use it in texts recited by the warriors (CUSA IV, and RABA V) as part of their war chants. It is transmitted from generation to generation along with all the sacred lore of the lubas. The Borana pronounce it "Baréettum(a)," but there is no doubt that it is the same as one of the versions that Bahrey recorded, namely "Bäräytuma." The convergence of this version with what appears in Orma ethnography and with the term found in current Borana ritual texts indicates that the ancient name of the junior moiety was "Baréettum(a)" rather than "Barentu" or any of the other seven variants recorded to date among the eastern Oromo.

In short, the phonemic properties of the ancient moiety terms can be summed up as follows. The senior moiety is properly rendered as "Boorán(a)"—the "o" is a long vowel, the second vowel "a" is accented and the terminal vowel "a" is optional: it is dropped in phonologically restricted environments. Hence, the common spelling of "Boran," in Kenyan ethnographies and archives is a legitimate variant. It is always rendered as "BORAN(A)" in European languages or Borän(a) in the Ethiopic languages and by the current descendants of the moiety in central, western and southern Ethiopia. In the manner the word appears in Ethiopian Borana sacred texts the name of the junior moiety is pronounced as "Baréettum(a)," where the 'ée' is a long accented vowel, the 'tt' is geminated and the terminal vowel 'a' is optional. That, I believe, is the ancient form of the name. Other forms are probably deviations.

Incidentally, it is worth noting that our discovery of the ritual text in which Borana warriors shout "Baréettuma!" as the name of their brave ancestors, raises a totally unexpected question. Why are Borana singing war songs in which they cry out "Baréettuma!" in memory of their warrior ancestors? Do all Borana sing this song or is it a sacred text for only one segment of Borana society? Is it possible that some Borana are actually BARETTUMA? This is the tangential but very provocative question that arose from the simple phonological issue we have been examining, but more on this later.

The immediate question we are concerned with here has to do with the dynamic qualities that the junior moiety seems to exhibit. It appears that the name of the junior moiety, and the reality it represents, was historically unstable. Virtually all the descendants of the Borana call themselves "Booran(a)," wherever they are in Central Ethiopia, Southern Ethiopia, or Northern Kenya. That is not the case with the descendants of Barettuma: Their collective name has virtually disappeared as a term of self-designation among most of the descendants of that moiety, except the population of Harar. If it exists in vestigial forms elsewhere we do not know what the vestiges are. Even in Harar we cannot be sure what the term is since it takes on such a wide variety of forms.

We must, therefore, turn to the Orma for an answer. The important finding here from the perspective of ethnogenesis is this:

> **Of all the Oromo peoples who are thought to be of BARET-TUMA descent, it is only among the Orma of Kenya that the term 'Barettuma' has been preserved not as a regional term or as the generic name of the people, but as the name of a moiety counterpoised against another moiety which is clearly of BO-RANA descent. This evidence strongly suggests that in the parent system—before the great migration—BARETTUMA was indeed a moiety, not a tribe, and that this property has been preserved among the Orma.**

In trying to understand the parent system of the Oromo, both Borana and Orma are, thus, of critical importance. By relating this evidence with historical materials we get a more complete picture. We, therefore, turn to the historic record and what it tells us about the moieties, the Gada institution, and the great migration?

## The Old Oromo Gada/Moiety System and the Great Migration

The fundamental message of Bahrey's History is that the Oromo in the 16th century were one nation organized as two moieties. He does not say that BARETTUMA and BORANA have two separate Gada institutions. No, he says both "BARTUMA and BORAN together" established their fighting force after the circumcision of their luba. There is no evidence that, at this stage, Bahrey was describing two "tribes" that had become self-governing, with two separate Gada institutions and two separate armies. That important historic-ethnographic fact must be kept in mind, at all times, as we look at the history of the moieties.

In Bahrey's account of Oromo warfare, the fundamental structure was simply this: a group of three lubas were mobilized for a national campaign, and each had the same kind of organization that is based on genealogical generations that cut across both moieties. This is a direct parallel to what occurs in the Borana life cycle and military organization today. The three lubas that are involved in warfare are ranked hierarchically, from the class in power (*gada* in Borana, *luba* in Bahrey), to the married warriors (*raba* in Borana, *quandala* in Bahrey) and to the unmarried warriors (*cusa* in Borana, *guarba* in Bahrey).

## *BORANA head west, BARETTUMA go east?*

The standard approach that has been adopted by most writers who have dealt with the migration of the Oromo moieties is to assume that the two "tribes" drifted apart, one went north and west toward Tulama (Shoa) and Macch'a (Wallagga->Ghibe) and the other went east and north toward Arsi, Harar, Awash valley, Wollo, and Rayya-Azebo. Cerulli, Huntingford and Trimingham began this style of analysis and the recent writers such as Lemmu Baissa, Tesemma Ta'a and Mohammed Hassen have continued the same pattern of thought. As a typical example, we might cite Tesemma Ta'a :

"The Barttuma settled in what are today the Bale, Arsi, Hararge and Welo administrative regions. The Borana, on the other hand moved toward the north and northwest, leaving the lower Omo and Gibe River basins to their left. They divided into Tulama and Macha by the Awash River on the west. Yet another branch of the Borana still occupies regions of southern Ethiopia and northern Kenya." [The author then cites Trimingham (1976) and Baissa Lemmu (1971)] [8]

At the beginning of this chain of scholarly events, there was a statement made by Enrico Cerulli—one of the most important pioneer observers of Oromo social organization—who recognized the significance of moiety exogamy in Oromo dual organization. Nonetheless, he stated that the "tribes" drifted apart and settled, after their migration, in different territories.

Among the Galla tribes of Shoa, exogamy is no longer in force, a feature which—as I have explained elsewhere—is conserved among the Galla of Kenya Colony, in a most interesting form. The old division of Galla tribes into Borana tribe and Baraituma tribe, concerning exogamy, no longer has relevance for the tribes of Shoa, where Borana groups alone have settled according to the folk history of the invasion. [9]

Cerulli, like most researchers who followed him, calls them "tribes" but, to his credit, suggests they were initially bound together as exogamous moieties and that, later, they separated. [10]

In these and many other such descriptions the various sections of the Oromo nation are treated as discrete "tribes," who went to particular territories, and became self-governing entities. The possibility that both moieties might have migrated side by side, as two competing halves of the same society, was never considered.

In this chapter we do not seek to invalidate Cerulli's style of analysis which has yielded so many valuable insights and is often backed up by impeccable scholarship. We simply offer an alternative interpretation that brings the historic-ethnographic evidence into better alignment with each other than is otherwise possible.

Mohammed Hassen pushes the Cerulli-Huntingford-Baissa-Ta'a style of analysis to another level by arguing that the "separation" of the BARETTUMA and BORANA had occurred even before the great migration began—as early as the 14th century. Following the lead of Haberland, he presents the BARETTUMA as a predominantly agro-pastoral population living in the cool highlands of Bale, and the BORANA as a full-fledged pastoral people living at lower altitudes in what is today Guji and northeast Borana territory southwest of the Gannale Doria river. In other words, they had separated from each other not only sociologically and politically, but also in their habitats and subsistence economies.[11]

What does "separation" mean in this context? If it means territorial separation, it is a problematic proposition in view of Bahrey's evidence on BARETTUMA and BORANA and all the ethnographic evidence on the Oromo polity showing that the moieties are/were dynamically linked to each other. If it means divergent social formations, i.e., a dual organization or moieties consisting of genealogical groups or confederacies that were living in adjoining territories before the 16th century (as in the cradleland maps) and participating in the same political-military-rituals systems, it is a proposition that can be better supported with ethnographic/historic evidence.

### *Regionally one moiety predominated over the other*

The data reviewed in this chapter indicate that both moieties migrated into many of the areas occupied by the Oromo, but that, in the course of migration, one moiety predominated over the other in some regions and, as a result, the region and all the people who migrated to it accepted a common regional designation deriving from the name of the dominant moiety. We do not know why the name of one or the other moiety becomes dominant in different regions. We know that the Borana and Barettuma identities predominate today in the western and eastern regions of Ethiopia respectively. That simple fact cloaks a very complex reality linked to dual organization that is central to their democratic life and has far-reaching implications for their pattern of migration, for the character of their military campaigns, and for the level of integration or fragmentation at different stages of their history.

The fundamental historic questions raised in this chapter cannot be answered adequately unless there is a methodical and in-depth collaboration between *anthropologists,* who have a better grasp of social structure, and *historians,* who are better equipped with the analytical tools and resources needed to examine the transformation of society over time. The issue is decidedly *interdisciplinary.*

## The Moiety Thesis: Ethnography and History

So long as our historian colleagues continue to use concepts like "tribe," "clan," and "confederacy" but not the concepts of "moiety" or "dual organization" in analyzing the history of Oromo institutions, there is room for serious mis-reading of the ethnographic evidence. We, the anthropologists, do not use the term "moiety" frivolously. *Moiety is a fundamentally different concept from tribe.* The most important difference being the fact that tribes are self-governing, moieties are not. A tribe is a territorial entity whereas moieties need not be and often are not. The Oromo moiety is a structure that cuts across territorial groups. It is a non-territorial concept. That, most assuredly, is the case in Borana and Orma—the two most conservative descendants of the ancient moieties.

The preliminary formulation of the moiety thesis is in the form of a proposition to be tested empirically. The proposition is this:

> **If we are right in thinking that the 16th century dual organization of the Oromo was a non-territorial type of social organization and if the two parts of the Oromo nation were moieties that were interdependent, we would today expect the descendants of those moieties to exhibit some of those properties. Both moieties should be widely dispersed in the eastern and western regions. In other words, we would expect the clans and lineages descended from both the ancient moieties to be present, in significant numbers, across the entire Oromo nation. We would expect that kind of *cross-distribution* to occur, whether the region identifies itself as being nominally Borana or nominally Barettuma or even when the moiety terms have completely disappeared.**

In the form that the organization takes among the southern Borana and Orma today, the moieties are not localized, and cannot be localized, although they are often confused with particular territories, because the leaders of the two moieties reside in one or the other territory. Donaldson Smith made exactly that error when he first visited Borana in 1896. He observed that the Qallu of the Gona lives in Liban in the east and the Qallu of the Sabbo lives in Dirre in the west. He inferred, mistakenly, that the Gona moiety as a whole lives in Liban, and the Sabbo moiety lives in Dirre. The fact is that the two moieties are present in both territories, in significant numbers, as demonstrated by this writer with abundant survey data.

The important realization here is that it is very easy to "localize" a social group by simply placing it on a map—even if the group has a non-local distribution.[12] This is the kind of mistake that was made again and again by observers who wrote about the Oromo dual organization. In the form that they take among the Macch'a, today, there are no indications that they are localized: the two great divisions of Macch'a society, Gabaro and Borana, are territorially intermingled. The Orma case is very similar to that of the Borana: the moieties were, historically, exogamous and dispersed. Today it appears that the men in one moiety tend to take their wives from the other moiety, by preference if not by prescription.

In short, in contemporary Borana or Orma, there is no such thing as "moiety territory." There is no Sabbo-land or Gona-land in Borana, nor is there Barettuma-land or Irdida-land in Orma. Similarly, before the great migration, there is no evidence that identifies BARETTUMA-land or BORANA-land as recognizable territories of the ancient moieties.

Only in the fragmentary evidence we have on Arsi do the moieties—Sikko and Mando—appear to be localized, mainly because Haberland placed them on a map, with a boundary line between them, a line he drew halfway and left the rest open with a question mark at the end of the line. (Perhaps he had second thought about it). Suspecting that Haberland may be making the same mistake as Donaldson Smith, I interviewed an Arsi elder, Haji Idris Mahmoud, to try to clarify this matter.[13] His testimony suggests that the Arsi moieties are no different than the other moieties we have seen in Southern Ethiopia: the names "Sikko" and "Mando" are indeed associated with two broad territories. Nevertheless, the constituent clans of Sikko and Mando are present in both regions.

Evidence presented by Abbas Haji Gnamo suggests that the localization of the Arsi moieties may have been an internal development, a transformation of the ancient dispersed moieties that resulted in one or the other territory being identified with one or the other moiety. It is still necessary to find out if the two halves of Arsi are ethno-genetically linked to the old Oromo moieties, and whether they retain any of their moiety characteristics.[14]

Surprisingly, Emperor Menelik and his regional governors seem to have understood the non-territorial nature of the Borana moieties and made dual appointments of administrative intermediaries *(balabbats)* in every part of Boranaland, and at every level of the administrative hierarchy. In each district and sub-district of what was then called "Borana Province," later called Sidamo, one balabbat represented the Sabbo and the other represented the Gona. That is an extraordinary adjustment that Menelik's administration made to this aspect of Oromo society. He appointed the leaders of the moieties, chief balabbats of Borana, with the rank of Fitawrari, and was not bothered by the completely overlapping territories over which they were given dominion.

### Interdependence of moieties: kinship & political factors

If moieties are exogamous, every family would be part BORANA, part BARETTUMA. In the BORANA half of the society, the father of a family is necessarily BORANA, the mother would then have to be BARETTUMA and vice versa. The dualism reaches down to the internal structure of the individual family. As such, the moieties could not be separated without playing havoc with their kinship and marriage rules and their democratic dialectic.

Moieties were not only the two sides of the Oromo family, they were also the right and left arms of Oromo government. Hence, we cannot think of the right arm going east, the left going west, without having to worry about the viability of those severed limbs. We can, however, think of offspring being born, with their limbs intact, in the newly occupied territories, i.e. by a process of "replication."

Our proposition is this: Wherever they went, Oromo took the moieties with them, but modified them to accommodate the altered political environment, created by the assimilation of aliens, in the newly occupied territories. The design remained the same, but *some* components were altered, mainly by accretion or name change.

## Bahrey's Epic Chronicle

An extraordinary aspect of Oromo history is that it contains one of those rare moments in Africa when the 16th century history of a non-literate society was recorded in some detail, using their own chronological framework. The reason why we have this document is because Oromo warriors raided a monastic community and one monk, named Bahrey, who lost all his possessions, escaped, got to know the Oromo quite well, and documented their history in Geez, the sacred and archaic language of the Ethiopian Orthodox Church. Bahrey's interest was to explain to his king why Oromo were so victorious and to let him know what he can do to rectify the situation.

He opens his brief story with a description of the two "tribes," BAREYTUMA[15] and BORAN, along with a genealogy of their "descendants" i.e., clans and lineages. Please note what the BARETTUMA (A) and BORANA (B) are doing in this amazing history.

Table 4.1  Bahrey's Chronology, 1593, in five *gogessas* (columns)

| CURRENT GENERATION | | | | | |
| --- | --- | --- | --- | --- | --- |
| Name of Abba Gada | | | | | |
| MOIETY | | A & B | A & B | [B] | A & B |
| Gada period | | 1586-94 | 1578-86 | 1570-78 | 1562-70 |
| cyclic name of luba | | Mulata A Mulata B | Birmaje A Birmaje B | Robale | Harmufa A Harmufa B |
| PRIOR GENERATION | | | | | |
| Name of Abba Gada | | | | | |
| MOIETY | [A] | [B] | [A] | [B] | [A] |
| Gada period | 1554-62 | 1546-54 | 1538-46 | 1530-38 | 1522-30 |
| *cyclic name of luba* | *Mesle* | *Bifole* | *Kilole* | *Mudana* | *Melba* |

(Dates as in Mohammed Hassen, *Oromo of Ethiopia,* 1994.)
(Moieties A & B transferred from the Borana chronology)

## Chronicle of the first generation (hemicycle of 40 years)

The 1st luba, Melba [1522-1530] began the invasion of Bali.
The 2nd luba, Mudana [1530-38] crossed the River Web [Shebelli]
The 3rd luba, Kilole [1538-1546] fought a war in the lowlands of Dawaro against an Abyssinian military colony and its subjects.
The 4th luba, Bifole [1546-62] devastated Dawaro, made war on Fatagar.
The 5th luba, Mesle [1554-62] fought against an Abyssinian rebel general and killed his troops. For the first time, Oromo occupied the conquered territory and took war captives.

### Transition in the life cycle to the second generation

[During the last 40 years, the children of the first generation were going through childhood, youth, and young adulthood.] The oldest among them were now circumcised, i.e. became a luba. When a luba is formed, it was required to attack an area which none of its predecessors had attacked.

Those who are uncircumcised abandon their children. After circumcision, they begin to raise sons; they begin to raise daughters some years later.

### Transition on the war front: periphery to center

[All the wars until now were in the Ethiopian periphery. Now the Oromo warriors go into the heartlands of the Christian Kingdom.]

## Chronicle of the second generation [incomplete hemicycle]

### 1st luba [1562-70]

A. Harmufa, the sons of Melba, devastated the countries of Gan, Anguat and Amhara. The best known among the warriors were from the BORANA tribe. [This is the first time in the narrative that 'tribes' are mentioned by name, associated with different wars.]

B. Harmufa of the BARETTUMA made war on Begemeder [Gondar] and killed a general who had rebelled against the king [Sartsa Dengel].

### 2nd luba [1570-78]

Robale, the son of Mudana, devastated Shoa and made war on Gojjam. Later, the king, Sartsa Dengel, scored a major victory.

### 3rd luba [1578-86]

A. Birmaje of the BORANA, the son of Kilole, attacked the Maya [mercenaries in the service of the kingdom]; he also killed members of the royal family.

B. Birmaje of the BARETTUMA made war on Dembia, killed members of the royal family and a Bahrnegash or "ruler of the maritime province" [later called Eritrea]

A. Birmaje of the BORANA, surrounded Damot and enslaved the men, including one prince. A major counter-offensive killed many of the BORANA warriors.

### 4th luba [1586-94]

A. Mulata of Warr Daya [of the BARETTUMA] attacked a territory [in Gojjam] under Ras Wolde Kristos, whereupon the Ras put up a fierce resistance.

B. Mulata of the BORANA, the son of Bifole, devastated the Christians of Damot and brought the whole population under his submission.

Bahrey ends the chronicle with the statement that he wrote the book on the seventh year of the government of Mulata [i.e. 1593]

### [Postscript]

For the benefit of his king, Bahrey adds a sociological analysis that explains why Oromo are victorious. He describes the Christian Kingdom as having ten social classes of which only one fights and the Oromo as having ten social classes [i.e. gada] all trained in warfare, all not afraid to fight. There, in his view, lies the problem. There is an implicit warning that unless the king mobilizes his nation on the same scale as the Oromo had done, they could not be stopped.

## Bahrey's Evidence Re-examined

This chronicle documents how the Oromo nation, starting from a relatively small area South-west of the Webi Shebelle River, occupied a major part of the Ethiopian periphery, and made significant inroads into the Christian Kingdom. All that was accomplished over a period of 72 years. The chronicle also states, in no uncertain terms, that the driving force behind their expansion was the Gada institution, organized as regiments, and led by Gada leaders.

On the whole, Bahrey's history is a remarkably precise document. If he makes errors, they are usually errors of omission and rarely errors of commission. On the subject of the Gada System, its role in warfare and its contribution to the expansion of the Oromo nation, his information is rich. It has withstood the test of time. On the subject of the Oromo kinship system his evidence has significant gaps on both the BORANA and BARETTUMA sides. Not only is he silent on the subject of moiety exogamy, he also neglects to inform us about the moiety affiliation of all the Abba Gadas who ruled the nation and led the campaigns during the first five gada periods he describes. Nevertheless, what little he tells us of moieties in association with the Gada institution is precious and will be so treated. We begin this analysis by re-reading Bahrey's evidence, armed with all the understanding we have been able to gain of the structure of the Oromo political system. We will use the contemporary chronology and political idiom of the Borana to get a deeper understanding of Bahrey's language.

| CURRENT GENERATION | | | | | |
|---|---|---|---|---|---|
| Name of Abba Gada | Jaldessa Liban | Madha Galma | Guyyo Boru | Aga Adi | Bule Debbasa |
| **MOIETY** | **GONA** | **GONA** | **GONA** | **SABBO** | **SABBO** |
| Gada period | 1960-68 | 1952-60 | 1944-52 | 1936-44 | 1929-36 |
| *cyclic name of luba* | *Fullasa* | *Makhula* | *Birmaje A Birmaje B* | *Sabbaqa* | *Libasa* |
| PRIOR GENERATION | | | | | |
| Name of Abba Gada | Arero Gedo | Liban Kuse | Boru Galma | Adi Doyyo | Liban Jaldessa |
| **MOIETY** | **GONA** | **SABBO** | **GONA** | **SABBO** | **GONA** |
| Gada period | 1921-29 | 1913-13 | 1906-13 | 1899-06 | 1891-99 |
| *cyclic name of luba* | *Darara* | *Mardida* | *Fullasa* | *Makhula* | *Moggisa* |

Table 4.2, Borana Chronology, 1963

The table below (4.2) is an abridged version of the Borana gada chronology. It covers ten gada periods or a complete gada cycle comparable to the nine gada periods which Bahrey's history covers. (The complete Borana chronology appears in Appendix I). It is important to note that the four items of information given in the table have specific meaning for Oromo chroniclers, beginning with (1) the name of the Abba Gada who was in power at each period of history, (2) the moiety he comes from, (3) the years according to the Borana calendar when he was in office, (4) the seven cyclical names of gada periods in italics. These seven names *(maqabasa luba)* are listed against the five columns *(gogessas)* so that the same name returns to the column after "eight" (i.e. seven) generations. Permutation is the method they use to check the accuracy of their oral records.

If Bahrey were to write a description of the "War of Madha," a war waged by Borana in 1950 against the Marrehan Somali, Bahrey might have written: "Makhula of the Gona, the son of Mardida, attacked the Marrehan and returned home with much booty."

### The war of Madha as if described by Bahrey

Had Bahrey written the above statement what would it have meant? It would mean that an Abba Gada whose cyclical luba name (maqabasa luba) is "Makhula," who belongs to the Gona moiety, whose father's gada bears the cyclical name of "Mardida," attacked the Marrehan Somali. The actual name of the Abba Gada is not Makhula but Madha Galma. In writing this history, Bahrey would not tell us the proper name of the Abba Gada but would use the cyclical name of the luba as if it were the personal name of the leader. Indeed he would describe the whole luba as if it were a "person," whose "father" was in power 40 years earlier. In the case of Madha, his father's luba, Mardida was led by a man (Liban Kuse) who was *genealogically unrelated to him* and, in fact, belonged to the opposite moiety (Sabbo). In Gada idiom, father and son need not mean actual father and actual son, but merely "luba father" and "luba son," i.e., any one who belongs to one's father's gada class is one's *abba luba* or "luba father." Hence, *"father" and "son" in Bahrey's chronology need not belong to the same moiety,* i.e., the son could be BORANA and the father BARETTUMA. That understanding fundamentally alters the way we have read Bahrey to date.

Furthermore, the war of Madha would be described as a "Sabbo victory" because Madha, the leader, is Sabbo. However, Madha drew his fighting force from both the Sabbo and Gona moieties. Bahrey's description implies that each of the first five Abba Gadas who led the campaigns during the great migration drew their fighting force from both the BORANA and the BARETTUMA.

Bahrey's chronology (Table 4.1) covers nearly two generations. It covers nine not ten gada classes, because from the start of the cycle of wars he is documenting until the time when he wrote the book (1593), only 72 (not 80) years had elapsed. In other words, the second generation had not completed its 40 year hemicycle. Nevertheless, the underlying design of his chronicle is perfectly intelligible. We know, for instance, that the father-son pairs he describes when recounting the wars of the second generation are in fact *gogessas* or "patriclasses," shown on the chronology as five columns. Men patrilineally related to each other belong to the same gogessa. Bahrey treats these as "father/son" pairs: that is legitimate use of gada idiom as long as we know it refers to *luba paternity.*

### Bahrey's data: one luba, one name, one army

We should note also that half way through his story, he switches models: he leaves the gada chronology to write about the gada life cycle. He implies that if we, as a young luba, started out as Melba's children when Melba came to power, at the start of his chronicle, we would now—40 years later—be ready to be circumcised, become a luba and enter the grade of power with our leader Harmufa, the son Melba. Bahrey makes this statement at the end of a forty-year period, in which five gada classes waged wars, and then he very clearly marks the *transition to the second generation* and describes the military campaigns of another four gada classes.

The contrast with the first generation is, thus, fairly clear. Until the generational transition, a unitary luba, representing both "tribes," was conducting wars at each gada period. In other words, he was telling the story of a nation that was at once "united and divided" (q.v. Triulzi, 1994) and the "unity" takes the form of joint military campaigns. It is only when they begin launching separate wars in very different locations that identifying them by "tribe" [i.e. by moiety] becomes necessary.

One of the most telling pieces of evidence in Bahrey is the statement on the formation and naming of the gada class and the emergence of a fighting force within it. Describing the transition between the two generations, he says that when they are circumcised, BARETTUMA and BORANA give themselves a collective luba name that he compares with the names of Abyssinian armies; he says that the group that is thus established as an Oromo army then makes war on lands never attacked by its predecessors.

He is emphatic in stating that *the luba of the entire Oromo nation has a common name and implies by the collective language* *he uses, that it is a single force.* It is important to note that in the two generations in Bahrey's history, the "tribes" behave in different ways, *fighting as one body in the first generation* * *and as two bodies, in the second.* Starting with the first luba of the second generation he describes two separate armies from the two moieties fighting in entirely different locations. What are the periods that Bahrey has thus identified for us? The early phase was from 1522 to 1562. In this period, there is no indication of separate armies.[16] Beginning in 1562 with the Harmufa luba (1562-1570) and again with Birmaje luba (1578-86), and the Mulata luba (1586-94) he describes the luba of one moiety and of the other moiety as separate entities, bearing the same luba name but fighting in different regions.[17] This interpretation of Bahrey's history is also justified by the fact that he prefaces the whole story by saying *Oromo "tribes" were initially together and later separated.* They migrated in different directions, like Abraham and Lot.[18]

---

*It seems that a recent translator of Bahrey's work has taken this matter lightly. Getachew Haile, the contemporary Ethiopian historian/linguist, has recently translated Bahrey's History into Amharic and English ( *Yä Abba Bahrəy Dərsätoch,* 2002). It is a most valuable contribution that makes this classic accessible to all who read Amharic. We should, however, note that on the specific question of the two halves of the Oromo nation in warfare, which we are discussing here, he makes a critical error by adding, in parenthesis, an infix to the Amharic text that is not in the Geez text and thus changes Bahrey's statement completely. In describing the formation of the luba, its circumcision and naming, Bahrey states (p.66) *"yawätsə'u səmä lärə'somu kullomu Bärtuma wä Borän."* His Amharic translation (p. 80) *"Bärtuma nna Borän hullum lä(yä)rasachäw səm yawät'allu."* His English translation (p, 200) "Bertuma and Boren each gives itself a name," versus Huntingford's translation (1955:115) "...all the Baraytuma and Boran give themselves a *collective* name." Huntingford is on target, Getachew has missed the point. His translation gives the impression that Bahrey is describing *two tribes with two armies* when, in fact, his evidence indicates that Oromo, at this stage, were under *one ruling luba, with one luba name, and one army.*

### Bahrey's problem: difficulty with non-local groups

It is, in my view, a mistake to think of the ancient dual organization described by Bahrey—BAREYTUMA and BORANA—as tribes rather than moieties. The fact that Bahrey calls them *nägäd* or "tribes" is not important. What else could he call them since there was no word in his language that could capture the concept of moieties, a concept so alien to the super-territorial Amhara and Tigrayans?

The word "moiety" was not yet invented by anthropologists in the days of Bahrey, and anthropology did not even exist as a discipline. But contemporary historians have an obligation to go beyond the language of the 16th century, and re-read Bahrey's document armed with his substantive observations about BARETTUMA and BORANA, and interpret what he says in relation to what we know today about the structure of Oromo moieties.

### The first part of Bahrey's history of the two moieties fits into one gada chronology

The history of the first five Abba Gadas whose exploits are described by Bahrey's epic story make up *one* gada chronology. Hence, it is very likely that the Abba Gadas sometimes came from one moiety and sometimes from the other. That is what we would expect if indeed the two moieties were sharing power, as they do today among the Ethiopian Borana. The names of moieties A and B that appear in the Chart (Fig. 4.1), Bahrey's chronology, are, of course, transposed from the Borana chronology. The pattern A,B,A,B,A implies that the moieties alternated in assuming power. It could just as easily have been an A,A,B,B,A pattern. All we know is that the moieties were sharing power and that each probably assumed the top position of leadership roughly as often as the other.

### Historic-ethnographic parallels

The reason why we chose to read Bahrey chronicle using the contemporary Borana chronology as reference material was because it is *one and the same gada idiom that is being used in the two instances* and we have to know what the idiom is. The parallels are justified because what is happening in Borana today is comparable to what the Oromo were doing in the first part of Bahrey's history. The Oromo, at that time, were one and the same people governed by two cross-cutting organizations: one Gada institution and two moieties.

The Borana today in Southern Ethiopia are one and the same people governed by two cross-cutting organizations: one Gada institution and two moieties. Among the southern Borana today the age-regiments are drawn from the Sabbo and the Gona moieties; they always go to war as a single force, not as two separate "tribes" called "Sabbo" and "Gona." That, for instance, was the situation in the war between Madha Galma's regiments and the Marrehan Somali. Madha was Sabbo, but his regiments were Sabbo and Gona: *it is, nonetheless, said to be a "Sabbo victory," because it was commanded by a Sabbo war chief.* In the first phase of Bahrey's history, it is clear that gada regiments, made up of fighters from both moieties, did their fighting not as two tribes with two parallel armies, but as a single nation governed by the same political and military institutions.

All this is not to deny the fact that, as the great migration progressed, Oromo peoples broke up into self governing communities. The only point of our thesis is this: (1) the separation *did not occur by moiety* and *(2) it did not occur during the first generation covered by Bahrey.*

### Compensatory processes

Even as the fragmentation progressed, however, there were two compensatory processes at work. One was the well-known and amply-described process of *forming confederacies.* That, happened, for instance, in Tulama (Shoa) on a grand scale, encompassing the ancient moieties, as well as the Oromo/Gabra dual organization, the latter serving as one of the keystones of the larger confederacy. It is a very complex system. (Macch'a, by contrast, offers a lop-sided picture, in which the Oromo/Gabra dualism has completely supplanted the moiety organization.)

But it is the *moiety replication and rebuilding* process that we are focussing on here, not the Oromo/Gabra dichotomy. Moiety replication had two consequences: (1) It permitted the continued use of the moieties as a power-sharing framework; (2) It gave rise to widespread moiety networks, so that a Borana and Barettuma from Tulama still retained ritual and kinship ties with the Borana and Barettuma in the cradlelands.

The replication and rebuilding of moieties was part of the Oromo assimilationist, integrative, and re-integrative strategy that played an important role in keeping the Oromo nation together, even as the nation spread out over a huge area and broke up into separate kingdoms, territorial groupings, or confederacies that were autonomous political entities.

## The Cross-Distribution of Moieties: Empirical Evidence

If the BARETTUMA and BORANA of the early 16th century were indeed moieties, we would expect to find a substantial amount of intermingling of the constituent clans and lineages throughout the Oromo nation today—a situation that would cast considerable doubt on the notion that the descendants of the ancient BORANA occupy the western regions of Oromo country and the descendants of BAR-ETTUMA live in the eastern region. We expect to find elements of the BORANA moiety in the east and elements of the BARETTUMA moiety in the west, contrary to the common picture presented in the historical and ethnographic literature. In other words, there should be a significant degree of *cross-distribution*. Here are a few examples.

> *Borana in Zwai:* As was suggested in my first work on the Gada System, an examination of Beguinot's *Chronaca Abbreviata* reveals that elements of the ancient Borana moiety occur in Damot[19], in Gojjam[20] in the western region—as expected—but also in Zwai in the eastern region which is contrary to expectations.[21]

> *Borana in Wollo:* The same pattern of cross-distribution also occurs in Wollo. Why, for instance, are there major groups known as Borana within Wollo—a region that is thought to be a segment of the Oromo nation that is of BARETTUMA descent? In view of such evidence of the cross-distribution of clans across the two great territories of the Oromo nation, we have to re-think our assumptions.

> *Macch'a are not really Borana?* When we find such strange bits of information suggesting that the Macch'a are not really Borana but the "brothers of Borana"[22] should we simply dismiss it as an aberration? In the words of Atsmä Giorgis:

>> Thus Macch'a is not Borana but the Borana had occupied before the Macch'a the Walal hill which was originally called Seyon Dur at Zigam. They also say the Borana is the father of all the Galla...born on top of Walal;"[23] "...Borana and Macch'a were brothers. In fact, Macch'a means alien, and it seems that they have no relationship with the Teloma."[24]

It is possible that Atsmä is describing here a situation where Borana and Macch'a are descendants of different moieties. Indeed the Macch'a-Tulama pair may itself be part of the old moiety system abandoned when the two branches became autonomous and the Macch'a began replicating the dual organization in the form of the internal Borana-Gabaro pair. If they are, we cannot tell which one, Macch'a or Tulama, leans more heavily toward BORANA or BARETTUMA or if both contain elements of the two ancient moieties, and that the Borana identity has become dominant in Macch'a, while both moieties have been preserved in Tulama.

*Macch'a in Barentu and Arsi:* In Mohammed Hassen's map there is a section of Arsi society that is referred to as Macch'a. More significantly, Macc'ha is one of the ancestors of the Arsi on their clan genealogy, putting them on the BARETTUMA side of the great divide. We may ask "What are Macch'a doing in the heart of Barettuma country and at the trunk of their genealogical tree?"

*Barettuma ancestors of Ghibe kings:* Many bits and pieces of such evidence were beginning to surface since the publication of Beckingham and Huntingford's *Some Records of Ethiopia.*[25] In the genealogical record of Ghibe kingdoms (Gera) there are ancestors who are of Barettuma origin, in spite of the fact that the people as a whole are said to be of BORANA origin.

*Cross-distribution of Karrayyu:* Perhaps the most dramatic evidence of the cross-distribution of clans is the case of the great clan known as Karrayyu. We have found that this clan is the most expansive and dynamic part of the Oromo nation. In our record of Marsabit Elders, Karrayyu was one of the vanguards of the southward migration of the Borana into Kenya. Evidence compiled by Haberland also suggests that it existed in the Awash valley in what is presumed to be Barettuma country, as well as in western Wallagga, presumed to be Borana country and as far south as the Tana river in Kenya, among the Orma.[26]

All this suggests that the assumption that the east is BARETTUMA country and the west is BORANA does not hold water. It is a huge simplification of a complex reality, in which moieties were not drifting apart, but rather they were reproducing themselves everywhere.

The simplification begins with Bahrey's Abraham and Lot story that was taken to mean a separation of the moieties in their entirety. Once it was decided that the west was BORANA country and the east was BARETTUMA on the basis of this feeble prompt from Bahrey, how much of the contradictory evidence was swept under the rug and continues to be so treated to day?

We must keep in mind that Bahrey is using biblical idiom in which all history comes in personified images: the luba is like a king, and refers to it as "he," and the moieties are like Abraham and Lot, brothers drifting apart? In this perspective, it is difficult to see that Abraham and Lot are not two 'tribes,' but that *each is made up of 'twins' who migrate as inseparable pairs*. Neither Bahrey nor his interpreters, anthropologists and historians alike, envisioned such a possibility.

## Compelling Evidence: The Borana/Oromo Concordance

The most compelling and most surprising evidence that we have uncovered so far comes from the southern Borana, the part of Ethiopia where this writer gathered his Ethiopian field data. As indicated earlier, the contemporary Borana are divided into two moieties called Sabbo and Gona. The Borana people as a whole have been assumed to be descendants of the ancient BORANA moiety who remained in the homelands when the great migration began. All the authors, myself included, assumed that the Borana were BORANA, a seemingly natural assumption. By far the most important fact that I now recognize is that a major part of Borana is not BORANA at all but BARETTUMA and that there is significant concordance between the clan structure of the Borana moieties of today and the pan-Oromo moieties of the 16th century.

The clan structure of the moieties reveals that there is a clear *ethnogenetic linkage between Bahrey's BARETTUMA/BORANA division and the southern Borana's Gona/Sabbo division*. That is a totally unexpected phenomenon. It became apparent to me only after I had completed all the above re-examination of Bahrey, although the evidence was in my field notes ever since 1963. Most of the above correspondences occur at the level of major clans, some—the indented items—refer to lineages of various magnitudes. The data are from Beckingham and Huntingford's genealogy of the Oromo, tabulated from Bahrey's account, matched with the moiety, clan, and lineage record of the Borana of Ethiopia from my records.

| PAN-OROMO MOIETIES | | BORANA MOIETIES | |
|---|---|---|---|
| 16th CENTURY | | TODAY | |
| *Moieties* | *Clans & Lineages* | *Moieties* | *Clans & Lineages* |
| **BORANA** | | **Gona** | |
| | Macc'ha | | Macch'itu |
| | Jidda | | Warri Jidda |
| | Dacch' | | Dacch'itu |
| | Galan | | Galantu |
| | Konno | | Konnitu |
| | Bach | | Bacchitu |
| | Jelle | | (Jillitu, Jilliccha) |
| **BARETTUMA** | | **Sabbo** | |
| | Karrayyu | | Karrayyu |
| | Obo | | Obbole |
| | Suba | | Sibu |
| | Liban | | Libano |
| | Itu | | Itu |
| | [Digalu]* | | Digalu |
| | Ilu | | Ilu |
| | Uru | | Aru |
| | ? | | Matt'arri |

*\*Digalu is missing in Bahrey, present in Susenyos chronicle.*

Table 4.3  Concordance of 16th Century Oromo Moieties
and today's Borana Moieties

Most of the correspondences occur at the level of major clans, some—the indented items—occur at the level of lineages. The data are from Bahrey's genealogy of the Oromo, as translated by Beckingham and Huntingford, matched with contemporary Borana genealogical records.

## *The concordance interpreted*

Table 4.3 reveals the very close correspondence between the Gona (Fullelle) clans of the Ethiopian Borana today and the BORANA moiety in Bahrey's account. This is fully expected since the Borana are commonly believed to be a section of the ancient BORANA moiety that had stayed behind during the great migration. What is remarkable about these data is the degree to which the two lists of Borana clans are virtually identical; there is an extraordinarily close duplication of clans between the ancient BORANA and the contemporary Borana of the south, but the parallels are with one, not both, moieties. In other words, the BORANA moiety of Bahrey corresponds only to the Gona moiety, Fullelle sub-moiety, of the southern Borana and the parallels are these:

Macch'a in one is Macch'itu in the other, Dacch'a in one is Dacch'itu in the other, Konno in one is Konnitu in the other, Galan in one is Galantu in the other, Bacch in one, Bacchitu in the other. In other words, one set is a simple grammatical variant of the other. They are otherwise identical. This parallelism is as expected, but the closeness of the two systems is quite striking in view of the fact that the two bodies of evidence are four centuries apart.

What is unexpected is the presence of one major Barettuma clan, the Karrayyu, inside the Borana kinship system, under Sabbo. Digallu is missing in Bahrey but two of its lineages, Ilu and Aru, appear in Bahrey's genealogy under Wollo and Morowwa. Bahrey also identifies Itu as a major clan but it appears as a lineage in Karrayyu today.

At this point we should note that Sabbo—the junior moiety—consists of three great clans: Karrayyu, Digalu, and Matt'arri. Karrayyu and Digalu lineages are reflected in Bahrey's genealogy but none of the Matt'arri lineages are part of that historic record.

### *Why is the Digalu clan missing in Bahrey?*

It is surprising that Bahrey does not include the Digalu in his list of Barettuma clans. They are the dominant "secular" clan of the junior Sabbo moiety today. Politically they hold an important place in the Gada System. Over a period of three and a half centuries they have held the office of Abba Gada more often (31%) than any other clan of either moiety (see Appendix II). The absence of this clan in Bahrey's genealogy is, therefore, an important deficit. If, however, we set our mind to searching for evidence concerning the role of this major Barettuma-Oromo clan during the great migration, the evidence begins to surface. There are, for instance, some instructive references to the clan in the Susenyos chronicle—a document written about two decades after Bahrey's epic history. The chronicle helps to complete the gap in Bahrey's account. The two references in the text suggest that Digalu was a very powerful clan that launched two major campaigns against the army of Emperor Susenyos:

> In one instance, the chronicler describes a war between the forces of Susenyos and the Digalu regiments. He describes the celebrations that followed the king's victory. The magnitude of the celebration suggests that it was a major confrontation.[28]

> The second reference is an account of a war in which the Digalu were probably victorious. The chronicler does not say that but instead talks about the arrogance of the king and how he was humbled by God. This is chronicler language that means that the king was badly defeated by the Digalu.[29]

> In the index, Pereira adds: "Digalu era o nome de una tribu de Galla, que provavelmente pertencia aos Baraytuma. Esta tribu nåo e mencionata na Historia dos Galla [Bahrey]"[30]

Pereira is guessing the moiety affiliation of the Digalu as belonging to BARETTUMA, not BORANA, but his insight is consistent with what is suggested by contemporary ethnographic evidence of the Borana. Karrayyu and Digalu belong to the same half of Borana society and we now have evidence that the Karrayyu are BARETTUMA as they so pointedly say in their ritual texts.

### *Borana moieties (Sabbo/Gona) retain big parts of BARETTUMA*

Our evidence so far indicates that the moiety organization of the southern Borana of today retains very substantial elements of both of the Oromo moieties of the 16th century. In other words, it is clear that Sabbo and Gona are, in the main, a replication of BORANA and BARETTUMA, with Sabbo corresponding to BARETTUMA and Gona corresponding to BORANA (Fullelle). In both these situations it is BORANA and its derivative Gona that serve as the senior half.

Since making these discoveries, I have taken the issue back to the Borana elder, Galma Liban, who commented extensively on these chapters. One of the questions I raised was the matter of the Barettuma presence in southern Borana society and culture. I asked him to tell me what he knew about it. He said that he knew very little, but added that he remembered a passage that is part of the blessings that Karrayyu elders recite on ritual occasions:

> *Nu warr Dayyu dullaccha, nagenni kenna dullachum duri,*
> *Nu warr Bareettum(a), barin kenna nagaya.*

> We are the ancient Dayyu people, our peace is older than old,
> We are the Bareettuma people, our morning is peaceful.

The speaker, who is a member of the Dayyu lineage of Karrayyu, says that they are Barettuma people. This is corroborated by text in Raba rituals that identifies Karrayyu in its entirety as Barettuma.[31]

The Karrayyu, who are calling themselves an ancient part of Barettuma, are not a small refugee clan attached to a big Borana moiety. They hold a dominant place in the moiety, and lead in both the Gada and Qallu institutions. Naturally, they are by law excluded from the top office of Abba Gada, because their clan is empowered to elect that most senior officer of the nation. As a result there are virtually no Karrayyu Abba Gadas in the entire 360-year long chronology. Only one such Abba Gada turned up in the record.[32] On the other hand, Karrayyu have permanent representation in the senior Gada Council.

Furthermore, when we look at the level of Karrayyu participation in all the three gada councils of Borana—namely, the Adula (senior), Garba (junior), and Meddhiccha (lateral) councils—they have a dominant presence. Between 1891 and 1968, Karrayyu held gada office 33 times, compared with the other two clans of the moiety—Digalu and Matt'arri—who held office 25 and 23 times respectively. The Karrayyu also held, and still hold, one of the two key ritual offices of the Borana—the office of Qallu—by hereditary right. In view of the dominant role Karrayyu play in the moiety, they cannot be viewed as assimilated aliens or as second-class citizens, still yearning for equality.

## *Replication of the ancient moieties in Borana, Ethiopia*

The data in Table 4.3, above, show concretely how the ancient moieties were replicated among the Borana people who remained in the cradleland region, during the 16th century migration. At first glance, this population seems to be a section of the ancient BORANA moiety that was left behind, a fact strongly suggested by the word BORANA—the name of the ancient moiety—that has become the name of the people who remained in the homelands. The facts that have now surfaced indicate that the situation is quite different.

The Borana people who remained in the cradleland contain substantial elements of both moieties, not merely of the BORANA moiety. The Karrayyu clan of Borana is undoubtedly of BARETTUMA origin. It is the most expansive clan in all of Borana and, possibly, in the entire Oromo nation. It is not an appendage of the Sabbo moiety, but stands at its political and ritual core.

The Susenyos chronicle suggests that the second dominant clan, Digalu, was very powerful during the decades following Bahrey's manuscript. Today, it holds a position in the junior moiety which is no less important than Karrayyu. It is a paradox, however, that the Karrayyu are spread across much of Ethiopia and Kenya, but the Digalu clan seems to have vanished. We have found no historic or ethnographic evidence that would allow us to place it anywhere on the current map of the Oromo speaking nation outside of Borana. Fortunately, two of its minor lineages, Aru and Ilu, show up as major lineages among the Barentu of Harar, as well as in Macch'a and Wollo, suggesting that a closer examination of the component lineages may reveal that the Digalu clan continues to exist in these branches of Oromo, under a different clan or local groupings.

Finally, the third clan of the Sabbo moiety, Matt'arri, appears to be a latecomer into the moiety. That is suggested by the fact that they have three minor Qallus of their own. It is very likely that they are Sabbo by assimilation, not by genesis. They pay homage to the most senior Qallu, i.e. the head of the Gona moiety, in addition to performing their own lesser Muda rituals. In Oromo history, such peripheral rituals in minority populations often indicate that the people in question are still in the process of achieving equal status. This proliferation of Qallus, however, is only a vestige of history, for Matt'arri today are fully integrated into the Gada institution. Their representation in Gada councils is only slightly smaller than that of

Karrayyu or Digalu. Incidentally, Matt'arri clan also shows up in the Orma clan list, but in a similarly marginal position. Kelly calls them the "Galecha clan," [ a word derived from *galalcha*, "to delay" i.e.,"late comers"].

Kelly says that its major lineages were, curiously, attached to two different moieties: Metta and Karare to Irdid (Boran moiety), and Garjeda to Barettuma, (see Appendix 4, and Hilarie Kelly personal communication). Both Borana and Orma data suggest that Matt'arri are stragglers in the assimilation process.

As matters stand now, it appears that a major part of Borana is not BORANA but BARETTUMA, emerging mainly by ancient ethnogenesis. Only in one instance, Matt'arri, does a major clan appear to have been assimilated. Once again Borana turns out to be not an insignificant offshoot of the Oromo nation, as Huntingford once thought. On the contrary, Borana seems to represent the Oromo nation in proto form, encompassing Gada, in its entirety, and both the old moieties in significant measure.

Finally, it is worth noting that there is one strong indication that all the clans of the Sabbo moiety are viewed as "late comers" into the Borana moieties. All three clans of Sabbo, not merely the Matt'arri, are known as "Galalcha Saden." Asked to explain the phrase, Borana say *galalcha jecchu, warr galgala dhufe*, "galalcha means people who arrived in the evening." That probably refers to ancient ethnogenesis. At present the Galalcha Saden are full partners with the Gona in the political domain, hold a dominant position in warfare and expansion, and a secondary position in ritual.

### Related Concepts of National Identity & Transformation: Oromo, Ilman Orma, Oromsu, Boransu vs Orma, Ormu

The name "Oromo" appears as the collective name of the ancestral clans in many parts of the Oromo nation. Hence, the term probably has considerable antiquity. However, its specific genesis as the common name for all Oromo speakers needs to be carefully documented, in the same way that we have done for the moieties.

Here, parenthetically, is an ethnographic paradox that has bothered me for decades. Borana—the people I selected, after one year of exploratory research, as the most distinctive and most conservative representative of the Oromo nation—do not call themselves Oromo, but only recognize the name as referring to their kinsmen who are spread out far and wide. Some of these kinsmen, such as the Macch'a and Tulama, maintained contact with them through the institution of the Muda pilgrimages.[33] Others, notably most of the Barettuma-dominant groups, migrated not only beyond the reach of Muda pilgrimages, but completely abandoned the cradlelands. Prominent among these are the Orma. One part went south into Kenya, past the Lorian Swamp, and settled on the right bank of the Tana River; the other part went deep inside Somali territory and then migrated south to settle on the left bank of the River: they are known as Bararetta and Kofira Orma respectively. (Turton 1975, p. 531 and A. Legesse, "Preliminary Orma Field Notes," 2006, p. 8.)

In addition to the term "Oromo" and "Orma" the phrase "Ilman Orma" also seems to have become a collective name for the growing nation. Here too, the genesis of the phrase and who began using it as the general name for Oromo speakers is a matter of great interest for ethno-linguists. One early record that I came across of people calling themselves "Ilman Orma" is the case of the Yejju and Rayya who went in the opposite direction from the Orma and almost as far as they did. They called themselves "Ilman Orma" as recorded in Antoine d'Abbadie's account of the great ancestors of the northernmost Oromo.[34] That instance and the many instances like it when the phrase becomes associated with a widely shared identity needs to be documented and mapped out.

I am compelled to think back to the beginning of my field research and recall a conversation with my key Borana mentor, Arero Rammata. I asked him what the word "Orma" means to Borana and he said "stranger." Indeed, the verb form of the word *Ormu* means "to become estranged (vi.)" or "to banish (vt.)." I then asked if Borana consider themselves to be Orma and he said, "No we cannot be Orma, we are still here aren't we?" At that time, the statement no sense at all. What does "being here" have to do with "not being Orma?" Now, in retrospect this conversation begins to make sense, because Borana were telling me they were not "Orma" because they did not leave the cradlelands and the Muda rituals, whereas the Orma did.

Although Borana do not call themselves Oromo, it is remarkable that they use the word *Oromsu*, "to Oromize" to describe the assimilation of aliens into *their* society. Historically, even the assimilation of slaves into Borana was described in the same language: *garbiccha Oromsite*, "Oromized a slave." They also have a lineage in Karrayyu-Danqa, called *Oromtitti* paired off with another called *Gabarttitti*, reflecting the Oromo/Gabra division that occurs in Arsi and many other branches of the nation. In these vestigial but critically diagnostic forms the *Oromo identity is part of the identity of the Borana.*

Conversely, Borana consider themselves to be deeply connected to the wider nation, including the "Orma strangers," by virtue of the fact that they are its ritual leaders, its most senior segment, and the "first born" (*angafa*). Far from abandoning their culture—as their Barettuma kinsmen have done—they have maintained their Gada and Qallu institutions, and used both to build up the Pax Borana, thus expanding the influence of their culture into neighboring territories, converting two Somali clans—Garri and Ajuran—into bilingual Oromo-speaking allies. Among all the Oromo, the Borana are least likely to trade their identity for some other identity. Hence, *Borana have become the sole remaining custodians of Muda shrines.* As such, Borana is a fully embedded part of the identity of the Oromo nation.

Of their own children who go to cities and schools, in distant places, and come back behaving like strangers, Borana say *Ya nyap'e inni!* "He has become an alien or enemy!" To make sure that the children are not totally alienated, they make good use of their return visits to immerse them in rituals. The thinking about emigrants is somewhat similar. People become estranged (*Ormu*) through emigration and are, therefore, welcomed to the Gada rites of passage and the great Muda ritual, through which *Oromo renew their cultural roots and rediscover their lost identity.* In short, for the Borana, *Ormu* stands for "estrangement between brothers," *nyap'u* for "total alienation" (joining the enemy) and *Oromsu* stands for "re-integration"—over and above its second meaning of "assimilation of aliens." When Borana assimilate other Oromo groups it is described by the narrower term *Boransu*, "to Boranize." It is worth noting, however, that BARETTUMA have no such specific term meaning "to Barettumize." They employ only the generic term *Oromsu* (vt.), "to Oromize," or *Oromoomu* (vi.), "to become Oromo."

## Moiety Replication or Rebuilding: the Twin Nation

One of the deepest aspects of Oromo heritage that is shared by the entire Oromo nation is the pair of concepts, BARETTUMA and BORANA, that together define a fundamental aspect of their identity. The fact that the dual organization is also shared with Somali and Afar further suggests that this is an ancient aspect of East Cushitic social and political structure.

In other words, *the identity of the twin nation is at least as old as the Oromo identity, if not older.* In Borana the moieties evolved from the ancient moieties, without going through the destruction and rebuilding process. The ancient BORANA moiety became Gona, the ancient BARETTUMA became Sabbo, and they are still with us today.

In other areas, Oromo populations migrated too far apart to be able to share a common government, a common military organization, and a common moiety system but, as they were separated, they took with them both the Gada and moiety institutions and changed them to fit their new conditions. However, unlike Borana or Orma, where the ancient moiety structure was preserved, but renamed, there was some breakdown and rebuilding of the moieties.

The evidence from present-day Arsi—the cradleland of the ancient BARETTUMA moiety—is very scant. Part of the reason is that Arsi institutions, both Gada and Qallu, were destroyed during Menelik's conquest and in the subsequent Islamization of the people. These historic processes are epitomized by one of the traditional leaders of the Arsi who had the extraordinary name of "Mohammed Gada Qallu." (Abbas Haji, personal communication). Assailed on all sides by new forces that overwhelmed his society, it seems that this leader was trying to preserve in his person the two great institutions of his ancestors along with his newly acquired religion.[35]

Among Arsi and other Oromo who have converted to Islam, we may also be facing what Günther Schlee calls *l'islamization du passé* or Mohammed Hassen labels the "fabrication of Islamic genealogies" by Oromo societies such as Yejju.[36] Islam is a religion that does not permit the celebration of pre-Islamic history or institutions. Instead an Islamic past may be invented for the new converts—in much the same way that the Somali constructed a genealogy for themselves that makes the whole nation descendants of the Quraishitic lineage of the Prophet Mohammed, a most prolific lineage, indeed.

As a result of the extensive Islamization of the Barettuma world (Yejju, Wollo, Barentu, Arsi), the only Barettuma-dominant branch who have preserved the moieties today are the Orma of Kenya, although they too have now converted to Islam, as documented in Hilarie Kelly's ethnography titled, appropriately, "From Gada to Islam." They too are in the process of relaxing the exogamous rules.[37] How far they have gone down that road is a matter that must now be determined through further field research.

### The Tulama Case

One of the most interesting cases which I have not been able to analyze adequately in this book is the case of the Tulama in central Ethiopia. They are a Borana-dominant group who have preserved their Gada institution and some aspects of the dual organization, despite the fact that they live at the center of the country, around the capital city. Like the Macch'a, they have the Borana and Gabaro sections. But the more important fact is that their clan list also contains two groups called *Saglan Borana, Torban Barentuma,* "The Nine Borana and the Seven Barentuma." This suggests that the BORANA/BARETTUMA division is represented in their social structure. As yet I do not have a list of the constituent clans needed for more detailed comparison.

The Oromo/Gabra dualism occurs in Tulama also occurs in most other Oromo areas. It surfaces with the root form of Orm*/Gbr* in Barettuma-dominant groups, or the Brn*/Gbr* in Borana-dominant groups. The terminology differs but the process seems to be the same. It refers to the partial but progressive assimilation of aliens. Moieties, on the other hand, represent an ancient assimilationist dualism, which goes back to a deepest layer of Oromo ethnogenesis, antedating the beginning of the Gada Chronology, when both moieties were present among the founders of the Gada institution.

### Extending the thesis: Schlee's Approach to Ethnogenesis

The history of the destruction and rebuilding of moieties must now be carried forward to the present time in those areas where a dual organization exists and whatever form it assumes. This is a difficult task and will require the collaboration of many scholars with specialized historic and anthropological knowledge of the different parts of Oromo society. It may also require the contributions of historical linguistics and the specialized branch of anthropology that uses clan identities as the critical basis for the study of ethnogenesis. In this regard, Günther Schlee (1985:23-30) has demonstrated how the Cushitic speakers of Northern Kenya evolved from a common base, diverged from each other, or merged with each other over the centuries.

His main analytical tool is what he calls *inter-ethnic clan equivalences* i.e. clan or lineage names that are cognates. These can be assumed to be of *common* origin but always keeping in mind that the similarities can also result from *lateral influences* due to conquest, alliances, mass adoption, and ritual or linguistic assimilation that are themselves defensive responses to the threat of conquest. He has developed a number of diagnostic tools to distinguish one from the other, comparable to the methods linguists use to distinguish genetically related *cognates* from *loanwords*. Hence, his contribution to our work on Oromo ethnogenesis is not only methodological but also substantive.

On the specific topic of the genesis of the Oromo moieties, he writes one paragraph that is packed with insight. He says that the BORANA moiety of Bahrey ". . . has formed the core of the Gona moiety of the modern Boran, while BAREYTUMA has become a moiety of the Tana Orma. The products of this split must have each rebuilt the moiety system by incorporating groups of different origin as the second moiety, thus enabling them to continue moiety exogamy and moiety balance or ritual functions."[38] He has further stated that one of the moieties of Orma is derived from the ancient BARETTUMA and is called "Barettuma," whereas the other moiety, called "Irdida," has connections with the BORANA.[39]

The data we have presented here is in fundamental agreement with Schlee but with three qualifications. (1) Borana moieties were not, in the main, rebuilt because most of their clans, in both moieties, are directly derived from the ancient moieties; (2) Throughout the four centuries of their history; they never ceased to function as the balanced halves of the political community; (3) The part that has been added on to the junior moiety, namely Matt'arri, is a marginal part of Sabbo. They also appear in a similarly marginal position in Orma moieties, their lineages strangely attached to two different moieties. Their lineages are also missing in Bahrey's genealogy of the moieties. Hence, they are, in all probability, aliens assimilated in recent centuries. Such annexation is a normal part of the extrinsic growth of moieties.

### Summing Up

The specific linkages between the moieties of Orma, Arsi, Barentu to the Borana of southern Ethiopia and to the ancient moieties of Bahrey have been tabulated, and the results are reflected in Fig. 4.1 and in Appendix III. The connection of Arsi Mando to the old BARETTUMA moiety has been amply demonstrated. However, the linkage of Sikko and the old BORANA moiety cannot be demonstrated at present time, because the Arsi data (Haberland's) are inadequate.

The chart below is a graphic summary of the evidence presented above and in Appendix III. Solid lines represent known linkages, broken lines represent probable connections. The Orm*/Gbr* or Brn*/Gbr* dual organization is a different layer of ethnogenesis. That is the main form the dualism takes in Macch'a, but it exists superimposed on moiety structure in Tulama, Borana and Arsi.

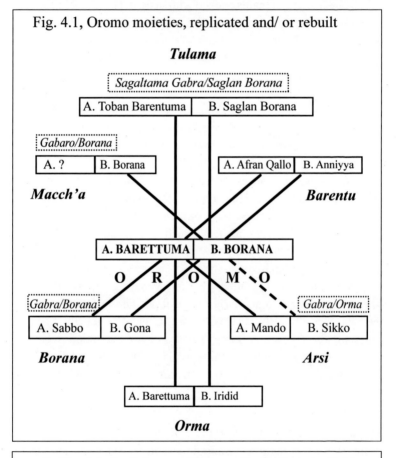

Fig. 4.1, Oromo moieties, replicated and/ or rebuilt

In Fig. 4.1, the linkages of Borana, Orma, Barentu, Tulama to the ancient moieties have been demonstrated with varying degrees of certitude. The strongest linkages are those of Borana and Orma moieties with the ancient BORANA and BARETTUMA moieties.

Another member of the Barettuma-dominant group who do not appear in Fig 4.1, because no clan list is available for them, are the Warr Daya—a people who went as far away from the homelands as the Orma. The effect of the emigration on their society has been very destructive, particularly for those who ended up under Somali domination. On the Tana River basin, they are part of Orma, but they do not appear on the Orma clan lists. Nevertheless, the Orma describe them as their kinsmen and neighbors. A major part of their clan got separated from Orma and now lives in the Juba valley, Somalia, apparently under miserable conditions (A. Legesse, Preliminary Orma Fieldnotes, 2006 and Appeal of Wardey Elders to the International Humanitarian Community, Nairobi, 2006).

Warr Daya are recorded as the last *luba* (Melba, 1586-94) in Bahrey's history when they fought against Ras Welda Kristos of Gojjam. At that stage, they were obviously a potent force.

### Some Old Roots of the BARETTUMA in Orma & Warr Daya

It is worth remembering that the Orma have some very ancient properties that should be kept in mind in re-thinking Oromo ethnogenesis. They have retained as their name, the name "Orma." Similarly ancient features also appear in other regions. One clan in Barentu (Harar) bears the name of "Oromo." Arsi on the other hand refer to themselves as "Orma" when contrasting their society to Gabra. Mohammed Hassen suggests that the Orma cradleland is Tullu Nama Duri, "the hill of the ancient people."[40] I too have records, in my Borana field notes, indicating that Borana view Tullu Nam Dur to be a most ancient cradleland.

Warr Daya are allies and kinsmen of Orma. A useful fact that should be kept in mind in tracing their ethnogenetic connections is that their name appears in four different forms: Warra Daya, Warr Dae, Wardai, Wardey. They do appear in the Borana clan list not under their own name, but as a minor lineage of Karrayyu, called Wayyu.

A most significant fact about their history is that the Borana credit them with having excavated most of the great wells *(tula)* in their territory. They are said to have dug the wells and lived in the area with their herds for generations, before being driven out of Borana territory by Abbayyi Babbo, Abba Gada, 1667-74. This was one of several waves of Orma/Warr Daya migration southward.

In all my research, the Ethiopian Borana have emerged as the conservators of a major part of the Oromo heritage. It now seems that the Orma/Warr Daya too should be seen in the same light, on the Barettuma side of the great divide. As an initial step, however, all the precious evidence, both historic and ethnographic, on Orma and Warr Daya must be assembled and analyzed, before these converts to Islam invent an Arab genealogy for themselves, and delete Oromo history from their oral traditions, as their kinsmen in Wollo have done (Trimingham, 1965:198-99).

## Stages in the Development of Moieties

The most rudimentary stage in the development of moieties happens when Oromo rapidly adopt or incorporate aliens on a large scale. It takes assimilated aliens some time to gain full citizenship. During that transitory stage, they may be excluded from key Oromo rituals and/or institutions, they may create their own rituals, they may have their own Qallus, and they may have only a partial role in Gada, or they may have their own Gada. In other words, their transitional situation may be revealed in *partial* or *parallel participation* in Oromo institutions.

The best example of an advanced moiety system is that of the Borana, where the two halves are interlinked through the rules of exogamy and political-demographic balancing. From the brief descriptions offered by Alice Werner, Hilarie Kelly and Günther Schlee the Orma moieties too were at a similarly advanced stage, since they had ritual balancing and, until the 1920's, moiety exogamy.[39]

### *Gabaro: a moiety in formation*

The Oromo/Gabra dimension represents relatively recent assimilation of aliens. The root form of the word Gbr* originally referred to slaves, and its derivatives are now applied to assimilated aliens, and various low status groups among many Cushitic, as well as Semitic speakers.

In Macch'a the situation of the Gabaro, in relation to the dominant section called Borana, is complex and changing. It has been described at different stages of history by different writers. From these descriptions we get two quite different profiles. The first description, concerning the early 17th century, is presented by Mohammed Hassen. The second is by Lambert Bartels, based on many years of research in the mid 20th century.

In the early 17th century, the people who were conquered by the Macch'a did not readily accept their subjugation, despite the opportunities given to them for incorporation into Oromo society. In the words of Mohammed Hassen "The Oromo adopted the Gabaro en masse, giving them clan genealogy, marrying their women, and taking their young into service for herding (p. 63)." Men were recruited for military service. When they joined the Macch'a cavalry as mounted warriors, they were honorably referred to as "Yahabata." They were given the right to form their own Gada (p. 68-69).

There were times, however, when their rights were "trampled," says Mohammed Hassen. That became the reason for an uprising that led to open hostilities with the Borana. Some of the Yahabata broke away from the Borana of Macch'a and joined the army of Emperor Susenyos, who, of course, welcomed them. The emperor offered to settle them in Gojjam, across the Blue Nile, and told them to accept Christianity. Amazingly, they asked to be given time to complete their *butta* ritual—a most important rite that occurs in the middle of the gada life cycle (p. 64, 69). Their concern indicates that they had been immersed in Gada culture, before they crossed the Nile and were absorbed by another society.

Parenthetically, it is worth noting that this is one piece of evidence we have of *mass adoption by an Emperor.* Significantly, the emperor who did that was himself captured as a child and raised as one of their own children by the Oromo. He had first-hand knowledge of their culture and had in some measure become Oromized. He was using Oromo techniques of mass adoption and military strategy to reverse Oromo expansion and to try to bring them under his dominion.

The early period in the development of the Gabaro in Macch'a society was a period of turmoil that contrasts sharply with their situation in contemporary Macch'a. The study of *Oromo Religion* presented by Father Bartels contains much evidence about the junior status of the Gabaro vis-a-vis the Borana, but that is only part of the picture. The other part reveals that Borana and Gabaro are one and the same people, not masters and servants, not autochthons and half-assimilated aliens. The language in which all this is described is, of course, *ambiguous,* but that is the characteristic of the language of moieties. Statuses that are being altered by political bargaining between coordinate groups cannot be sharply defined. *Ambiguity* is the anti-structural feature that *creates room for maneuver and a legitimate framework for give and take.*

The decidedly senior position of the Borana is exhibited in many areas. To begin with, the Borana leads in all rituals. He also has more land, more leisure, and more opportunity to assume leadership roles. As the first-born son does for his younger brothers, the Borana always opens the way for his juniors in ritual, political, and economic activities.[41] Seniority, so defined, is not merely a symbolic matter; it has practical consequences. However, there is no evidence indicting that this status differentiation has resulted in sharp economic stratification between Borana and Gabaro.

In Bartels' presentation, the most telling language they use is the idiom of "older brother" and "younger brother," which is not the same as "master" and "servant" (p. 148). Even more telling is the fact that the Borana claim common ancestry with the Gabaro. When asked where the Gabaro came from, they answer "Gabaro and Borana are all the children of Rayya"—the first ancestor of the Oromo according to one Macch'a tradition (p. 163). It is clear that there is much in their political idiom that presents Borana and Gabaro as "brothers" and "equals," even if the ritual seniority of the Borana is still intact.

In short, between the exploitation, turmoil, and rebellion that was in evidence in the early 17th century and the relatively more balanced situation recorded in the 20th century, a basic process of transformation has taken place, in which inequality and conflict have been replaced by ritual give and take, shared citizenship, and a common ancestor. This process of transformation of the Gabaro suggests that they were well on their way to becoming a moiety on par with their Borana countrymen, when the process was sidetracked by new forms of stratification resulting from incorporation of Macch'a as a whole into the Ethiopian Empire.

### *The Barentu case: analysis in progress.*

Every one of the sections of the Oromo nation examined above, except Barentu, has yielded some evidence on dual organization so far. For Barentu, we now have two published sources that give us some valuable clues, namely, de Salviac and Trimingham. Martial de Salviac, suggests that the Warra Bokku/Warra Qallu dual organization was still at work at the time that he lived in Harar. It should be remembered that the Warra Bokku are the "ruler-warrior" half of society; Warra Qallu are the peaceful ritual leaders. More relevant is his statement that Harar pilgrims go to Mormoro where they form two groups called Warra Barentou and Warra Kallo.[42] This terminology immediately suggests that the Warra Kallo are not Barentu. That, however, turns out to be a dead end lead.

The only available clan list that divides Barentu into two major sections, Ania [Anniyya] and Kallo [Afran Qallo], is Trimingham's (1965, p. 206). Based on this source, a comparative chart for Barentu,

Borana and Bahrey has been prepared (See Appendix III). It reveals that the Afran Qallo have four major links either to Borana/Sabbo or to the ancient BARETTUMA moiety (Bahrey), Anniyya has three major linkages to Borana/Gona and to the ancient BORANA moiety. In due course, this analysis will be strengthened with more detailed but less structured data contained in the works of G.W.B. Hunting-ford (1955) and Mohammed Hassen (personal communication).

## *Dual organization in the Oromo periphery: Gabra & Guji*

According to William Torry, The Gabra have a complex dual organiza-tion consisting of the Lossa-Yiblo division that exists *within* the clans. Instead of a pattern where the moieties are divided into clans, we have here a situation in which each clan is divided into "halves."[43] Most of the Gabra pay tribute to the Borana Qallus, and they have three kinds of links *(tiriso, hori fina, or dabare)* with Borana moieties. Alganna and Sharbana are linked to Sabbo, whereas Gara and Galbo are linked to Gona. These are relationships of alliance, not descent. (See Torry's chart on p. 47). None of the Gabra clans, except Alganna, are descend-ed from the BARETTUMA and BORANA ancestors of the Oromo, but were rather bonded en masse to one or the other Borana moiety and remained part of the Pax Borana until the late 19th century, when the British colonists went to work trying to actively dismantle the Borana confederacy.[44] They were suspicious of all inter-ethnic mergers such as those that occur on the border of Somali clans. It is called "the She-gat Problem" in the colonial archives, because such mergers tended to confuse the boundaries colonial rulers had imposed on the popula-tions. Gabra describe their merger with Borana as follows:

> Very long ago Borana came to our country and divided us up. "What section are you from, and you?" they asked. They then told us we would become fellow clansmen, some of us being assigned to the Konnitu clan, others to Dambitu, etc. They called this new relationship imposed upon us *tiriso* and it involved mutual aid and blessings.[45]

Please note that the Gabra/Borana or Gabra/Orma relationship is not part of the BARETTUMA/BORANA division (Fig. 4.1). It is superimposed upon it, forming a layer of alliance and incorporation, that is different from the ethnogenesis we are examining here. There are indications, however, that the Oromo/Gabra phenomenon may also be an early phase in the formation of moieties.

On the other hand, Guji were not included in this study of the history of dual organizations (Fig. 4.1) for structural reasons: because the top levels of their kinship and Gada systems are very different from the patterns analyzed in this book. They have a triadic rather than dyadic organization that cannot be readily compared with the moiety systems. That is a marked deviation from the general Oromo pattern. There is one Qallu for the whole society and he stands above the three divisions (clans), each with its own Abba Gada—a reversal of the positions of Gada and Qallu. Throughout most of the Oromo nation there is one Abba Gada and a plurality of Qallus, whereas in Guji there is one Qallu and a plurality of Abba Gadas.

Of course, Borana too has a triadic organization. It exists in the form of the Gada Triumvirate that makes up the top half of the Gada Council. However, the Council as a whole is bilaterally organized —a feature that preserves the balanced opposition aspect. What further distinguishes the Guji system from Borana is that it has evolved into a *territorial* organization among a people who live in and around a luxuriant rain forest and practice a more sedentary, less nomadic form of agro-pastoralism. In that context, it is reasonable to expect the clans to become more *localized*, as indeed they are.

Despite the incidental analogies between the triadic Gada leadership of the Guji and the Gada Triumvirate of the Borana, we should recognize that the balancing features have been eliminated in both Guji institutions: on the one hand a singular Qallu has no adversary and, on the other hand, among three the Abba Gadas there is little possibility of balance—more likely it will be unstable coalition dynamics that would dominate their relationships, if and when they operate in one political arena.

These are all variations in the evolution of Oromo institutions which must, in the final analysis, have a place in our model, if the moiety thesis is to account for all aspects of the evolving system.

### Dualism among Eastern Cushitic nations: Afar & Somali

Just as dual organization is virtually universal among the Oromo, so also is dualism a feature of other Eastern Cushitic nations. Thus, the Afar consist of two tribal halves called Asaimara and Adoimara, and the Somali people consist of Somal and Sab. In the Afar case they evolved a common name that encompasses both tribal halves, in the Somali case, the name of the senior half became the name of the nation. Both patterns occur in the evolution of Oromo moieties.

## *Moieties versus dual organization*

Throughout the above analysis we have used both the concepts of moiety and dual organization to describe the highest levels of the Oromo kinship system. It is necessary to clarify the distinction. The moiety system is a sub-set of dual organization. Any pair of social groups can have the quality of a dual organization if the members of the pair maintain culturally formalized linkages and interact with each other in regulated fashion. It is possible that in the earlier development of the Eastern Cushites, Oromo, Afar and Somali nations dual organizations served as the foundation of the balancing principle underlying their democratic life, possibly antedating the creation of the Gada institution and the rules of exogamy which are believed to have come into being at the same stage of history, prior to the beginning of the great migration.

## Muda, Pilgrims, Moieties, and Cradlelands

The practical consequence of the moiety replication/rebuilding process is that the moieties became an evolving but shared basis for creating and maintaining linkages across the widely dispersed nation and, at the same time, preserving the balancing mechanism that was so important to their democratic way of life. Our re-reading of Bahrey suggests that the Oromo were one nation until the early 1560's and that they maintained positive bonds across the nation, for some unspecified, and as yet to be determined, time after the great migration. It is likely that through the network of the moiety linkages branching out to all the autonomous regions, some degree of integration persisted. Such integration occurs not merely in the generic sense of going to the cradlelands for spiritual and cultural renewal, but also in the more specific sense of maintaining moiety networks.

The pattern of cross-regional bonding is most obvious in the ritual field, where the pilgrimages allowed the far-flung communities to return to one or the other cradleland to renew their links with their cultural and genealogical roots. The integrative role of Oromo pilgrimages and the respect the pilgrims were accorded as they went across regions that were often at war with each other, has received adequate attention in the literature.[46] However, the specific moiety linkages that were the basis of the pilgrimages are still unknown.

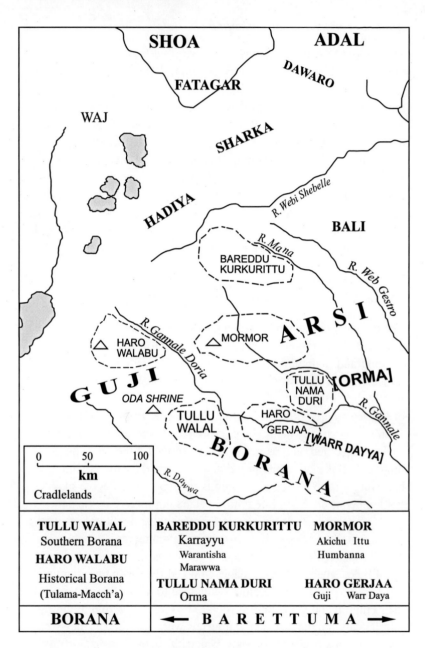

Fig. 4.2 Oromo Cradlelands
Adopted from Mohammed Hassen

The question we must now ask is this: did the pilgrims make the pilgrimage by moiety or was the choice of one or the other cradleland a random event or perhaps based on the seniority, or the reputation of particular Qallus—possibly a charismatic effect? If by moiety, we would expect the pilgrimages to follow the network displayed in Fig. 4.1. If that is the case, it would not be the people of eastern Oromo who would go to the ceremonial grounds in the Arsi cradlelands (e.g. Mormor, Tullu Nam Dur, Dallo Baruk, Debanu) and the people of western Oromo who would go to the BORANA cradlelands (e.g. Haro Walabu or Tullu Walal).[47] Rather, the people from each Oromo region would go to one or the other cradleland following their historic moiety linkages: the descendants of the BARETTUMA moiety (the A's in our chart) would go to the BARETTUMA cradlelands, and the descendants of the BORANA moiety (the B's) would go to the BORANA cradlelands, regardless of their location in Oromo country, and regardless of the over-arching regional identities that have developed as a result of the nominal dominance of one or the other moiety in each territory. In this perspective, Muda networks are seen as a *genetic*, not a *territorial* phenomenon.

Looking at the moieties from his Harar base, Martial de Salviac is very conscious of the fact that there were two cradlelands that the Oromo recognized, one at Mormor (Arsi) and the other at Walabu (BORANA).[48] He then makes a statement that associates the BARETTUMA with Mormor and "all the rest" with Walabu. "Harar pilgrims go to Mormoro where they form two groups called Warra Barentou and Warra Kallo. All the rest of the nation went to Barrake (the blessed land) among the Walabou-Galla, at the foot of Mount Walabu (p.155)." Salviac's description preserves the image of the two cradlelands for the two branches of the Oromo nation, one for the descendants of the BARETTUMA, here represented by the Arsi, and the other for the descendants of the BORANA. Interestingly, he also describes the BORANA cradleland as *more inclusive in its outreach*. This resembles the pattern in Borana of south Ethiopia where the Muda of the Gona moiety is inclusive, all Borana take part, and the Muda of the Sabbo moiety is for that moiety alone. In other words members of the junior moiety go to two different Muda rituals.

There is no indication in the ethnographic or historical literature that the Muda ritual today continues to be performed by any of the Barettuma-dominant populations, i.e., Yejju, Barentu, Arsi or Orma—all of them having become adherents of Islam. The only place where Muda is still a major on-going periodic event, that serves as an inclusive ritual regardless of moiety affiliation, is that of the Gona-Borana. Because of its historic and ethnographic significance, this ritual should be recorded every eight years, so that students of Oromo culture will have a cumulative record of it. This is the only remaining window on the old rituals of "Abba Muda."

At present, the Muda ritual of the Gona-Borana is the key event. It is performed in honor of the Qallu of the Oditu, the senior Qallu of the Borana. It takes place at the Oda shrine, not far from Negelli town, located within the ancient cradleland area on the map (Fig. 4.2, p. 184). It lies south-west of the Dawwa River. Its most likely date is in the middle of each gada period, and thus the next occurrence will be on the 4th or 5th year of gada Ilman Gobba, in the year 2012 (or 2013, if it is delayed). It draws pilgrims not only from all Borana— Gona and Sabbo—but also from any branch of the Oromo nation, and from the allied peoples in Ethiopia and Northern Kenya.

This model suggests the possibility that, historically, some very senior and prestigious Qallus may have attracted pilgrims from beyond their own pan-Oromo moieties; they may have appealed to all Oromo regardless of their sectional loyalties. At the same time, lesser Muda rituals may continue in which junior moieties anoint their own Qallu, in addition to anointing the national figure. In other words, the institution had different layers which are not mutually exclusive.

### Outstanding research task:  the question of moiety exogamy

Before concluding this chapter, one question should be given some attention, that is, the question of exogamy. We know that in the two conservative Oromo groups whose moieties are descended from the ancient moieties—southern Borana in Ethiopia and the Tana Orma in Kenya—the exogamous bonds linking the moieties were preserved. In the case of the Orma, however, we do not know the extent to which exogamy has declined since their conversion to Islam.

What is the sociological significance of moiety exogamy? It offers the *most extensive level of societal integration that can be achieved through marriage,* without going beyond the boundaries of the society itself. It is the antithesis of the Arab pattern of first cousin marriage, which permits unions between the children of brothers (first cousins), and has the potential of giving rise to a proliferation of small endogamous patrilineages. *The Arab patterns fragments society, the Oromo pattern aggregates it to the highest levels.* The outstanding research question now becomes: Are there exogamous tendencies or, minimally, a pattern of preferential marriage between the re-built moieties in the Oromo world?

With regard to Borana/Gabaro exogamy in Macch'a, the options we need to consider are these: (1) If there is no Gabaro-Borana inter-marriage, it would indicate the lowest level of integration—a wholly atypical situation for the Oromo that happens only with *endogamous* oc-cupational castes. (2) If the relationship between Borana and Gabaro is *hypergamous*—Borana more often taking Gabaro wives, but the obverse being less common—then that becomes added evidence of stratification and partial exogamy, i.e., a modest level of integration—a situation that is characteristic of Oromo groups undergoing a process of assimilation. (3) If the relationship is reciprocal, or if it exhibits a pattern of *prefer-ential marriage* across the Borana/Gabaro boundary, it would indicate a more advanced stage in the moiety re-building process, a tendency toward (4) the ancestral Borana-Orma ideal of equalizing and linking the moieties. In this advanced stage, the moieties are interdependent and bound together by powerful affinal links that makes all the members of one moiety the in-laws of all the members of the other moiety.

An extraordinary Sibu saying recorded by Jan Hultin and quoted in Triulzi's "United and Divided," goes as follows: "Borana must not marry Borana, as their union would lead to sterility."[49] That suggests that the ideal of large-scale exogamy may be at work in Macch'a: it suggests that the two groups in their dual organization—Borana and Gabaro—may be developing exogamous bonds. And more im-portantly, for the nation as a whole, the statement opens up the pos-sibility that Oromo may have *beliefs about exogamy that are genetic in the biological, not merely ethnohistoric sense,* encompassing such factors as *hybrid vigor* and the dangers of *inbreeding.* It also raises the possibility that marriage entirely outside their society may also be seen as genetically advantageous.

Such beliefs may lie at the root of the general preference for large-scale exogamy and affinal ties with conquered populations. It would not be surprising if a pastoral people who are accomplished selective breeders of livestock, applied the same genetic knowledge to their own society. This will be examined in my forthcoming book titled *A Pastoral Ecosystem: Field Studies of the Boran and Gabra of Northern Kenya.* It is worth remembering that Mendelian genet-ics was first discovered in the cross breeding of flowering plants and later applied to animals and, finally, to humans. It is a natural progres-sion, since one can experiment with plants and animals—a strategy that cannot be applied, ethically, to humans..

### The Moiety Thesis: Summary of the Evidence Presented

The description and interpretation of the moiety replication and rebuilding process presented in this chapter has obvious implications for the history of Oromo migrations and for the underlying structure of the Oromo nation as a whole, after the great migration.

A. At the earliest stage of the great migration, the BORANA and BARETTUMA were moieties that formed part of one and the same social-political system. Moiety structure was one of the foundations of Oromo democracy and of the pattern of mutual regulation between institutions.

B. During the first phase of Bahrey's history—1522-1562—the ancient moieties were both players in the *same political arena* and were, in all probability, engaged in electoral competition for the same top gada office—one moiety winning it at one stage and another moiety becoming victorious at another stage, thus tending toward a rough pattern of alternation.

C. During that phase of history, the Oromo moieties were also players in the *same military arena.* They were one nation organized as two competing moieties, with one joint army under the leadership of a single Abba Gada. Conversely, there is no indication, in all the historic evidence reviewed, that the Oromo were, at that stage, two societies that had become self-governing entities, with separate Gada-military organizations, and separate territories.

D. The assumption that Oromo moieties drifted apart, as separate "tribes," during the great migration receives very little empirical support. On the contrary evidence has emerged suggesting that *each local branch of the nation migrated carrying both moieties within it,* and, if necessary, boosting the weaker moiety by rapid assimilation of aliens.

E. *Where one moiety had disappeared,* as in Macch'a, another prospective moiety was created through the assimilation of aliens. In this case, the moiety properties of the junior branch are still in formation, showing successive stages of societal integration.

F. The southern Borana of Ethiopia, who are thought to be remnants of the ancient BORANA moiety, who were left behind during the great migration, have been shown to consist of descendants of both moieties. Evidence has also been presented demonstrating that there are ethnogenetic linkages of the moieties of Orma (Barettuma/Irdida), Arsi ([Sikko]/Mando), Barentu (Anniyya/Afran Qallo) with the Borana moieties (Sabbo/Gona) and with the ancient Oromo moieties in Bahrey (BARETTUMA/BORANA).

G. Our analysis has raised questions about how we should interpret the idiom of *"the few and the many."* Regardless of how few the Borana of Macch'a are thought to be, compared with Gabaro, the problem of moiety balancing must still be raised as a problem of Oromo democracy and demography. In any case, *we should not make demographic inferences from an idiomatic expression,* but rely on survey data, instead, to determine whether there is demographic imbalance or not.

H. The thesis also suggests that pilgrimages may not have been *random* or *regional* events, but may have followed *moiety networks,* taking the pilgrims to their ancestral shrines and allowing people to renew their moiety roots. In this process, the senior moiety often holds the fort, culturally, if the junior moiety falls a prey to alienation.

I. The *presumed fragmentation* of the Oromo, after the great migration, was not as extreme or as early as is assumed in the historic or ethnographic literature. Even as the fragmentation progressed, there were compensatory factors of re-integration by *moiety networks,* and *large-scale exogamy—within and between nations—*in addition to the well-known processes of *Muda pilgrimages* and the formation of *confederacies.* In other words, the presumed fragmentation of the nation must be measured against their *complete arsenal of re-integration.*

J. Above the moiety level, pilgrimages also performed an integrative function for the nation as a whole regardless of moiety affiliation. That happened especially after the destruction of the Qallu institution and its shrines in Arsiland, the cradleland of the BARETTUMA Oromo, as a result of the double impact of the conquest by Menelik and Islamization. It also happened because one of the two Qallus (BORANA in Oromo, Gona in Borana) was always placed at *the pinnacle of the ritual hierarchy,* so that people coming from distant regions paid homage to him, regardless of moiety affiliation.

**Concluding Note**

It is clear that the heart of this chapter is not an organized body of facts but an exploratory thesis. Some of my most respected colleagues, both historians and anthropologists, who feel that they must always stand on solid ground as they conduct their analyses, will, no doubt, declare that the moiety thesis is "not proven," as they have said about my earlier theses concerning the instability, demographic pressures, internal transformation, and adaptive responses of the Gada System.

Sometimes it is necessary to swim in very unsteady waters to get to an island—equally solid ground once we get there, but separated from where we are by a turbulent sea. The most important criterion for judging an exploratory thesis is not whether it is proven or not. Rather it must be judged by its usefulness in opening up new vistas and in allowing unexpected relationships to surface.

The moiety thesis is not a syllogism that can be proven in a series of logical and quantitative exercises, as in the simulation experiments. Rather, it is a new perspective on the history and evolution of neglected institutions, which will encourage researchers to gather evidence that puts the thesis to test. Pro or con, the evidence that is generated is useful.

This chapter has shown how facts begin to make sense after the formulation of a thesis—facts which lie dormant in our field notes or scattered about in the scholarly literature, as fragments of observation, gems in their own right, but meaningless in the aggregate.

I am thankful for feedback received from colleagues who have already devoted much thought to the issues concerning moieties, exogamy, the Muda ritual and the Qallu institution, that were raised in the limited preliminary edition of this book, published in 2000. I hope that these institutions and the relationships between them and the Gada System will be firmly established in Oromo Studies as important fields of historic and sociological inquiry that can greatly deepen our understanding of the Oromo nation and its genesis.

# NOTES

1. Alternatively the Gabaro/Borana pair can be seen as an entirely different layer of Oromo ethnogenesis which, at its deepest levels, appears as a GABRA/ORMA pair in Arsi or GABRA/BORANA pair in Borana, and in Tulama. It exists superimposed on the BARETTUMA/BORANA division, in Borana, Tulama and Arsi, but by itself in Macch'a.

2. Mohammed Hassen, "The Relation between Harar and the Surrounding Oromo," (B.A. thesis, Addis Ababa University, 1972); In *The Oromo of Ethiopia*, Mohammed Hassen standardizes the term as "Barentu."

3. Triluzi in "United and Divided," p. 261, contrasts *angafa* with *qutt'isu,* or the Qube equivalent *quxxisu.* Borana use both terms, *mandha* and *qutt'isu,* with different meanings: *mandha* refers to all children other than the first born, and *qutt'isu* to the last born.

4. Lambert Bartels, *Oromo Religion* (Berlin: Dietrich Reimer, 1990), 162.

5. In all 671 adults were selected of which 560 were *household heads.* The latter evidence was analyzed to determine the relative size of the moieties, across the whole of Borana territory, regionally in Dirre and Liban and nationally, in the population as a whole.

6. Bartels, *Oromo Religion*, 163 ff.

7. Günther Schlee, *Identities on the Move: Clanship and Pastoralism in Northern Kenya* (Manchester: Manchester University Press, 1989).

8. Tesemma Ta'a, "The Political Economy of Western Central Ethiopia: from the Mid-16th Century to Early 20th Centuries," p. 21.

9. Cerulli, *Etiopia Occidentale*, v. 2, 55, (italics added, translation mine).

10. Cerulli has indicated that "Among the Gullallie of Shoa, those who wished to achieve the status of pilgrim *(jila)* went to the Abba Muda of the Arussi." Enrico Cerulli, *Etiopia Occidentale*, vol. 1, (Rome: Sindacato Italiano Arti Grafiche, 1933), 60; this author's translation.

11. Mohammed Hassen, *The Oromo of Ethiopia: A History 1570-1860* (Trenton N.J.: Red Sea Press, 1994), 4-6.

12. Donaldson Smith, "Expedition through Somaliland to Lake Rudolf," *Geographical Journal,* London, 8 (1896): map sheet 3.

13. Asmarom Legesse, "Conversations with Haji Idris Mahmoud," Addis Ababa, 1995.

14. Abbas Haji Gnamo, "Egalitarianism, Justice and Democracy in an Oromo Polity," in *The Oromo Republic* ( forthcoming), pp. 13-14.

15. Bahrey, Chapter 1, paragraph 1.

16. Bahrey, in C. F. Beckingham and G. W. B. Huntingford, *Some Records of Ethiopia, 1593-1646* (London: The Hakluyt Society, 1954), Ch. 17, 18. He does not identify the BARETTUMA by name here but instead he refers to the Mulata of the Warra Daya. The moiety affiliation of Warr Daya is known from current ethnography: it is Barettuma.

17. Bahrey, *History*, 125.

18. *Ibid.*, 112.

19. Francesco Beguinot, *Chronaca Abbreviata* (Rome: 1901), 37.

20. *Ibid.*, 43.

21. *Ibid.*, 36.

22. Bairu Tafla, *Atsmä Giorgis and his Work*, 707.

23. *Ibid.*, 707.

24. *Ibid.*, 703, emphasis added.

25. Beckingham, *Some Records*.

26. Haberland, *Galla Süd Äthiopiens*, 117.

27. Please note that in this analysis we ignored the Matt'arri clan, the third clan of the Sabbo moiety, who appeared to be assimilated aliens.

28. Pereira, *Chronica de Susenyos*, 83.

29. *Ibid.*, 93.

30. *Ibid.*, 384.

31. Asmarom Legesse, "Conversations with Galma Liban," tape 4, side B. In the Nyacchisa rite, marking the formation of the luba, the initiands sing a song with the refrain "Oh Raboma!" in which the phrase "Karrayyu Barettuma" recurs. (Source, Liban Jatani, 2006)

32. His name is Bidu Doqqe, a member of the Warra Kula Kurme lineage of the Dayyu-Bokkiccha sub-clan.

33. According to Mohammed Hassen, the Borana cradlelands—Walabu and Walal—are just west of the Gannale Doria river. The BARETTUMA cradlelands are east of that river. The key cradleland of the Barettuma is Mormor. Warra Daya or Orma are linked to two Barettuma cradlelands. Mohammed Hassen, *The Oromo of Ethiopia*, pp. 1-20, and map 3, p. 19.

34. Triulzi, "Toward a Corpus of Historical Source Materials," p. 323.

35. Abbas Haji Gnamo, personal communication.

36. Günther Schlee, "Islamization du passé," (1988); and Mohammed Hassen, "The Pre-Sixteenth-Century Oromo Presence within the Medieval Christian Kingdom of Ethiopia," in *A River Blessings*, 1994, 53-54.

37. Schlee, *Identities*, 35-36.

38. *Ibid.*, 35-36.

39. *Ibid.*, 35-36; Hilarie Ann Kelly, "From Gada to Islam," 59-69, 361, 431; and Alice Werner, "Some Galla notes," *Man* (1915):17.

40. Mohammed Hassen, *Oromo of Ethiopia,* 19.

41. Bartels, *Oromo Religion,* 133, 148-9.

42. P. Martial de Salviac, *Un peuple antique*, 155.

43. W. I. Torry, "Subsistence Ecology among the Gabra: Nomads of the Kenya/Ethiopia Frontier," (Ph.D. diss. Columbia University, 1973), 47.

44. See Schlee, *Identities*, 42-47.

45. Torry, *Gabra*, 52.

46. Knutsson, *Authority and Change*, 147-52; Bartels, *Oromo Religion*, 64-66, Mohammed Hassen, *Oromo of Ethiopia*, 7-9.

47. Mohammed Hassen, *Oromo of Ethiopia*, 8.

---

*Guyyo Boru (left),*

Abba Gada of all the Borana, 1944-52. He was the most distinguished mediator among all the living Abba Gadas—a man of peace and wisdom. He had an avuncular face and a soft soothing voice that tended to pacify the most acrimonious litigants who came before him. The speech he made at the *lallaba* ceremony (photo, p. xxxii, above), on the occasion of the election of his son as Abba Gada, was an eloquent example of how Borana leaders use history truthfully to persuade the nation to return their lineages to power.

*Adi Dida (right),*

a senior councilor in the gada of Guyyo Boru, whose role in the election of 1963 became a most contentious issue, because he had violated many aspects of Borana ethics *(Borantitti)*, such as refusing to assist the Abba Gada, Jaldessa Liban, when he was placed under house arrest by the national government for refusing to convert to Christianity. He had also bribed the council of electors and thus succeeded in having his son elected to the senior Gada Council, despite much vocal popular opposition. Such were the events that exposed the weaknesses of the Qallu Council and led to the constitutional reform that ultimately deprived them of their electoral authority.

*Chapter 5*

# PRINCIPLES OF OROMO
# DEMOCRACY
## Explorations in African Constitutional Thought

O
romo democracy is one of those remarkable creations of
the human mind that evolved into an indigenous political
system as a result of centuries of adaptive changes. It also
developed a formal body of laws governing all their institutions
because of five centuries of deliberate, rational, legislative transformation. It contains genuinely African solutions for some of the
problems that democracies everywhere have had to face. In viewing
this tradition as a potential source of ideas for our generation and for
those who will come after us,[1] it is probably not useful to think of
it as a literal blueprint. We should not assume that institutions that
reached their highest stage of development in the 16th and 17th centuries, can be transplanted wholesale into the 21st century, when the
Oromo nation will face new and awesome challenges. Nor should
we assume that this system of political thought belongs to the Oromo alone. It is an integral part of the age- and generation-based
political-military-ritual institutions that prevail in the eastern half of
sub-Saharan Africa, stretching from Ethiopia and the Sudan all the
way to South Africa. As such, all Africans can read these pages and
contemplate what it is that their ancestors have passed on to them.

It is not the structures of Oromo democracy but the underlying
principles that are most valuable for this part of our analysis. As
we saw in the preceding chapter, the structures are of the utmost

importance for historical and ethnographic analysis, whereas the principles are equally important for an exploratory study of constitutional thought.

## A Polycephalous Government

One of the features of democratic governments is that the polity is differentiated into separate components which are granted some measure of autonomous existence. Such a government is "polycephalous" in the sense that it has more than one "head."[2] In this type of democratic system there is no monolithic state, which crushes all power that is not hierarchically subordinated to it. Power is divided and shared. In Western democracies this pattern of power-sharing rests primarily on a territorial basis (federalism), on institutions that are functionally differentiated from each other and interdependent (branches of government), and on the vast array of voluntary associations and organizations that form the basis of political participation and competition (civil society). In Oromo, power-sharing, based on the division of roles among four different institutions, is clearly at work. Though they do not rely heavily on civil society organizations, as a medium for political participation or competition, they use their membership in three different institutions which cross-cut the nation along different associational lines as alternative means of political action, thus effectively working in a manner comparable to voluntary associations.

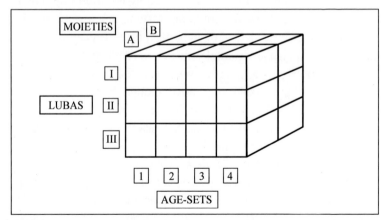

Fig. 5.1 Oromo Cross-cutting Organizations.
(There are many more clans, lubas and age-sets than shown here.)

As we have seen in earlier chapters, the three cross-cutting organizations are the moieties or clans, called *"gosa,"* the generation-classes called *"luba,"* and the age-sets called *"hariyya."* By "cross-cutting" we mean that members of each luba are in both moieties (& clans) and all age-sets; members of the moieties (& clans) are in all lubas and age-sets; members of each age-set are in all lubas and all moieties (& clans). The structure is presented above, Fig. 5.1, in simplified form.

## An Attempt to Define the Principles

The fundamental principles of Oromo Democracy, as they are reflected in the political life of the Ethiopian Borana, are outlined below. Whenever the information is available, the outline is also based on information from other parts of Oromo society—mainly Macch'a, Tulama, Arsi and Barentu—as well as the pastoral Oromo of southern Ethiopia and northern Kenya. In the main, however, the principles are based on years of dialogue with the Borana elders, leaders and ordinary folk representing each of the major institutions under study. They are also based on observations of many political and ritual events by myself, my assistants, and by colleagues who were kind enough to send me their eye-witness records of key events during the years when I was unable to return to Borana. The total eye-witness record is quite massive.

Four decades have elapsed since I began my research into Oromo political institutions. It is, therefore, possible that my recollection of the earliest phenomena I studied or witnessed has begun to fade, even though the evidence is embedded in volumes of field notes as well as diaries in the form of personal letters. This was my reason for returning to my original research base, once again, before completing this book and discussing the principles of Oromo democracy with a most knowledgeable Borana elder, whom I refer to as "Galma Liban," a pseudonym.[3] His testimony supplements and updates the evidence obtained from many other elders among whom the late Arero Rammata was the most important. Arero is no longer with us but his prodigious knowledge has been preserved for posterity and continues to enlighten us today. Both these men of knowledge served as advisers to successive National Assemblies.

The principles of Oromo Democracy are the following:

1.  The Laws *(ada-sera)* that Stand Above All Men
2.  The Principle of Accountability:
    the Role of Confession and Impeachment *(buqqisu)*
3.  Subordination of Warriors to Deliberative Assemblies
4.  Man-made Laws and the Great Lawmakers
5.  Supreme Authority of the National Assembly *(Gumi)*
6.  Government by Councils and Assemblies *(ya'a):*
    Seniority and Equality
7.  Term of Office and Measurement of Time
8.  Limitation of Office to a Single Term *(Gada)*
9.  A Period of Testing: Time Gap between
    Election and Investiture
10. Use of History as Ethical Guide and Precedent *(dhacch'i)*
11. Hereditary and Elective Leadership *(Warra Qallu & Warra Bokku)*
12. Staggered Succession versus
    the Convergence of Destabilizing Events
13. Alliance of Alternate Groups *(walanna* and *qadaddu)*
14. Bridges across Generations in the face of
    Political Discontinuity
15. The Principle of Balanced Opposition
16. Distribution of Power across Generations
17. Separation of Powers: Functional and Spatial
18. Separation of Ritual and Political Domains *(ebba* and *mura)*

Of these 18 principles, 17 were presented to Galma for comment, all, that is, except the 4th. That principle emerged during the course of our discussions concerning the role of the great lawmakers in history and in Oromo political life, provoked by a question raised by Alessandro Triulzi. The information came from Galma and there was no need to present it back to him. However, there was one area in which my thinking and Galma's were completely at odds with each other. This concerns the role of the Qallu in Borana political life. Based on my earlier field research, I believed that the Qallu and his lineage were empowered to oversee the electoral process and that the active or retired gada leaders did not have the right to oversee the election of their successors.

Galma's testimony reveals that this is one central aspect of the Oromo constitution that was altered during the many years that elapsed since I completed my earliest fieldwork in Borana. The change came about as a result of legislation by the Gumi Gayo assembly of 1980, held during the gada of Jilo Aga (1976-1984).[4]

Aside from the exception mentioned here, Galma recognized every principle presented to him as being one of the main ideas that serves as the basis of political conduct in Borana society and as the foundation of Borana political institutions. It is important to stress, however, that although nearly all the principles discussed were acknowledged by Galma, as I had originally formulated them, none were left unaltered after my discussion with him. Most were expanded, modified, re-phrased, illustrated, rendered more accurate, and, in some instances, radically altered. His remarks will be given below as a series of excerpts.

Here then is the unwritten constitution of the Oromo, an outline of the basic principles of Oromo Democracy, of the ideas and precepts that guide their political life and serve as the foundation of their political institutions.

## 1. The Laws that Stand above All Men

We start with the principle that the fundamental laws *(seera)* of the people are an enduring aspect of their life and that all men and women, including the leaders, are subject to those laws. The subject is also discussed  below under two other headings: "Principle of Accountability," and "Subordination of Warriors to Deliberative Assemblies." It is useful to examine both the legislative and juridical traditions of the Oromo so as to understand what the principles mean and how they are applied in practice.

Historic evidence indicates that respect for the law is reflected in the elaborate procedures followed in traditional litigation. By way of illustration, we might cite an example described by Martial de Salviac. In Arsi legal proceedings, a litigant is required not to attack, verbally or otherwise, the person of the adversary, but must, at all times, respect the person, and present the facts concerning his/her actions, as they relate to the particular case under adjudication. To remind the litigants of these obligations, the plaintiff is required to stand to the right of the judge and keep one leg bent and leaning against a tree, while the defendant is seated to the left of the judge, with one leg stretched out on the ground, and the other tucked under it. These physical constraints are reminders that litigation must be conducted with decorum. One must show *respect for the person of one's adversary*, and for the laws that bind the litigants, even as one engages in legal combat that can easily lead to personal violence.[5]

In his studies of the Gudru Republic, Antoine d'Abbadie describes a similar practice in the manner that the defendant and the plaintiff conduct themselves before the judge. He then adds that in seeing "how far our [European] advocates go in abusing their position in order to injure their adversaries," he wonders if it would not be better to have the advocates' legs similarly imprisoned.[6]

Oromo legal traditions are well developed. In contrast to what happens in most traditional African societies, the Oromo make a clear distinction between laws *(sera)* and customs *(ada)*. It is mainly the laws that are the subject of legislative action. The body of laws so developed are binding on all the people. There are no leaders whose position is so exalted that they stand above the law. In Galma's words:

> The Abba Gada himself is subject to the same punishment as all other Borana if he violates the laws: same laws, same punishments. That is the evidence that shows us that the law is above everybody, including the Abba Gada.[7]

A clear example of this principle is that the ruling Gada Council must appear before the National Assembly *(Gumi)*, in the middle of their term of office, and be evaluated. This does not happen very often. It happens only if the luba in power has committed some egregious offenses, e.g. if they have violated the laws, if they have failed to enforce the laws, or if they have enforced them with cruelty. If so, they can be removed from office.

I have discussed this principle with many Borana elders at many stages of my fieldwork. The resulting data, therefore, come from different sources and are discussed in *Gada* (1973) and nearly all the chapters of this book. I believed that I was thoroughly familiar with Borana ideas of the rule of law, until Galma volunteered information I had not anticipated, because I was focusing on *how the law constrains the political leaders.* He said that *the law does not only discipline the highest; it also protects the lowliest.* By way of illustration he suggested that dogs are among the lowliest creatures in Borana; nevertheless, there are laws that protect them from harm.

Borana say *Seeri mumme, seer sare!* "There are laws for everything, even for the dog." He explained the meaning of the law as follows: people are not required to raise dogs, some do, some do not; but those who do are constrained by the law of the dog. The law says that while the nomadic camp is in place, there is much leftover food and the dog is not exposed to hunger. But when the camp is on the move, or when it has moved to a new site and the camp is clean, the dog has nothing to eat. On such days, people must remember to feed their dogs, by setting aside some of the precious meat destined for human consumption. That is why they say "There are laws for everything, even for the dog."[8]

This theme of the *protection of the lowliest* came as a surprise to me because that is not a common theme in political anthropology. Hence, I was not prepared to ask probing questions immediately following the topic Galma had volunteered. Students of Oromo democracy should examine this matter in great depth and see if it leads to the study of the *rights of disadvantaged groups.* We need to know who all the disadvantaged groups are whose rights are protected by law, and what specific protections are given to them (q.v. the laws of *Siqqe,* p. 257, below).

## 2. The Principle of Accountability:
### the role of Confession and Impeachment *(buqqisu)*

Our main theme is not the rights of the weak but the constraints on the strong. In this regard, one noteworthy aspect of Oromo democracy is the extent to which the elected leaders of the class in power are accountable to their own generation and to other generations. This principle stands at the very core of Oromo democracy. It is so critical that we will go into greater detail in citing some of the ethnographic evidence at our disposal. This principle takes the form of a requirement that the luba in power should appear before the Gumi and let the people judge how well they have conducted themselves as leaders. If their leadership was inadequate, the National

Assembly will remove them from office or penalize them in other ways, such as barring them and all their descendants from holding the same office. In the very highest office, that of the Abba Gada, it is more likely that the Gumi will use its power of cursing *(abarsa)* to punish the man who violates his office and the curse, they say, usually results in his death. As Galma put it, *Abba gada hinijjesan male, hinbuqqisan, yo inni seera balleesse.* "The Abba Gada is killed rather than being uprooted, if he brakes the laws."[9] How he is killed will be explained later.

Similar constraints on leaders occur in other Oromo regions as well, besides Borana. That the National Assembly has such powers among the Oromo of central Ethiopia, i.e., Tulama and Macch'a, is indicated by the Ethiopian historian, Atsmä Giorgis, who wrote, at the turn of the 20th century, that the general assembly had the power to make laws, evaluate the luba in power or, as he put it, "to hear the historical and judicial report of the expiring eight years."[10]

In Borana, the luba in power is expected to face one of the *younger* and three of the *older* gada classes who sit in judgment of its actions in the Gumi Assembly, should that become necessary because of egregious misconduct. This happens on rare occasions. Most often, the Abba Gada in power presides over the meetings, assisted by the *Abbotin Gada*, "Gada Fathers" or *liccho dullatti*, the "old whips." Whoever presides over the Gumi is known as *Abba Sera*, "father of laws." Gumi leadership is thus made up of five groups of councilors from the RABA-GADA (V-VI) and YUBA (VI-IX) grades, i.e., the entire second half of the Gada Cycle.

All individuals who assume a position of political authority are answerable to the society which gave them the right to govern and to the National Assembly (Gumi) which has the right to oversee their activities. This right is exercised *during* the ruler's term of office, not afterwards. It is also exercised *before* the term of office begins, as a result of the twenty-one-year-gap between their election as leaders of their own luba and their assumption of power as leaders of all the people. If they are incompetent, the National Assembly can and does "uproot" *(buqqisu)* them from office. A group of qualified elected officers wait on the sidelines, always ready to take over responsibility from the deceased, disabled, or uprooted officers. Occasionally, a male kinsman may take over if the death or uprooting occurs during the final years of the leader's term of office.[11] These practices, which help to ensure the accountability of elected leaders to the people who elected them, are widespread in Oromo country.

One such practice among the Barentu Oromo of Harar is described by Martial de Salviac. He writes, "On the fourth year of their term of office, the magistrates [gada leaders] convoke the tribe, each one of them begins by confessing publicly and in detail the mistakes he made due to his inexperience, or his greed for wealth." He promises to make amends during the second half of his term of office and asks for God's forgiveness.[12]

The two methods of ensuring accountability described here were observed in two different parts of Oromo country. Confession depends largely on morality for its effectiveness, whereas the uprooting procedures rely on laws and sanctions. De Salviac, who is a clergyman, is obviously impressed by the role of conscience in political conduct, whereas more secular scholars may attach greater importance to the force of law. It is important to remember, however, that law that is not founded on morality is a flimsy structure. The following case which was described by Galma shows how moral and legal pressure work in tandem as elements of the same order.

Consider, for instance, the case of Jilo Boru, of the Matt'arri-Gadulla, who was a Meddhiccha councilor in gada Aga (1936-44). The assembly removed him from office because he was said to be uncaring toward the poor. The term that was used to describe what was done to him was *"hingoodhabsan."* When asked to define the term, Galma added *mura hark fuudhane,* "they took mura away from his hands." The concept of *mura,* as we have indicated earlier, stands for "decision-making." The following passage shows what kinds of powers were taken away from him. He was ordered:

| | |
|---|---|
| *Eela hinmurin* | Make no decision about wells |
| *Haara hinmurin* | Make no decision about dams |
| *Biyya waldubbatin* | Call no meetings of communities |
| *Daba ilma-niti hinmurin* | Make no decisions about welfare of women and children |
| *Daba ka busa gonofa hinmurin* | Make no decision about the walfare & protection of clansmen |

He was thus stripped of his authority and responsibilities. He was, however, publicly penitent and *asked for the forgiveness* of the Gumi. The Abba Sera told him "You have also offended your own clan: ask them for forgiveness." He did as he was instructed. He paid the penalties and was returned to his office. These records indicate that *the Gumi and the clan working together*, do remove a gada leader from his office but that if he is contrite and admits his offenses, he is given penalties and returned to his office.

The outstanding historic case of the uprooting of an Abba Gada is that of Wale Wacch'u, whose term of office was from 1722 to 1730. He was a violent man who had taken drastic action against the luba of his successor, while the latter was in the RABA (warrior) grade. He ordered them to go and fight an un-winnable war and the RABA leader and his councilors were all killed. Thereafter, Wale was removed from his office, partly because of what he had done to the warriors. But the final incident that provoked his dismissal was that a pregnant woman had come to his council and asked for water. He and his councilors told her that pregnant cows drink water on all fours and that she should do likewise—hands and knees on the ground. Denying a Borana, who has committed no crime, access to water is a crime. Denying a pregnant woman such help is an even bigger crime, because she carries a precious gift of God. The Gumi of Wale Wacch'u (1722-30) decided to have these *hayyus*, including the Abba Gada, chased out of the seat of luba government. They were exiled. They said to Wale Wacch'u *Warri ch'uf sitti orme*! "All the people have banished you!"

The primary example of an Abba Gada who was cursed by the Gumi and who died as a result of the curse is that of Halakhe Doyyo (1745-53). Outside of these two instances, which occurred in the 18th century, there are no Abba Gadas who were uprooted or cursed.[13] There are more recent cases of lesser gada officers who were uprooted in secular proceedings that did not involve the curse or the attendant threat of death. Two examples are Haro Ukkunna, Hawatt'u clan, in the gada of Adi Doyyo (1899-1906) and Dibloya Fach'i who was Garba councilor in the gada of Boru Galma (1906-13).[14]

Occasionally, the *Gumi also passes judgement against Ethiopian Government officials*. When that happens, they may face jurisdictional crises, if the officials who are summoned by the Gumi do not show up, or do not accept the penalties they have imposed upon them. In such cases, the Gumi does not have the legal clout to enforce their decision, as they do within the framework of the traditional society. Nevertheless the following case is most instructive:

Garbiccha Liban, who lived a short distance outside Megga town, was *qäbäle* (ward) chairman and a member of the Ethiopian Communist Party. The episode took place when the Ethiopian military junta, known as the Dergue, was in power in 1975-91. His offense was that he dug up Borana graves and thus desecrated them. The Gumi heard his case and ordered that he be brought before them. The officer said that he could not be summoned, because he was a Communist party official. There was much anger about this in Borana, and the gada leaders threatened that there would be serious repercussions if they were thus prevented from performing their tasks. While discussions with the party officials were in progress, the offender travelled to Kenya and was killed by the Gabra.

It is worth remembering that Gabra are members of the Pax Borana. Most of the Gabra are Kenyan citizens and live on the Kenyan side of the Ethiopia/Kenya border. They speak the same dialect of Oromo language as the Ethiopian Borana. The two peoples support each other in ritual and political matters. During the scramble for Africa, the Gabra sheltered the Borana immigrants under the pretext that they were "Hofte Gabra" and, therefore, "British subjects." Criminals who escape from Borana and take refuge in Gabra territory are apprehended by Gabra chiefs and punished. That, most probably, is what happened to Garbiccha Liban.[15] In this instance, the judgement was passed by one Oromo people and it was executed by their allies, whose territory lies outside of the jurisdiction of the government that sheltered the criminal.

### 3. Subordination of Warriors to Deliberative Assemblies

One interesting example of accountability has to do with the subordinate position of the age-regiments vis-a-vis the ruling Gada Assembly. This relationship is defined by the following constitutional formula that was mentioned in earlier chapters: "What the gada decides, the age-set carries out." A most important aspect of this law is also tied to the belief that the body empowered to declare wars should be different from the group that is authorized to wage wars. In all parts of the Oromo nation which are governed by Gada and for which we have evidence concerning warfare, we see that the declaration of war is a deliberative act, not the result of impulsive decision making by the warriors. It is the Abba Gada-in-Assembly, not the warriors who call the nation to arms. This fact is clearly illustrated by Enrico Cerulli who writes that when the independent Tulama-Oromo were facing the armies of Negus (later Emperor) Menelik of Shoa, the Gullelle Oromo—whose land is now part of Addis Ababa—found themselves under attack from Dejjach Weldie Baseyum. Cerulli says "The assembly of the Gullallie resolved to stand resolutely against the Amhara led by Weldie." He presents the following text of the resolution they passed (*Folk Literature,* p. 70-71):

| | |
|---|---|
| *Lugama fardatti inbasin,* | Do not remove the harness from the horse, |
| *Addu addarra inbufatin,* | Do not remove the headband from your head, |
| *Meddhiccha harkarra inbufatin,* | Do not remove the wristband from your hand, |
| *Tume seera,* | I have struck the law, |
| *Mure seera,* | I have cut the law, |
| *Seera abba lubati,* | It is the law of the luba fathers, |
| *Bokkudha,* | This is the scepter, |
| *Ch'affedha,* | This is the parliament, |
| *Ch'affe abba Gallaati,* | The parliament of the Galla fathers, |
| *Akka Chaffe kienna, balleessi!* | According to parliament, waste them! |
| *Amara agabusa olcha.* | Force Amhara to fast this day. |

The passage clearly indicates that it is the assembly, not a war chief, who made this decision. It invokes the universal symbol of Oromo democracy—the *bokku* or "scepter"—that represents elective gada leadership. It is here mentioned to symbolize the role of the gada leader as chairman of the Gada Assembly. The law is legitimized by invoking the authority of *abba luba*, the singular collective form for *abbotin gada* (q.v.) or *abbotin luba*, "the luba fathers." The decision is described as *tume seera* "I have hammed out the law," or *mure seera* "I have cut the law"—critical phrases that refer to law making.

The same pattern of decision making is also reflected in the detailed historic study of Arsi wars presented by Abbas Haji.[16] He says that the regiments who fought against the army of Ras Darghe and Emperor Menelik for an entire decade were mobilized by the clan assemblies and the decision to fight was made again and again throughout that period. In each instance, the right to declare war was not left to the warriors, but was made by the clan councils.

In addition to the requirement that the mobilization for war be ordered by deliberative bodies, another method of controlling the warriors is to require that the role of a particular war chief be limited to a particular war. In Oromo culture this is reflected in the customary expectation that each war should have its own leader *(Abba Dula)*. The military leadership of the warriors comes to an end after their gada class hands over power. Hence, there is little likelihood that the warriors will turn their military activity into a life-long occupation that stretches from decade to decade, well into middle age or old age. This custom inhibits the growth of a class of professional soldiers for whom war becomes a profitable career. Their ambitions may pose a political threat. That, I believe, is the reason for the anti-heroic and anti-gerontocratic factor in Oromo culture.

The entrenchment of the war chiefs in positions of political authority is, in fact, an ever-present danger in Oromo political life, particularly during the many decades when they were at war with their Abyssinian neighbors. It happened among the Macch'a, who fought a defensive war against King Teklehaimanot and Ras Deresu of Gojjam and Emperor Menelik and Ras Gobena of Shoa. Wars then became protracted and the war chiefs remained in power for decades. Great numbers of firearms became available. In this long confrontation, the war chiefs usurped the power of the gada leaders and turned their position into that of hereditary rulers *(moti)* whose lineages ultimately merged with those of the Ethiopian royal house. These are extraordinary situations resulting from the massive expansion of Menelik's dominions and the heavy militarization of society during the scramble for Africa—an era that is out of the ordinary in relation to the rest of Oromo history.

## 4. Man-Made Laws and the Great Lawmakers

One of the most interesting aspects of Oromo tradition is that laws are treated as a product of human deliberation not a gift of God or of heroic ancestors. There is little in Oromo thought that suggests that laws are natural and, therefore, immutable. There is even less that suggests that the laws are supernatural and, therefore, beyond discussion. Nevertheless, it is worth noting what Dinsa Lepisa has recorded concerning the concept of natural law, encapsulated in the phrase *dhuga genema* or "daybreak truth," i.e., "the truth [that was revealed] at the day-break [of history]." This is an intriguing lead and should be investigated in depth.[17] The present state of ethnographic knowledge does not permit us to include it in our analysis.

As indicated earlier, Oromo legislative tradition is an uncommon phenomenon in Africa. In most traditional societies laws and customs are not distinguished. Customary law is taken for granted and handed down from generation to generation. We rarely find deliberate traditions of "making and unamaking laws." Even if changes occur, they are not acknowledged, the present being projected back onto the past. In Oromo culture, laws are known as *"sera,"* customs as *"ada"* and it is the laws that are subjected to deliberate change. Occasionally when customs must change, they are elevated into the legal arena.

The procedures they follow in the National Assembly suggest that leaders may be inclined to abolish the laws and if they do the Gumi must resist such action. A most interesting procedure reported by de Salviac in his work on the Oromo of Harar can serve as an example. He says that at the start of the legislative session, the presiding gada councilor says that *the laws have been abolished.* The assembly then demands that the laws be reinstated and the presiding councilor acquiesces to their demand. In the words of de Salviac "The Abba Bokku announces Seri bue! 'The Laws have fallen.' People object saying 'The law, the law, we want the law!' The Abba Bokku then announces Seri bae! 'The laws have risen again.'"[18]

The language of the ceremony suggests that if the leaders were to abolish the laws, the assembled multitude would demand that they be re-instated. It is a ritualized reminder of how the people ought to conduct themselves if a ruler were to abrogate the laws. One variant of this practice has been recorded in detail among the southern Borana where the laws are recited one by one in the National Assembly. They are debated and, if need be, they are altered. If there is no need for change, they are reaffirmed.

This cultural tradition indicates that the people view the laws as being their own, not something imposed upon them by a divine force, by venerated patriarchal lawgivers, by a superior class of learned men, or by "Tradition" in the generic sense.

### The great lawmakers: Dawwe Gobbo and Makko Bili

There is, in some parts of Oromo country, the tradition of great law-makers who are believed to have created of the laws that serve as the foundation of the Gada and Moiety systems. Two well-known examples are Dawwe Gobbo in Borana and Makko Bili in Macch'a.[20] We should not imagine, however, that these were men who single-handedly made up laws and handed them down to the people, as Moses is reputed to have done, when he descended from the mountain with his tablets, after his encounter with God. The renowned Oromo lawmakers are not bearded old patriarchs with divine inspiration but gifted parliamentarians known for their wisdom and/or eloquence. They may also be influential men who are neither wise nor eloquent, but persuade the assembly to act by the force of their personality or their historically mandated persona.[21]

The following conversation with Galma Liban reflects Borana thinking about the "great law-makers." I posed a question to Galma to try and answer one of the interesting issues that Alessandro Triulzi raises concerning the role of Makko Bili in Macch'a legislative tradition. I rephrase his question to read "Are men like Makko and Dawwe individuals who appear as God-inspired men in history and invent or substantially alter long standing institutions?"[22]

Q. Let me ask you a question concerning Dawwe Gobbo and the Gumi. My understanding is that the Gumi represents all Borana and that it has the authority to abrogate existing laws and to make new laws. In history, however, we come across individual leaders, such as Dawwe Gobbo, who made many of the laws of Gada, and the laws of Sabbo-Gona [moiety exogamy]. What does that mean? On the one hand they say it is the Gumi that makes laws, on the other hand, individuals like Dawwe are said to have made many of the basic laws. How do we reconcile these two viewpoints?

A. You were not properly informed on this matter. Dawwe Gobbo is given credit for the work of the Gumi of which he was the leader. He was *abba sera,* [the presiding councilor of the assembly] but it is the Gumi that made the laws. In fact, Dawwe made many propositions: some were accepted, others were rejected. For instance marriage within Gona or within Sabbo is prohibited but a lover-mistress bond (*garayyu*) is allowed. Dawwe sought to prohibit the keeping of lovers within the moiety but the Gumi did not agree with him.[23] He was challenged by a councilor named Dubbe and he lost. About this confrontation the women sang:

| | |
|---|---|
| *ka Dubbe dubbuma* | Dubbe's is real talk |
| *ka Dawwe dawwuma* | Dawwe's is foolishness |
| *dudubbacchu feedha* | I want to relish again and again |
| *dubbi Dubbe tana* | this talk of Dubbe |

This is a stanza from a beautiful song-poem, in rhythmic rhyming couplets, that is part of Borana singing and dancing today, three centuries after the fact, for Dawwe was Abba Gada in 1706-1714. The critical song that women sing about one of his "foolish" ideas leaves no doubt that he is seen as a very mortal human being with very human shortcomings.[24] By this song, the great lawmaker stands humbled in perpetuity. Some of the laws he proposed or sponsored have become the foundation of the Gada and Moiety systems. He is presented as a good exemplar when he makes laws, but as a cruel exemplar when he enforces the laws. The Borana interpretation of Dawwe Gobbo is, therefore, critical, pragmatic, and egalitarian. Whether Macch'a would view Makko Bili in the same light is an open question for the students of Macch'a history.

## 5. Supreme Authority of the National Assembly

As indicated earlier, Gumi Gayo, the National Assembly, is the body that makes or abrogates laws and adjudicates cases of conflict including intra- but mainly inter-luba, -age-set and -clan affairs that cannot be resolved at lower levels of their judicial organization. As such, the Gumi does not stand on the same footing as the Gada, Qallu and clan institutions; it stands above them.

The position and authority of the Gumi can be described as follows:

In Oromo democratic traditions, the highest authority does not reside in the great lawmakers who are celebrated by the people, nor the rulers who are elected to govern for eight years, nor the electors and ritual leaders who hold their office for life by hereditary right, nor the clan organizations whose authority is limited to clan affairs, nor the age-sets and age-regiments who furnish the military force, nor the Abba Dula who lead their people in wars. It resides, instead, in GUMI GAYO, the National Assembly, planned, summoned, organized, and presided over by gada leaders—active (RABA-GADA) and semi-retired (YUBA). Qallus have no function in the convention. Clan leaders are represented as participants, but not as presiding officers, lawmakers or decision makers. They caucus separately and submit their recommendations through their representatives in the Gada Assemblies. The purpose of the meetings is to re-examine the laws, to reiterate them in public, to make new laws, and to settle major disputes that were not resolved at lower levels of the system.

We describe this National Assembly as "open" because any individuals who have views about the gada class in power, or about the laws of the land, and have the initiative and ability to articulate those views, may attend the great meeting, take part in the *preliminary sessions* of the Gumi and submit their recommendations. Similarly, *clans caucus separately during the main session*, and bring their recommendation to the assembly through their gada representatives. In the main sessions, however, *no one can speak unless permitted or invited to do so by the presiding Gada leaders.*

A remarkable aspect of the institution is that managing the assembly requires knowledge of laws, rituals, gada history, chronology and time reckoning. If the gada leaders do not have such knowledge, they must seek the advice of the men of knowledge *(bekuma)*. Borana experts, such as Arero Rammata, in the 50s and 60s, and Galma Liban, from the 80s and until the present, were consulted extensively in the *preliminary sessions* of the great meeting. I have been told that even friends of Borana from other lands, such as this writer, who have knowledge about their institutions would be welcome to participate in those sessions. These *pre-Gumi meetings* may last for as long as a *month*. In those sessions, the main issues to be presented to the Gumi are debated, and *propositions* are "hammered out."

The main session of the National Assembly, called *"Gumi Gayo"* is held in the vicinity of Gayo well and lasts about *eight days.* It is worth noting that all the great wells of Borana are centers of intense social-political activity. The meetings are dominated by the leaders of Raba-Gada and the semi-retired gada assemblies. Others have little or no opportunity to voice their opinions. If they do, they speak through their gada representatives with whom they share their thoughts in preliminary meetings or in clan caucuses.

After the conclusion of the Gumi, a third meeting is held known as *"Gumi el Dallo,"* located near a great well by that name. At that meeting, only active and semi-retired gada councilors (of the RABA-GADA and YUBA grades) take part and the outstanding resolutions of the Gumi are *finalized and proclaimed.*

### Conduct in the national assembly

The nature of conduct and the pattern of discourse in the National Assembly are well elaborated. To begin with there is no concept of a *quorum:* Gada assembly members must be present at all formal meetings and failure to do so is heavily penalized. That imposes severe constraints on the movement of leaders. (See *Sera Dawwe* concerning "travel restrictions" on gada leaders).

Secondly, there is no concept of a "majority" that can impose its will on a "minority." Debate must be continued until the councilors come to agreement. That does not mean, however, that their debates are endless. There are effective methods of pressuring the participants to refrain from adversarial talk for its own sake. Indeed, the participants in Gumi Gayo are forcefully reminded that clever disputation has no place in the meetings. Nor should people attempt to pull rank or resort to self-praise. These values are clearly reflected in the opening statement that is often made at the National Assembly as reported by Galma. The presiding gada officer usually admonishes the Gumi in these or similar words:

*Dubbin dubbi Gumi Gayooti,*[25]
Our talk is that of Gumi Gayo,

*Dubbin dubbi Gumiiti,*
Our talk is the affair of the multitudes,

*Dubbi qarumman dubbatani miti,*
This is not the place for clever talk,

*Warri qaro qarumman laf keyyaddha,*
Clever people! Leave all cleverness behind.[26]

*Fula tun, fula wan aadaa dubbatan male,*
This is the place for discourse on custom,

*Fula qarumman dubbatanii miti.*
It is not the place for clever talk.

*"An hayyu, an qaro, an dureessa" wabeekha jedhani;*
[People] say "I am Hayyu, I am clever, I am rich" and so on;[27]

*dubbin akkas akk hinjiranne.*
such talk is not allowed here.

*Dubbi kara aadaati;*[28]
[Our] talk is [about] the path of custom;

*Nam aadaa ch'aqasa!*
Listen to the man of custom!

The purpose of this exhortation is to advise the participants to give up verbal diatribes, clever disputation, or adversarial tactics and to focus their mental energies on reaching unanimous decisions that would be acceptable even to those who may have initially disagreed. Note that the word *ada* is used here in a generic sense to encompass law, procedure, and custom.

Gumi is not a debater's arena but a place for sober reflection. The basic guideline for the deliberations is simply this: *Do not look for the worst in what others have said in order to undermine their position and win an argument; look for the best they have to offer, so as to find the common ground.* This, in a nutshell, is what Borana elders, gada leaders, and men of knowledge have told me in many different ways. It represents an ideal in Oromo democratic conduct that people aspire to achieve. There are many practical strategies that have been developed to help people approach that ideal.

At the end of a long session of the National Assembly, if the *abba sera* who presides over the meetings is ready to formulate a decision *(murti)* that might be acceptable to most of the participants, and tolerated by the rest, he announces, "Would there be anything but peace if we came to such and such a decision?" If the assembled multitude overwhelmingly responds with "Peace! Peace! Peace!" it means that the presiding councilor has properly judged the proposition that reflects the "meeting of minds." If not, the discourse continues.

The *abba sera* may make concessions to the dissenters by modifying the proposition. Alternatively, *he may pressure the dissenters to follow the voice of the many by heaping blessings upon them;* and the Gumi chimes in *Ebbis! Ebbis! Ebbis!* "Bless! Bless! Bless!" I have seen this method work wonders on numerous occasions at Gada Assembly meetings. At best it is an effective way of building up consensus; at worst it may become a way of drowning the voice of the dissenters with a flood of blessings. It is, at any rate, better than silencing dissenters with guns, detentions, or torture as often happens in the "presidential democracies" of Africa.

### 6. Government by Council-in-Assembly: Seniority and Equality

The core of luba government is the Adula Council, a "committee" of six men elected to lead their nation for a period of eight years, one of them (the *Abba Gada*) serving as the presiding officer. The periphery is made up of the two junior councils (*garba* and *meddhiccha*) and the many assistants or the senior councilors (*makkala* and *jallaba*). This is the Oromo version of "government by committee-in-assembly." In this regard, their organization is roughly comparable to the Swiss system of government, where executive power is held by a seven-member Federal Council, each councilor elected for a four-year term by the Federal Assembly, and one of them elected by the assembly to preside over the council.

This type of institution stands in sharp contrast to the presidential governments that have evolved in much of postcolonial Africa superficially mimicking the American presidency—a pattern that has, on many occasions, led to despotic extension of the powers of the presidency. American style presidentialism which accords the leader vast amounts of power is exposed to serious dangers: the president is head of state, chief executive, and commander of the armed forces all rolled into one. Such a leader can usurp more power than is his due by provoking conflict, putting the nation on the war path, and himself in the saddle as the undisputed wartime chief. This is one of the great dangers facing this form of government. America's *"imperial presidency"* continues to work as a manageable institution mainly because of the deeply rooted system of checks and balances, the unquestioned authority of the Supreme Court to defend the constitution, the equally strong authority of

Congress to impeach the president, and the ability of the press to uncover official misconduct—a task it pursues relentlessly. All this is a formidable bulwark against the inherent threat. The introduction of presidential rule in Africa without well-established checks on the abuse of power has proved disastrous during the first half century after independence (1957-2000). Some elected leaders became "presidents for life" as in the case of Dr. Kamuzu Hastings Banda of Malawi (1971), and some military heroes usurped political power and crowned themselves in the style of Napoleon I, as in the case of "Emperor Jean-Bédel Bokassa" of the Central African Republic (1977). Today Africa is faced with elected leaders who refuse to handover power and "transitional military governments" that keep their nations in limbo for decades. Such are the constitutional threats that have bedeviled African nations.

In the Oromo polity, there is no "president" who looms large on the political horizon. No heroic war chiefs are left in office long enough to damage to the democratic institutions. The ruling Gada Council consists of six men elected equally from the two moieties by their respective electoral councils. The most senior individual among these, the Abba Gada, holds the position as *hayyu fit'e* or "apical councilor" and is treated by his peers as *primus inter pares* or "the first among equals." That is also how he appears to outside observers in his language, dress, and conduct.

Whenever we speak of the Abba Gada deciding anything, we mean the Abba Gada-in-council. Leaders hardly ever make any decisions alone or against the wishes of their peers. When critics of Oromo government single out the gada class or age-set *as a whole* and declare that they have no power, because they never meet "as sets," they are stating a meaningless fact (Baxter, 1978:154). Sets do not need to meet "as sets," since they have representative councils delegated to speak for them. Furthermore, if the Abba Gada is "powerless," it does not mean that the Gada Assembly or the Gumi of which he is the presiding officer is also powerless. Assemblies have great authority of a political, judicial, and military kind. I would even argue that they have power over life and death, but the instrument they use to punish high crimes is the curse, not the electric chair or the hangman's noose. To understand what happens after the curse is a matter that requires insight and astute observation.

What then is the nature of the authority of this "powerless" Abba Gada who has no gavel to wield, no sabers to rattle, no weapons with which to terrify his "subjects" into submission?

> The Abba Gada's role is to (1) summon *(lallaba)* the Gada Assembly or the Gumi together for meetings, (2) to ensure that all assemblymen are in attendance and to take disciplinary action against absentees *(Sera Dawwe)*, (3) to oversee the deliberations as they "hammer out" the laws *(tuma sera)*, (4) to determine when there is a meeting of minds *(wali galte)* and present it as a proposition at an opportune moment, and bring the discussion to an end with a resolution *(murti)*, and (5) to pressure dissenters to accept it, using a variety techniques of which the blessing *(ebba)* is the most important, (6) and to proclaim *(lallaba)* the laws in public.

To facilitate his ability to communicate with the assembled multitude, he is assisted by men with powerful voices, referred to as *qonqo Abba Gada,* "the voice (literally, throat) of the Abba Gada," who repeat his statements loud enough so they can be heard by the massive crowds. This is the kind of leadership and modes of communication Oromo have evolved after centuries of trial and error.

### Seniority and equality

Seniority is one feature of Oromo democracy that is badly misunderstood. Because Oromo society is ordered by seniority, it is thought to have a hierarchical structure that contradicts the egalitarian ideology which the people profess. It is true that all Gada and Qallu Councils are ordered by seniority, as are the individual members in each. These seniority positions are most important in matters of ritual *(jila)*. At political and adjudicative meetings, however, seniority does not play an important role. It is only the order in which the members speak or perform ceremonies that are so determined. On the whole, the councilor's influence or prominence is a function of his abilities not his seniority. Nevertheless, some commentators, such as Gudrun Dahl, believe that seniority is rank and that Oromo egalitarianism results not from gada ideology but from some other forces, such as ecological pressures.[29] As I have indicated earlier, in the account of the seniority of moieties, Borana accept seniority as a natural fact but reject arbitrary inequality based on extraneous factors such as wealth, as a violation of their egalitarian ethic.[30]

Seniority is nothing more than a *queuing device*. In situations where individuals or groups must perform activities or get access to resources in sequential manner, they do so in the "order of their birth." This metaphor is applied to many aspects of social organization, i.e., not only to brothers, but also to lineages, clans, moieties, as well as age-sets and gada classes. All these have an "order of birth." There is no doubt that seniority confers some advantages in social life, but they are minor advantages that give rise to ephemeral inequalities. These inequalities can be readily altered by the diligence and creativity of the junior members. In my observations of the Gada Assembly, there were some clear situations when the junior councilors eclipsed the senior councilors in their fund of knowledge. The one member of the assembly who watched my data gathering most attentively, and to some extent benefited from it, is a junior member of the junior council. The senior council actively solicited his extensive mastery of facts, treating him more or less as an expert. However, his actual decision making authority was much below that of the senior councilors.

Readers who believe that the principles of seniority and equality are contradictory are advised to contemplate, for a moment, the concept of *primus inter pares* or "first among equals"—a phrase sometimes used to describe egalitarian leadership in Western assemblies or councils. Even if such a leader is assigned responsibilities that are important for the management of deliberations, such as those presented earlier in reference to the roles of the Abba Gada in meetings, when it comes to making critical decisions, all members of the ruling council have equal voice: that is the sense in which the concept of "first" and "equals" are reconciled.

## 7. The Term of Office & Measurement of Time

One of the key methods of regulating power is to delegate authority to elected leaders for limited periods of time. In the Oromo case, the term of office of the elected leaders is limited to eight years beginning and ending with a formal power transfer ceremony, known as *balli* in Borana or *jarra* elsewhere. This rule is universal in the entire Oromo nation. The place and date of the handover is fixed by law. The people know the place and the approximate time of the ceremony but they must be informed by "people who know the stars" *(nami ka urjii beeka)* as to when the actual day falls. For the outgoing or incoming gada classes, failure to be present at the designated time and place is a type of lawlessness whose consequences are deeply feared. The worst that people do is to show up late, but there is no instance, in four centuries of Borana history, when an Abba Gada extended his term much beyond the 8 years allowed by law. Nevertheless, a major source of criticism of gada leaders in the National Assembly concerns their failure to maintain the ritual schedule.

> **Regardless of the delays that distort the ritual-ceremonial-legislative calendar, the time-reckoning experts who advise the leaders go on saying "this is the month of the handover ceremony" or "this is the year of the Muda ritual," whether the event takes place at the expected time or not. In that manner they try to avoid compounding the errors from one era to the next. The discrepancy between the expected and the actual time is a perpetual source of tension between the men of knowledge and the men of power. Criticism about careless delays in the schedule of rites and political ceremonies is a theme that often becomes a factor in elections.[31]**

There is one case in the twentieth century when the handover ceremony was significantly delayed: that was on the occasion of the Italian invasion of Ethiopia in 1935 that deeply disrupted the political life of the Borana. Since gada leaders had led a campaign of resistance against the Italian army, they were "wanted men" and it would have been suicidal for them to gather at one place to perform the power transfer ceremony.[32] The time and place of the ceremony is so widely known that the Italian military rulers would have used the occasion to round up the leaders and take them to the firing squad. The resulting three-year delay in the handing over of power is seen as one of the great aberrations in the periodicity of Borana political life. Characteristically, the Borana re-set their historic clock by abridging the gada period by three years and requiring the Gada Assembly to hand over power, in phase, on the fifth, rather than the eighth, year of their term of office. In this manner, they prevented the error from building up from one period to the next.

As explained in the previous chapter, part of the reason why the Oromo put so much emphasis on their astronomic calendar is because their political system depends upon it.[33] They have also developed a system of naming the individual gada period after the man who was in office at the time. Out of the system of periods thus named, they have constructed a historic chronology that covers three and a half centuries (see Appendix I ). The chronology is governed by many ingenious internal checks that prevent it from being distorted by faulty memory.[34] The complete chronology is known to time reckoning experts and historians, but it is not esoteric knowledge that is jealously guarded.[35] Anyone can learn it and many do. Ordinary men and women do not know the entire gada chronology. They know it only in simplified, abridged, and practical forms.

## 8. Orderly Succession and Limitation of Office to a Single Term

The practice of allowing an individual leader to be elected again to the same office, which is common in Western democracies, is totally prohibited in Oromo democracy. Gada classes *(luba)* succeed each other in assuming power, and the leaders are elected entirely from within each generational cohort. Once the cohort has completed its term, it must leave the military and governmental functions to the subsequent group, but it continues to participate in rites of passage, as well as the legislative-adjudicative meetings of the National Assembly which take place once every eight years and continue throughout their years of partial retirement. They also take part in the national election contests. They campaign on behalf of their sons, as each group of sons reach the third grade in the gada cycle. (See lallaba ceremony, p. xxxii.) Not only is there no concept of a "second term," the very thought of extending one's term beyond the eight-year limit is morally offensive and legally prohibited. Hence, the problem that has arisen again and again in African democracies where elected leaders declare themselves to be "presidents for life," after they have had a taste of political and military power, does not arise except in situations, such as Macch'a, where Oromo institutions were severely distorted by extreme and sustained militarization during the colonial wars.

For approximately four centuries, Oromo passed on power from one gada class to the next in an orderly fashion—they still do today in those areas where Gada is still a living institution. Most often it is the incoming luba that drags its feet because it fears that it may not be ready to assume the burdensome responsibilities. In any case, the law of succession is well defined and the assumption of power is devoid of civic turmoil. Furthermore, there is no abrupt loss of power and prestige when handing over gada office. In the first half of the gada life cycle, power is achieved in incremental steps; in the second half, power is given up after three decades of participation in the National Assembly. It takes decades to climb up the ladder and an equally long time to climb down. To be more precise, 21 years are spent on the way up (CUSA and RABA grades) and 27 years on the way down (YUBA grades). In both these transitions the members of the luba are deeply engaged in their society. There are no periods of "waiting" (q. v., Baxter), no barren stretches in their lives—tortured years spent in the adolescent "search for identity" or equally aimless years spent floundering because of the loss of the sense of purpose that comes with retirement.

## 9. A Period of Testing:
### Time Gap between Election & Investiture

It is not possible to judge the political merit of candidates for elective office on the basis of the self-advertising speeches they make in election contests. A more reliable method is to elect people to a lesser office and watch them perform as leaders, before they take the higher office. The principle, simply stated, was that there was a period of two and a half gada periods between the time an individual was elected as leader of his luba (gada class) and the time that he was invested into office as leader of all the people i.e. of all the gada classes. In Borana this period of testing was 21 years. In other words the leaders were in charge of the apprentice warrior grade (CUSA IV) for 8 years and the warrior grade (RABA V) for 8+5 years before they assumed leadership of the GADA (VI) grade. During these 21 years the leaders can be removed from office by the pan-Borana assembly. They are judged for their prowess as warriors and hunters, their patience in times of crisis, their wisdom and eloquence, their moral qualities, their skills in mediating or adjudicating cases of conflict, and their knowledge of law, custom, and historic precedent.

In Western democracies there is no mandatory period of testing for political leaders. Men and women who are able speakers but have no political experience can be elected to the highest offices. The people may not have seen how the candidate behaves in times of major crises or in the face of many temptations. Sometimes, people have no basis for judging their conduct except what they see of them in the election contest. That is hardly an adequate basis for electing an individual to high office. In the words of one Borana elder, who heard my description of Western election practices, "electing a man after hearing him give self-praising speeches is no wiser than marrying a woman after watching her sing and dance in the company of a crowd of admiring warriors."

## 10. The Use of History as Ethical Guide and Precedent *(dhacch'i)*

The pattern of leadership that is recorded in the Gada Chronology (Appendices I and II) is part of the on-going political discourse. The chronology covers more than four centuries, but the part that is considered relevant to the present is 360 years long including the present generation. Beyond that, history has no political significance, through it has much cultural meaning.

Built into this chronology are recurrent historic events believed to revisit the land in cyclic or epi-cyclic fashion and deep lessons in political ethics that help the people to anticipate and judge the conduct of their leaders, on the basis of the accumulated wisdom of eight generations. They include the present in the historic record, i.e., the precedent of "eight" (in reality, seven) generations ago, exerts pressure *(dhacch'i)* on the current generation.[36]

The aspiring leader who is seeking political office, or the leader who has been elected and is presently in office, is expected to be familiar with the lives of important historic figures. If he is not, he must surround himself with knowledgeable assistants *(makkala* or *jallaba)* or, from time to time, secure the services of the men of knowledge, historians, and time reckoning experts. The people who seek the advice of these men of knowledge are not merely the men in power but also their critics and adversaries. In this regard it is clear that men of knowledge have a special place in Oromo political life, because they serve sometimes as defenders of one or another side in adversarial politics, and, at other times, as arbiters who judge the conduct of all leaders—aspiring, active, semi-retired, or historic—and their ancestors. Often, they are people who are inclined to speak the truth when the leaders find it inconvenient to do so, particularly those who have serious blemishes in their political careers or skeletons in their ancestral closets they wish to hide.

The role of historic precedent is especially important in regard to negative examples of conduct. Sometimes, they also contain positive examples the leaders are encouraged to emulate. The life history of leaders who have distinguished themselves in warfare or lawmaking is an integral part of gada chronology. It is recited again and again in songs, poems, legends, and stories celebrating events that are sometimes three or four centuries old.

Some of the historic precedents were periods of misfortune. For instance, it was believed that the misfortunes of Gobba Alla (1688-1696) would revisit the land in the era of Gobba Bule (1968-76), his 8th lineal gada descendant. Hence, Gobba Bule was urged to fulfill all his ritual requirements, in order to mitigate the *dhacc'i* impact of his cyclical predecessor. He did so meticulously. Aside from his personal misfortunes—he was once gored by a bull—the nation, they believe, was spared.[37]

Dawwe Gobbo (1706-1714), another major figure in Borana history, is reputed to have killed children who violated the laws. His career as a cruel and ruthless leader is told again and again as a cautionary tale.[38] The same man is also celebrated as a leader who introduced some of the fundamental laws of the Gada System and of moiety exogamy. It would seem that the evil in his record outweighs the good, since none of his descendants were ever again elected to the same office. (See Appendix II, the fourth gogessa.) It is likely that the saga of Makko Bili—the renowned lawmaker in Macch'a, central Ethiopia—also played the role of a model for the conduct of future lawmakers. He lived in the second half of the 16th century. He is reputed to have established the system of ten gada classes, the duration of the term of office (8 years), the generation interval (40 years) and the rules governing the Borana-Gabaro relationship—the two sections of Macch'a dual organization.[39] His record appears less ambiguous and more heroic than that of Dawwe Gobbo.

In Borana, the life histories of many such leaders are an integral part of political and historic ethics. Prospective leaders must have an intimate familiarity with both the heroic and anti-heroic figures in history. They must appreciate the reasons for their successes or failures and be guided by them. In seeking public office, the able leader invokes the lives of the heroic figures as a model for his own conduct. If he can claim, further, that these figures are not only his *luba* predecessors but also his genealogical ancestors, the impact is even greater. With the aid of experts, he can construct a pedigree and political persona for himself out of the raw materials that history offers. The veracity of the constructed persona is, of course, always subject to challenge by his adversaries and by the experts.

## 11. Hereditary and Elective Leadership: Complementary Roles

The pattern of leadership is based on both the hereditary and elective principles. On the whole, leadership is hereditary in the sphere of ritual and elective in the political sphere.[40] The balancing of these two principles is useful because the elective offices become responsive to the public will and are constantly under its influence, whereas the hereditary officers contribute to the continuity of institutional life and exercise their duties without being constantly exposed to external factional pressures.

The division of labor between ritual and political roles, whereby the hereditary groups are assigned mainly ritual functions and the elected leaders are assigned mainly political functions, was violated in regard to national elections, because the hereditary leaders of moieties had the authority to organize, oversee, and decide the outcome of elections. Hence, in this limited political sphere, hereditary leadership had a direct influence on political life. In a society that has no access to ballot boxes, the Qallu lineages served as neutral, apolitical bodies who could determine the people's choice. They did so until the constitutional reform of 1980.

It is, however, true that the office of Qallu is sometimes exposed to corruption. As a result, some candidates who do not have the support of the public will find their way into public office, as was demonstrated in the case of Adi Dida which I have described in some detail elsewhere, in connection with the gada election contests.[41]

If one insists that all leaders should be elected, then one is involved in a vicious cycle: the entire political system becomes unstable. Western democracies introduce a degree of continuity and stability into their governments by granting *lifetime tenure to their most senior judges*. Sometimes, as in northern Europe, they also retain a *constitutional monarchy* that serves as an enduring institution—its rituals playing a useful role in national integration. In this limited area, Oromo democracy shares a very important feature with the constitutional monarchies. For that reason the Qallu is often mistaken for a "king" or "sultan" in the descriptive literature.

The Oromo themselves occasionally use the term *"moti"* to honor the Qallu, a term that has come to mean "king" in the Ghibe kingdoms and in other parts of the Oromo nation where monarchic or quasi-monarchic governments emerged in the last two centuries. In Borana the word means "leader" or "conqueror," not "king." It does not exist as the title of an officer, but it is an integral part of the self-praising speeches gada leaders make as they advertise their accomplishments while seeking political office. The formula they use is *An qaro! An mo'a! An moti!* "I am capable! I have conquered! I am a ruler!" This is a permissible type of self-adulation in gada culture—mainly in the context of political contests. The term *"moti"* is applied to the Qallu in the same fashion, as a term of adulation not as the title of an office holder.

Hereditary and elective leadership often differ in terms of their *legitimacy*. In Western constitutional democracies, it is the elected leaders who need to legitimize their position by proving themselves to be equal to the office for which they were elected. Monarchs, by contrast, have ancient, mythological legitimacy and do not have to do anything to merit their high offices. Such legitimacy is taken for granted unless the monarch violates the ethical-legal code.

*The mixing of hereditary and elective leadership is a source of discomfort for all democracies. It is for the Oromo too.* It takes the form of questioning the legitimacy of the Qallu: because they are not judged by the same rational yardstick as all other leaders, because they are secretive, because they accept "bribes" in return for the political services they render, because they did some illegitimate power grabbing during the Menelik era and later, because they think they are *moti,* "kings," because they are supposed to be peacemakers but have internal factions who spend much of their time, effort and resources in litigation. These are but a few examples of the litany of complaints that are made against them.

In Oromo political culture, it was not the elected leaders but the hereditary leaders whose legitimacy was in question. This has been a subject of contentious debate throughout the years of my research. This is also the aspect that has now undergone change made by the National Assembly during the gada of Jilo Aga (1976-1984). According to Galma Liban, who has served as adviser to the gada assemblies, the Qallu has been removed from his position of overseer of gada elections. On the fateful day when the Gumi was to introduce this change, the assembly invited the provincial representatives of the Marxist government of Ethiopia to witness their debates and to acknowledge the final determination, lest the Warra Qallu use their considerable political assets in the provincial government to regain their lost prerogatives.

What kind of effect this will have on the pattern of mutual regulation between institutions remains to be seen.[42] Since the Gumi of Jilo Aga, in 1980, two gada classes have completed their terms of office and no attempts were made to reverse the decision. However, the fact that the Qallu's role is now mainly ritual does not mean that the office is no longer politically relevant. For instance, the new legislation has nothing to say about the Muda ritual which, historically, played an important role in the preservation of Oromo identity and in the maintenance of ritual networks linking diverse sections of Oromo society, that are geographically very far apart from each other. Hence, the role of *the Qallu is likely to still have over-arching significance in the realm of political ritual that has some meaning across regional, gada class and clan loyalties.*

## 12. Staggered Succession vs the Convergence of Destabilizing Events

The law of succession, which we have already mentioned as a factor of continuity in government, is not an obvious feature of the political system and has confused many students of Oromo social-political organization. Hence, there is need for a slightly more extended presentation here. One major problem of continuity that a democracy faces is this: If the entire political system were to undergo successional transformation at one and the same time, the disruption would be too great to handle and would expose the people to transitional crises or *interregna*: i.e., the time when there is no government because one government has left office, and their successors are not yet fully in charge. Like the no-man's land that lies between hostile states, it is a society in limbo—a threshold that is neither here nor there, a liminal interlude.[43]

In the Borana case, if all gada classes were to change status simultaneously, it would also mean that most other activities would be suspended. A hostile neighbor could then take advantage of the *interregnum* and launch an attack. This is an important consideration because rites of passage that take a month or more—such as the fatherhood ritual of the warriors (RABA V)—the men are in a totally 'feminized' state: they bear no arms and wear no trousers but instead cover their bodies with a toga-like garment and spend their days engaged in extremely ascetic and meditative rituals (See the *Dannisa* rite in *Gada*, 1973).[44] In that state, not only the warriors but the entire society whom they defend is in a vulnerable state. Hence, while the Raba are in an extended liminal state, the Gada are fully in charge and able to defend the nation.

These are some reasons why they have to stagger their periodic rites of passage and political transitions in such a way that the changes in different parts of the system occur in different cycles. When some groups are in limbo, other groups stay in place. When some types of political leadership are replaced, others stay in office. Hence, the terms of office are "staggered," in the sense that they occupy overlapping stretches of time.

The problem is exaggerated in the Oromo case because of the periodicity of all their transitional rites, ceremonies and conventions: if they had not made some special provision for staggered succession it is not merely the two gada classes who hold military and political power—warriors (RABA V) and rulers (GADA VI)—who would change roles simultaneously, *all the eleven gada classes, covering the entire human life cycle, would change status at once, resulting in a massive metamorphosis of the society.*

Among all the rites of passage and transition ceremonies, only one takes place outside of this eight-year cycle. That is the power transfer ceremony (known as *balli* or *jarra*). As a result, the luba in power (GADA VI) begins and ends five years later than all the other grades. (Incidentally, the circumcision of Gada (VI) in the 4th or 5th year coincides with all the other transition rites and ceremonies.) Throughout the Oromo nation there is evidence that the handover ceremony takes place four or five years later than all the other transition rites. As a result, the duration of all the grades (except two) is eight years: the grades that precede and succeed the power grade are longer and shorter respectively. I have observed and dated nearly all the rites of passage and transition ceremonies, whereas the handover ceremony took place two years prior to my fieldwork but was not observed. It is, nonetheless, equally well dated.

In the following charts, the ruling grade (VI) and the grades that precede and follow it are represented in boldface. The preceding grade, which is the stage of senior warriorhood (grade V), is longer than normal by five years; the succeeding grade (VII), which is the first semi-retired stage, is shorter by five years.

| Gada Grades | I | II | III | IV | V | VI | VII | VIII | IX | X |
|---|---|---|---|---|---|---|---|---|---|---|
| Duration | 8 | 8 | 8 | 8 | **13** | **8** | **3** | **8** | 8 | 8 |

This is the pattern that has been recorded in Borana. Elsewhere in Oromo country the staggered pattern was achieved by shifting the handover ceremony by 4 not 5 years.[45]

| Gada Grades | I | II | III | IV | V | VI | VII | VIII | IX | X |
|---|---|---|---|---|---|---|---|---|---|---|
| Duration | 8 | 8 | 8 | 8 | **12** | **8** | **4** | **8** | 8 | 8 |

This appears to be the more common pattern in the Oromo nation, and is seen as the normal pattern by some experts even in Borana.[46] This very important constitutional provision has been a source of much confusion in the literature on Oromo political organization because the suggestion is often made that the class in power is "abridged" to four years.[47] It is, in fact, the Raba-Dori grade (Vb) which appears "truncated" to the authors, because it is five years long in Borana, four years long elsewhere.

The result is that there are some periods of irregular duration (3,4, or 5 years) in the system which confuse the transient observer The power grade too is subdivided into two parts representing the parts that stand before and after the time of the other transition rites and ceremonies and their own circumcision ritual.[48]

The upshot of all this is that GADA (VI), which is the term of office of the luba in power, is eight years long, but it is not the same eight years as the grades of all the other lubas in the system.

> The practical consequence of the displacement of the power grades is that there is continuity in government: all the lubas remain in place while the governing lubas (RABA-GADA) transfer power. Conversely, the RABA-GADA remain in office while all the other lubas change grades.

## The convergence of destabilizing events

Oromo have dealt with the problem they face when their society is undergoing major, simultaneous transitions by resorting to the method of staggered succession. Other democracies have dealt with the problem in a different way. Thus in the United States the problem is resolved by granting unequal terms of office to representatives (2 years), the president (4 years) and senators (6 years): when the house elections are taking place, the senate and the presidency sometimes remain unchanged; when presidential elections are taking place, the house and the senate sometimes remain in place. From time to time, however, the elections of two different bodies will converge. As a result, a popular president may cause some incompetent or unpopular congressmen and senators of his party to be elected or re-elected, dragged into office, as they say, by the "bandwagon" effect or by hanging on to the "coat tails" of the president, not on their own merit.

Hence, unequal cycles do not minimize the convergence of destabilizing events as effectively as the Oromo system does. The method of staggered succession is a better strategy. Instead of giving the branches of government and the two houses of parliament unequal terms of office, the Oromo solution would be to give them all equal terms but have each branch begin and end its term on a different cycle: say, representatives 2000–04, president 2001–05, senate 2002–06. With that kind of staggered arrangement, the electoral cycles would never converge and the transitional crises would be greatly attenuated.[49]

## 13. Alliance of Alternate Groups

In African age- and generation-grading systems, adjacent groups are adversaries and alternate groups are allies. In this arrangement of successive cohorts, each group harasses its immediate juniors and is harassed by its immediate seniors. There is, thus, a pecking order in which the "enemy" of an "enemy" becomes a "friend." It is good-humored enmity, or—more accurately—it is regulated conflict.

The same principle is also applied to generations within the family and, by extension, in the wider society: fathers and sons are adversaries, grandfathers and grandsons are allies. This device converts a linear hierarchy into a pattern of balanced opposition and serves as a method of ensuring that the rights of lower groups are protected against arbitrary power exercised by higher groups. It is in this framework that we find evidence concerning Oromo ideas about the *rights of children.* Boys in the DABBALLE (I) grade are surrounded by a ritual buffer zone that protects them from angry, greedy, uncaring, or overly punitive parents who might do them harm. Grandparents GADA MOJJI (XI) and grandchildren, DABBALLE (I) are in a ritually sanctified liminal state and are allied to each other: two weak generations versus one powerful generation. The protection need not come from the biological grandfather: any member of that generation who is in the sanctified state can render that service.

This principle of alliance of alternate groups can have wide application *in any hierarchical system,* not simply age or generational hierarchies. This very principle is at work in the Gumi. When and if the luba in power is under review, the people who do the reviewing are the grades below and above it (Va & VII), both adversaries *(walanna).* However, their allies *(qadaddu)* too are in the same arena (in grade VIII and X), and more adversaries in IX. The allies ensure that the judgements of the adversaries are just, fair, and without malice.

This pattern of conduct seems to be widespread in Oromo land. In Borana it is referred to as *qadaddu* "allies" and *walanna* "adversaries." The pattern in Macch'a takes a somewhat different form because they name the alternate generations (*obo* and *ch'ora*) instead of naming the relationships. Adjacent generations exhibit respect and avoidance toward each other—they are said to have a *saffu* relationship.[50] Borana too have a ritualized type of relationship between age groups or gada classes that are *walana* (adversaries) to each other. It is a relationship dominated by avoidance (rather than respect), joking behavior, and harassment. These relationships have important function in *political socialization.* The junior members are always subject to discipline by their immediate *seniors,* while their *allies* protect them from excessive domination and cruelty.

## 14. Bridges across generations in the face of political discontinuity

The duration of democratic governments poses problems at both ends of the scale: If the governments are too short-lived, the system becomes unstable and a prey to dilettantism. If governments remain in office too long, they become unresponsive, arrogant, irrelevant, and entrenched—so entrenched that they tend to destroy the very system that brought them to power. All democracies must determine the optimal duration of government for their particular society.

Another problem that all democratic governments must deal with is this: after having created a system of institutionalized disjunctions, i.e., terms of office that are of reasonable duration, they must then devise methods of ensuring some measure of continuity. In other words, they must find *ways of sustaining the rule of law, transmitting political wisdom, and passing on the core values of the society from one period to the next, from generation to generation.*

In Western democracies there are some institutions that remain rock steady while the rest of the system is in man-made turmoil. Two outstanding examples are the *constitution*, which is seen as a virtually unchanging source of wisdom and justice, and *senior judges*, who are appointed for life and serve as the ultimate interpreters and defenders of the constitution. Similarly, *civil servants* stay in place while elected leaders and *political appointees* come and go. Civil servants are professionals with accumulated expertise, whereas the appointees are, on the whole, "politicians" who try to capture the shifting concerns of the electorate and translate it into "policy."

Here, as elsewhere, the Oromo have had to face the same kinds of problems that are faced by other democracies. Because Oromo government changes every eight years, it was necessary to devise methods that ensure continuity from one luba to the next. They have many such methods; we mention only a few salient items.

***The Oromo constitution, a lasting legacy:*** The basic constitutional principles described in this study make up the backbone of the political system and encompass the ethical foundations as well as the core values of the society. Some aspects of this system of thought and some of the rules that govern the Gada and Moiety systems have endured for at least four centuries and the underlying systems of age grading and time reckoning for much longer.

***Qallu's office, hereditary and for life:*** The Qallu contribute to institutional continuity because they are a hereditary group without any limitation on their term of office. Hence, as the ruling Gada Councils change every eight years, the Qallus stay in office. The rituals and myths that surround the institution are very powerful and have considerable staying power: they have endured even where Gada has been disrupted by colonial "chiefs," hereditary *motis*, "kings," or *abba lafas*, "lords of the land."

***Staggered Succession:*** The method of "staggered succession," which we have already described, is another procedure for ensuring continuity in the face of the periodic changes in government. It is a method for maintaining continuity, despite the inherent instabilities brought about by democratic transitions.

***Junior councilors, elected by one luba, to serve with the next:*** One of the junior councils of the Gada institution, known as the Garba Council, is elected by the outgoing government and serves with the incoming government. This particular measure appears to be deliberately crafted to create a bridge between the outgoing and the incoming generational cohorts.[51]

***The Men of Knowledge:*** "Elders," young and old, who have deep knowledge of history and time reckoning, contribute to the preservation and synchronization of traditions, rituals, knowledge, and institutional arrangements. The time keepers and historians are the custodians of tradition who judge the present generation of leaders by comparing them with their worthy and unworthy predecessors. Their counsel and their time is highly valued.

***Elders who oversee each gada cycle ritual or ceremony:*** When going through the rites of passage and political transition ceremonies at the beginning and the end of each grade of the Gada System, elders from previous generations guide the luba. At each stage of its career, the luba is going through a phase of life it has never experienced before—hence, the need for guidance.[52]

***History as precedent and ethical guide:*** The use of history as precedent, which was described above, is an important factor in ensuring continuity in cultural values and political ethics from generation to generation, from one period of history to the next.

***Dhacch'i, unto the eighth generation:***  Finally, and most importantly, each generation is responsible to the generations that preceded it
and to those that succeed it until the "end of time." This belief is a
philosophical premise that is at the heart of the Gada institution. It is
associated with the concept of *dhacch'i*—the belief that the conduct
of gada leaders affects its successors for eight generations.[53] That concept imposes a lasting *moral burden on the gada leaders* now in power,
and on those who are waiting or aspiring to take over. It also imposes
an *obligation on the men of knowledge,* requiring them to keep track
of history for a minimum of eight generations or 360 years.

## 15. The Principle of Balanced Opposition

Justice and fairness can be preserved if power is exercised by groups
that stand in opposition to each other and regulate each other's authority. Power cannot be checked unless the groups who exercise it
are balanced in numbers and strength. In the West, this is achieved
by having two major political parties, or coalitions of parties, standing in opposition to each other. The winners form the government,
with or without the support of other parties; the losers join the ranks
of the loyal opposition. Similarly, adversarial procedures in litigation fulfills a similar purpose of ensuring justice and fairness.

In party politics, the danger is that one party may gain a position of overwhelming dominance, in which case the system will be
thrown out of balance. When one party stays in power for decades,
it inevitably distorts the system of checks and balances.

In Oromo democracy, justice and fairness are achieved by ensuring that the gada cohorts and their leaders succeed each other every eight years, and by dividing the nation into two societal halves
or moieties that are counterpoised to compete for gada office. The
political offices are distributed equally between members of the two
halves of the society: in particular that is true in the case of the
ruling council (Adula) which is always made up of equal numbers
from each moiety. However, the problem of entrenchment arises in
regard to the presiding officer of that council (Abba Gada), who is
elected from one or the other moiety. Members of one moiety, clan
or lineage may succeed each other in office for generations (i.e.,
forty-year cycles). Given the vagaries of the election contests, the
danger of entrenchment of particular lineages is always present.

The principle of balanced opposition also surfaces when the successive gada classes or age-sets ally themselves as alternate groups thus converting an inherent hierarchy (X) into a dual organization (A & B), i.e., two groups whose numeric, political, and ritual power is roughly balanced. This principle, which was presented in the previous section is presented more clearly here in the form of a table:

| X➤━━➤ A | | B |
|---|---|---|
| 1 | 1 | |
| 2 | | 2 |
| 3 | 3 | |
| 4 | | 4 |

Table 5.1, Alliance of alternate groups:

A device for converting hierarchy (X) into balanced opposition (A,B): 1 and 2 are adversaries, 1 and 3 are allies, 2 and 3 are adversaries, 2 and 4 are allies.

It is a mark of the virtuosity of Oromo lawmakers and a remarkable aspect of the African genius that our ancestors invented a method of *converting any hierarchy into balanced opposition* and thus limiting the excesses inherent in a hierarchical organization.

It is clear, however, that *hierarchy* and *opposition, discipline* and *equity, rank* and *egalitarian values, structure* and *ambiguity* have their proper place in human society. They exist in Oromo life within well circumscribed frameworks that draw boundary lines between the lives of *assemblymen* and the lives of *warriors.* This structural differentiation allows each group to perform its tasks in a manner that is appropriate to its domain, making room for *dialogue* in one sphere and for *discipline* in the other.

### Balance in politics, hierarchy in warfare

Balanced opposition is the preferred mode of operation in the political system, but hierarchical principles prevail in their military organization. We have already seen how the balancing of forces is reflected in gada assemblies. We need only mention in what form hierarchy appears in the life of warriors.

There is a clear pattern of subordination in the manner they order age-regiments *(ch'ibra)*. In major wars approximately nine regiments may be called to action. The ideal, but feared, number is always nine. The fear comes from the fact that Abbayyi Bobbo (1677-74) fought with nine regiments and faced disaster after disaster.

Every regiment is headed by a leader called *abba ch'ibra*. All regimental leaders are under the command of a single war chief called *Abba Dula*. Furthermore, the entire complex of regiments is subordinated to the Gada Assembly, as far as the authority to mobilize the nation, commandeer supplies, levy rifles and horses is concerned. The relationship between these three levels of their political organization constitutes a clear hierarchy.

On the macro level the Oromo polity as a whole was divided into two equal halves or moieties that were perpetually opposed to each other and competed for the top office of Abba Gada. At the same time, however, the moieties had a joint military organization, a unitary army under a single war chief. That was the situation in the first phase of the great migration (1522- 1578) before the fragmentation of the Oromo nation began as it spread over vast territories. That was also the situation of the moieties and the age-regiments among the Borana-Oromo of southern Ethiopia in the 20th century.

A most revealing corollary of these two approaches is that even numbers have a special place in the political arena and odd numbers prevail in the military arena. This is not the product of magical or astrological thinking: it is so by design, and it has practical implications for decision-making processes. The Gada Council consists of six men, three from each moiety. So organized, it is obvious that the council can be and is often deadlocked, e.g., in matters concerning the equitable distribution of political offices, resources, privileges and obligations between members of the two moieties.

However, a deadlock is not seen as being particularly undesirable or disabling. Faced with a deadlock, the Gada Council simply works hard to try to find the common ground. They use their highly developed methods of persuasion, mediation, and ritual intervention to bring the two sides closer and closer together, until they reach a compromise position acceptable to all or nearly all. This precludes the possibility of using a single swing vote to reach a decision—a method they consider unreasonable and unfair when it is described to them. Hence, they prefer even-numbered councils.

That is not the case in military life. In the historical and contemporary records there are indications that the fighting force in national campaigns ideally consisted of nine regiments, when the full force is mobilized. A meeting of the regimental leaders would, therefore, become a council of nine men. Similarly, scouts *(doya)* who are sent to spy out enemy territory are organized in two groups of seven. The spies are known as *torban lama*, which literally means "two sevens." These two groups worked separately and gathered independent bodies of evidence to be submitted to the Abba Dula ("war chief").

There are also a few areas of ritual, political, and social life where odd numbers make an appearance. It is not clear if these domains have any features in common with the military organization. Odd numbers and dualisms in the kinship system should be compared in this regard.[55] In any case, the data suggest that Borana may use majoritarian procedures in the age regiments to arrive at quick decisions in warfare, in contrast to the consensus procedures employed in councils. Our guess concerning military decision-making must, however, be verified by further research.

## 16. Distribution of Power Across Generations and Age Groups

Compared with Western democracies, the age- and generation-based democracy of the Oromo, does a far better job of distributing power across generations and age groups. They make sure that people who are of age have an opportunity to play a legitimate role in political life. In Western democracies, the young and the elderly are pushed aside and do not have a stake in political institutions. By contrast, the autonomous self-governing age- and generation-groups of the *Oromo are extremely effective in keeping people actively involved in the affairs of their people, during a major part of their adolescence, adulthood, and old age.* Hence, describing these generation-

and age-organizations as *gerontocracies* or "government by elders" is, in the Oromo case, a gross mis-representation of the reality. It gives the false impression that age, per se, confers power. In the works of Baxter and Bassi, cited earlier, the role of junior warriors, senior warriors and gada leaders is severely down played, and all authority is seen as belonging to the semi-retired elders. That is done so that the ethnography can conform to the *a priori* dictum handed down by Radcliffe-Brown that gerontocracy is the governing principle in all age- and generation-grading systems. But it is necessary to keep in mind that Radcliffe-Brown and his contemporaries had an ax to grind. From the perspective of colonial Britain, which they sought to serve, *gerontocracies are perfectly safe and innocuous, African warriors, on the other hand, are not.* That is one political motive behind the glowing image of gerontocratic government and the demeaning language employed in describing most African warrior organizations.[54] It is part and parcel of the "pacification" strategies of the colonialists, but not a particularly truthful method of describing African institutions.

### 17. Separation of Powers: Functional and Spatial

Among the Oromo, power is not an undifferentiated entity that is exercised by a hierarchically organized monolithic state. It is shared by various political groups that stand in a coordinate relationship with each other. In other words, political power is held by different kinds of officers-in-councils, who have different kinds of authority, and the groups are sometimes on the same footing, not above or below each other. Thus gada leaders are responsible for war and for adjudication of matters concerning the luba. The Qallu lineage was, until recently, responsible for organizing the election of gada leaders over and above their principal role as ritual leaders of their people.

Functional differentiation among the four institutions does not preclude relations of subordination. The age-sets are definitely under the authority of the gada leaders and all three institutions are under the authority of the National Assembly. At these two levels, the functionally distinct bodies are also ordered hierarchically. Similarly, the relationship of the war chief, and regimental leaders also exhibit clear patterns of subordination.

Within the context of the National Assembly, which is led by five gada councils (grades V-IX), the gada leaders *(abbotin gada)* exercise their highest authority over the affairs of gada classes, age-sets, and clans. Some conflict that is not revolved in their respective councils, is taken up by the Gumi.

### Mobile Gada and sedentary Qallu

A most unusual aspect of the separation of powers in Oromo democracy is that the different institutions are not only different in the
kind of work they do, but they are also different in their territorial
organization. Thus, the Qallu councils are totally sedentary communities. As such, they are not viable pastoral communities and must
depend on the gifts they receive to maintain their herds and their
subsistence economy. Most of the time, they are far removed from
the gada councils who are required to travel, periodically, during
their term of office on a prescribed course around their territory and
thus to remain directly in contact with their people.[56]

It is also mandated that *Qallu and Abba Gada stay out of each
other's paths for the entire length of the latter's term of office*, except on the occasion of three very important events. The two leaders
confront each other directly at the great Muda ceremony in which
the gada leaders "anoint" *(muda)* the ritual leaders and, in return,
receive their blessings *(ebba)*. There are also two political events
when they cross paths. One is the *lallaba* ceremony when the newly
elected gada leaders are proclaimed before their fathers' gada class
and are blessed by them. The other is the Gumi Gayo national convention. In both these events, the Qallu have a place of honor but
they have no decision-making role in the proceedings.[57]

### 18. Separation of the Political and Ritual Domains: *Mura* and *Ebba*

Borana make a clear distinction between ritual and political activity,
a distinction that is completely lost in the accounts of ethnographers,
such as Baxter or Bassi, who have never seen the Gada Assembly
or the National Assembly in action. Behavior in the two domains is
sharply distinguished in *language, gear, taboos, and conduct*.

In political transition ceremonies, such as *lallaba* and *balli* or
in political meetings such as those of Gada or Gumi assemblies the
participants bring their weapons (spears and rifles), whips *(liccho)*,
and ceremonial staffs *(ororo)* to the ceremonial grounds. No taboos
are in force, other than the guidelines on decorum and proper discourse. In the lallaba ceremony, which is a political ceremony, not
a ritual, the children carry whips, and bring spears which they lay
down on the ground pointing away from the assembled group. By
contrast, in the ritual domain participants speak a ritual argot known

as *afan seeda:* they are prohibited from using words that refer to violence. They are prohibited also from carrying weapons, but they carry ritual paraphernalia instead, such as bouquets or wreaths of leaves taken from sacred trees. In some rituals, such as the father-hood ceremony, the behavior of the warriors is ascetic and medita-tive. Each warrior wears a toga-like garment, but no items of cloth-ing, such as trousers, that are particularly masculine. Weapons are kept some distance away from the ceremonial grounds.

The highest ritual leaders are men who have authority to bless (v.t. *ebbisu*). They are distinguished from political leaders who, col-lectively, can punish those who violate the law. They have the power (1) to make laws *(tuma sera)*, (2) to decide in cases of conflict *(mura)*, (3) to curse *(abarsa)* and thus to kill, or (4) to kill by more direct methods, without recourse to the curse. The Abba Gada's sphere is, therefore, primarily political-legislative-juridical. The great majority of his time is spent in conducting meetings of the Gada Assembly, which are secular in character. By Borana definition, they are not *jila*, "rituals," but *cora*, "meetings," and thus not necessarily peace-ful, and may require the use of legitimate force, to be used as last recourse, when peaceful means of persuasion have failed.

Ritual leaders have fundamentally peaceful, non-violent, roles. They are completely barred from ever bearing arms, shedding blood, or inflicting punishment. On the other hand, gada leaders who are in power are not barred from giving blessings. We have seen, for instance, how the Abba Gada used blessings to open assemblies, to end debate, or to regulate the conduct of participants in meetings. It is only when the ritual experts of his own luba, such as Bokku, or national ritual leaders such as the Qallu are at the center of the ritual space that he retreats to the periphery. He does not give the blessings, he receives them. In short, *the Abba Gada's ritual role is entirely secondary and does not define the nature of his office.*[58]

The distinctions of ritual and political domains should not be confused with Western ideas of the separation of "church" and "state." Ritual, in Oromo life, has important political functions. The separation of the ritual and non-ritual spheres becomes relatively sharp only in regard to warfare, bearing of arms, shedding of blood, the making of laws and the punishment of crimes, from which ritual leaders are totally excluded. Outside of these domains there is much give an take between the ritual and political spheres.

# NOTES

1. This proposition is no stranger than the British using the Magna Carta (1215 A.D.) as a source of constitutional ideas and as the most celebrated of all historic precedents in Britain. The Great Charter embodied some fundamental ideas that progressively led to proclamation of the Bill of Rights in 1688. Nevertheless, in its initial formulation, it was not much more than a shaky and convoluted contract between the king and the barons of England and, as such, it had, a much narrower compass than the Oromo constitution as we have come to understand it. George Burton Adams, *Constitutional History of England*, chap. 5.

2. See the discussion of monocephalous, acephalous, and polycephalous political systems in chapter 1, above.

3. At present, the pseudonym is necessary because of the current unstable situation in Borana and along the Ethiopia-Kenya border.

4. All my field research in the latter period was done among the Boran of Kenya, Marsabit district, where the traditional political institutions were no longer in operation because they were replaced by colonial institutions. My research in Kenya was mainly, but not exclusively, ecological rather than political, in character and is, therefore, not directly relevant to our present discussion. However, some of the information I gathered from Marsabit elders was on oral history of traditional institutions and thus political and military rather than ecological in character. The evidence was furnished by first generation immigrants from Ethiopia, who grew up under the Gada regime but also witnessed the clash of institutions concerning Borana warfare, horsemanship, and hunting, under British rule.

5. Martial de Salviac, *Un peuple antique au pays de Menelik, les Galla: grande nation africaine* (Paris: H. Oudin, n.d.), p. 201.

6. Antoine d'Abbadie, "Sur les Oromo, grande nation africaine," *Annales de la Societé Scientifique de Bruxelles* 4 (1889):187.

7. Asmarom Legesse, "Galma Liban," tape 2, side B.

8. *Ibid.*, tape 2, side B, heading "Seera sare."

9. *Ibid.*, tape 2, side B, heading "Uprooting."

10. Bairu Tafla, *Atsmä Giorgis and his Work: History of the Galla and the Kingdom of Shäwa* (Stuttgart: Franz Steiner), 133. Atsmä is right about the event but wrong about the timing: it occurs in midterm: in other words, it is a report of the expiring 4, not 8, years.

11. "Si un président du parlement oromo meurt dans l'excercise de ses fonctions, le bokou passe a son fils, et, s'il n'en a pas laissé, la femme du defunt...proclame les lois. Le président est inviolable en sa personne; tant qu'il est en fonctions, les vengeances nationales ou de famille ne peuvent l'atteindre." Salviac, *Les Galla,* 187.

12. *Ibid.*, 186.

13. The same kind of mystery that surrounds Shilluk regicide may also be present in regard to the uprooting, cursing, and killing of the Abba Gada. The death of Abba Gadas, after they have been cursed by the national assembly, is an ethnographic problem that should be studied with care, keeping in mind Evans-Pritchard's insights on regicide and Abbas Haji's contribution on the subject of the power of blessing and cursing titled "Le pouvoir de benir et de maudire," *Cahiers d'etudes africaines*, 146, 37-2 (1997): 219-318.

14. A third man, whose name Galma was unable to remember, is from the Halchayya clan and the gada of Dida Bittata. Asmarom Legesse, "Conversations with Galma Liban," tape 2, side B.

15. The reader is advised to link this evidence with what was said in Chapter 2, above, about aspects of traditional conduct that have been prohibited or criminalized by the state.

16. Abbas Haji, "Les Oromo-Arssi: continuité et évolution des institutions d'une societé éthiopienne," (Thèse de Doctorat de l'Université de Paris I, Panthéon-Sorbonne, 1990)

17. The Oromo National Assembly was a public event which was of interest to the Ethiopian emperors and their spies. The emperors who had to fight continuous defensive wars against the Oromo were aware of the key political ceremonies. Thus, Susenyos was told about the "laws of the Mu'alta and how and when the Luba was appointed, new laws and new proclamations were given. Thus, whenever the Luba was changed the emperors used to send spies in

order to find out what was decided in the Ch'affe at that time." Bairu Tafla, *Atsmä Giorgis*, 175.

18. Martial de Salviac, *Un peuple antique,* 186-7.

19. *Ibid.*, 186-7.

20. Asmarom Legesse, *Gada*, 199; Alessandro Triulzi, "The Saga of Makkoo Bilii: A Theme in Mac'a Oromo History," *Paideuma*, 36 (1990): 319-327.

21. Asmarom Legesse, "Conversations with Galma Liban," 1995, tape 2, side B.

22. Triulzi, "Makkoo Bilii," 320.

23. Asmarom Legesse, "Galma Liban," tape 2, side B.

24. Asmarom Legesse, "Galma Liban," tape 2, side B.

25. The word "dubbi" has many meanings: literally it means "talk" "dialogue" "discourse" but it may also mean "business," or "affair." We translate it variously as the context requires.

26. Literally "should leave it on the ground."

27. This refers to the language employed in political campaigns by aspiring councilors.

28. The word *aadaa (ada)*, commonly translated as "custom," is used here to encompass both custom, law, and procedure.

29. Gurdun Dahl, "Ecology and Equality: the Boran Case," in *Pastoral Production and Society,* edited under the direction of L'équipe écologie et anthropologie des societés pastorales, (Cambridge: Cambridge University Press, 1976), 261-281. Dahl's arguments on this subject are somewhat inconsistent. At times she holds that Oromo are not egalitarian and at other times she says that their egalitarianism results from ecological pressures, not ideology. The reality is that gada egalitarian ideology is consistent with their mode of ecological adaptation, as can be seen so clearly in the way they regulate access to water resources: the method is based on seniority but its consequences are equitable and ecologically sound.

30. See chapter 4, above, section on seniority of moieties.

31. Asmarom Legesse, *Gada*, p. 189.

32. In fact, the retired Abba Gada, Arero Gedo, who was involved in organizing the resistance against the Italian invaders, was later placed under house arrest by the Italian colonial administration. His confinement was in the house of Guyyo Abba Sara, a Borana balabbat or "agent" of the central government. Asmarom Legesse, "Borana Field Notes," p. 562.

33. The calendar appears to be of great antiquity as evidenced by recent archaeo-astronomic finds. It is probably part of the ancient heritage of the Cushites in general, not merely the Oromo, although they appear to be the only people today who have preserved the full system of knowledge as a living institution. The Afar and the Somali have also preserved some traditions about and knowledge of the stars.

34. Asmarom Legesse, *Gada,* 92.

35. The abridging takes place segmentally. In other words ordinary folk know the full chronology in their own gogessa but are liable to abridge the remaining four gogessas.

36. Asmarom Legesse, *Gada*, 189-201.

37. *Ibid.*, 191,199.

38. *Ibid.*, 190-91, 199.

39. Antoine d'Abbadie, "Sur les Oromo," cited in Triulzi, "The Saga of Makkoo Bilii," 319-327. D'Abbadie's date of Makko's laws is 1589 which is near the end of Bahrey's history.

40. Bokku and Imu are ritual leaders of the luba, Qallu are hereditary ritual leaders of the moieties.

41. Asmarom Legesse, *Gada*, 206 ff.

42. Marco Bassi is completely unaware of the constitutional reform made by Jilo Aga in 1980. Bassi conducted his Ethiopian field research in 1989. Hence, he had ample opportunity to gather information on the subject. His belief that Gada is a purely ritual institution is clearly a mental handicap, in this instance. He carelessly states that Gada leaders are "appointed" (2005:61) completely ignoring the full-length case study I presented on the electoral contests in 1963 (Gada, 1973: ch. 8). Hence, the constitutional abrogation of the Qallu's electoral authority cannot, be part of his mental purview since one cannot abrogate an authority that, *presumably*, does note exist.

43. Turner, Victor, *The Ritual Process,* (Chicago: Aldine, 1969)

44. That *femininity* is associated with creating life and making peace and *masculinity* with taking life and making war is perhaps a type of symbolism that is shared with many other cultures.

45. For the analogous splitting of the power grades into sub-grades see for instance de Salviac's description that suggests that the term of office is divided into four years of dori and four years of "law." Salviac, *Un peuple antique,* 186-7. This is one indication that Salviac does not comprehend the feature of staggered succession.

46. Incidentally, the long grade of the senior warriors is internally subdivided into two parts consisting of 8 and 4 or 8 and 5 years which are variously named RABA and DORI or RABA DIDIQQA ("small Raba") and RABA GUGURDA ("big Raba").

47. Martial de Salviac does not even understand that RABA and DORI are two stages in the gada cycle, but thinks of them as two "magistrates" who assist the Abba Bokku and then adds that all three of them are called "Dori" as a general designation. *Un peuple antique,* p. 183. Cerulli cites these facts and is then led further astray by his informant Loransios who tells him that "Dori" is not the title of a dignitary but a personal name. Cerulli, *Folk Literature,* 32.

48. One writer who has stumbled upon this problem is Domenico Pecci. He realizes that there is a 3/5 year split in GADA VI but makes a mistake in identifying the GADA grade as RABA DORI in the first 3 years and GADA (VI) proper in the last 5 years: in other words, GADA VI is abridged to 5 years. Domenico Pecci, "Note sul sistema delle Gada e delle classi di età presso le popolazioni Borana," *Ressegna di Studi Etiopici,* 1 (1941): 309, 311. De Salviac too makes the same mistake (see p. 204, above).

49. Deborah Prindle and Scott Grant, personal communication.

50. Bartels, *Oromo Religion,* 309.

51. In Western traditions this is comparable to the role of the professional civil servants who carry on their routine activities in government while the politicians and political appointees come and go with each elected government.

52. These elders are sometimes referred to as *jars albati* because they are given extremely rich foods by the luba and may, therefore, have digestive problems.

53. Asmarom Legesse, *Gada*, 198-201. The impact of *dhacc'hi* can be clearly seen in the gada chronology. If we find that a lineage held gada office for two or three generations and then it never appears in the chronology, there is almost invariably a skeleton in their closet.

54. The attribution of gerontocratic properties to age- and generation-systems, advocated by Radcliffe-Brown, and repeated by many of his followers, is in keeping with this bias.

55. It is very likely that expansive clans will have odd numbered lineages and the more stable clans will have a dual organization, such as Warra Bokku and Warra Qallu sections, within.

56. Even after the democratic institutions had declined among the Macch'a, and after the Ghibe kingdoms had been established, some Ghibe kings retained important features of Oromo democratic organization. Thus, Abba Bagibo, the great king of Limmu-Ennaria maintained a complex of 15 royal residences around his entire kingdom, a practice reminiscent of the Borana tradition of requiring the gada leaders to visit a series of ceremonial sites in the territory during their term office. This requirement kept them in touch with the population. Mohammed Hassen, *The Oromo of Ethiopia,* 167.

57. This stands in sharp contrast with the three branches of the US government which are physically located within hearing distance of each other—a situation which permits each branch to breathe down the neck of the other branches. It is doubtful that the framers of the US constitution would have allowed the branches of government to be physically so close to each other had they known the outcome. Although this issue is of historic interest, it is now a moot point since modern communications have made distances less relevant, though not entirely so, because face to face contact still has far greater impact than electronic communication.

58. The notion that the hereditary leader is ritually superior but politically inferior to the elected leader is analogous to the relationship between the president and the prime minister in France, and the monarch and the prime minister in Great Britain.

---

*The Gada Assembly in Session*　　⟶

***Jaldessa Liban,*** Abba Gada of all the Borana, 1960-68, head of the Gada Assembly and one of the presiding officers of the pan-Borana Assembly during the author's period of fieldwork.

*Chapter 6*

# CONCLUSION:

## Retrospect and Prospect

What was presented in the preceding chapter does not constitute an exhaustive account of all the principles underlying the Oromo constitution. It is simply one stage in the development of our understanding of the system that begins with the work of Antoine d'Abbadie and Enrico Cerulli, followed by Alessandro Triulzi, Mohammed Hassen and this writer with many other authors currently conducting research whose contributions help to illuminate particular elements in the structure or genesis of the four institutions that make up the multi-headed system of traditional government. The institutions are *integrated under the supreme authority of the National Assembly* [1] and, because they have cross-cutting membership, they are, in combination, *fully representative of the society as a whole,*[2] more so than the single territorial platform (voting districts) on which Western representative institutions are built.

The Oromo constitution, though unwritten, is a rich source of ideas. Scholars will probably continue to probe deeper and deeper into its foundations for generations to come. Compared with the modern democracies, the Oromo constitution has a few unusual features. We examined some fundamental ideas that are not fully developed in Western democratic traditions: these are the period of testing of elected leaders, the assessment of the leaders mid-way through their term of office, the methods of distributing power across generations, the alliance of alternate groups, the method of staggered succession that reduces the convergence of destabilizing events, and the conversion of hierarchies into balanced oppositions. Two of these principles are again mentioned here for emphasis and comparison.

### Inter-generational equity: an African innovation

One major contribution of Oromo democracy is the way power is shared by the generations. This is a feature that occurs in some generational systems in Eastern Africa that are often assumed to be *gerontocracies*. Far from being a government of the elders, the Oromo system ensures that rights are distributed among fathers, sons, and grandsons: no generation that is mature enough to be able to bear the rights and duties of citizenship is prevented from taking part in political life.

Historically, Western liberal democracies failed quite miserably to achieve any semblance of inter-generational equity. The youth movements and the movements of the elderly that swept across the United States and Europe in the 1960s and early 1970s were attempts to correct the generational injustices that were, and still are, present in Western political systems.

### A period of testing: an Oromo innovation

Perhaps one of the most interesting ideas in Oromo democracy is the notion of the period of testing for elected leaders. It is true that in the West elected leaders do often hold a variety of elective or appointive offices before they makes it to the top as presidents or prime ministers, and that their track records are reviewed by academics, the press, and political parties arrayed for or against them when elections are in progress. In parliamentary democracies, the prime ministers are also members of parliament and, as such, they may have had ample legislative experience. In presidential systems, the leaders may have had both executive or legislative experience as governors and parliamentarians. They may also have had some military experience. However, none of these experiences are required as a precondition for the top positions of elective leadership. It is, therefore, quite possible for an inexperienced and untested individual to be elected to the highest office in the land.

## *What if they turn out to be fools?*

One of the methods I used to provoke discussions about Oromo democracy with Borana elders was to describe to them electoral procedures as they occur in other parts of the world. They listened to these descriptions with undivided attention and often made astute and, sometimes, surprising comments about them.

On one such occasion, I described American electoral politics to the assembly of gada Jaldessa Liban in 1962. More specifically, I gave them an account of the Kennedy-Nixon elections that I had witnessed with avid interest, two years earlier, in the United States. I told them that the country went through many months of intensive debate; that the prospective leaders traveled widely throughout the land—by train, car, and air—trying to persuade the people that they are the best individuals for the office, and that, at the end of this period, one man was elected *Abba Gada*. Some months later, I added, that he took *balli* and was invested into office as leader of the whole American nation, after swearing before the *Abba Sera* and before the people, to uphold and abide by the laws of the land.

They were particularly impressed by the oath of office. They were listening to all this with puzzled curiosity when, unexpectedly, a councilor asked "What if the man they chose turns out to be a fool?" I said, "The *Gumi* can uproot him after watching him as head of the *'luba in power'* for a few years." They retorted "By then he may have done a lot of damage!"

## Electoral fever: its effect on recruitment of leaders

Such dialogue with Borana elders has led me to believe that there may be many areas in which Oromo democracy has come up with ingenious solutions for some of the common problems of democratic society such as: (a) electing a man to the prototype of an office, many years before he is to be invested into the real office, (b) keeping the man under public observation while he is the leader of his generation cohort, (c) if necessary, removing him from that position before his investiture as leader of the nation, (d) reviewing his performance *during* his term of office, and "uprooting" him mid-way through his term of office if he is not equal to the task for which he was chosen by the people.

Surely, modern democracies have had many surprises in this regard when eloquent individuals of unknown character and negligible political experience captured the public imagination and were, in the heat of the election contest, swept into office. Aspects of their character then surface, which were not evident when they were publicly posturing before the electorate.

### Despotism in Europe: Hitler Elected Legitimately?

An astonishing demonstration of this phenomenon is the fact that Hitler became chancellor of Germany by constitutional, not revolutionary means. Step by step, he was able to build up unlimited power in his hands by giving the defeated, humiliated and fragmented German nation a new theme around which to rally. He melded together, into a single *Aryan volksgemeinschaft*, the most disparate elements of the nation, including two historic adversaries, workers and industrial capitalists. His movement promised to rebuild the devastated economy, to free the nation from the shackles of the Versailles Treaty, and to give the rebuilt nation *lebensraum* or "space for expansion."

After Germany's defeat in the First World War, the German "Weimar" Republic was faced with continued economic and political crises including the fiercest type of hyperinflation that made the Deutche Mark worthless (4.5 trillion Marks to the Dollar), collapsing businesses and industries, massive unemployment (6.5 million out of jobs), vast numbers of armed war veterans *(freicorps)* on the loose, new political ferment that unleashed the most extreme ideologies, with fascism and communism at the antipodes, and a very liberal presidential democracy at the helm—threatened, on the left and right, by violent political movements, some with private armies.

Under such circumstances, *a Hitler can happen in any modern democracy,* whose Achille's heel is the constitutional loophole granted to the president, to assume far greater powers than normal, to deal with *national emergencies,* and to confront *internal and external threats.*

Sadly, however, the threats *need not be real:* a president can provoke conflict, exaggerate the threat, whip up nationalism to paranoid levels, in order to assume "war powers," as happened in the United States after the terrorist attack on New York on September 11, 2001. G.W. Bush provoked a war on false pretexts (nuclear threat) and put himself in the saddle as the undisputed wartime chief, severely limiting the ability of Congress to reason its way out of the difficulty, and accusing his critics of disloyalty to the magnificent men in uniform. Yet another false pretext employed by Bush to provoke conflict and assume "war powers" was the claim that the Islamic fundamentalists behind September 11 attacks were the same as the leaders of Iraq—a secularist Baathist state. Far from being Islamists, they had a socialist orientation and occasional communist affiliation that had for a long time resisted the Islamist movement.

### *Probationary service: an antidote to political fever*

These are some aspects of Western democracy that demand rethinking in light of the political wisdom that evolved in Africa. Why not require all elected leaders of modern democracies to go through a probationary period, during which time they exercise real executive power, in an office that is a prototype of the one for which they are being groomed, and require them to remain under public observation throughout that time? If this period is long enough, the holier-than-thou mask worn by political aspirants on the campaign trail will fall, and the true face of the candidate will be revealed, warts and all.

### Functional Overlaps and Mutual Regulation

A highly developed aspect of democratic dynamics that has been elaborated in the United States is the system of "checks and balances." Finding anything remotely comparable to this feature of Western democracy in Oromo institutions was an unexpected development. The more I delved into the system, however, the more it looked like a parallel system of thought. I do not use the phrase "checks and balances" in describing the Oromo system because it is such a highly specialized feature of the American constitution. Instead I refer to it as a "pattern of mutual regulation between institutions" and draw some cross-cultural parallels that seem to be appropriate and instructive.

It is the characteristic of *"functional redundancy"* of institutions and the phenomenon of *"multiple affiliation"* of all Borana in three cross-cutting social groups that laid the foundation for this analysis. That naturally led to a renewed understanding of the pattern of *"mutual regulation"* between institutions. In rudimentary form, all that was elaborated in *Gada* in 1973.[3] None of these three analytical concepts mentioned here have direct parallels in Borana language.

Nevertheless, the political phenomena they represent, are an integral part of the living institutions. Stated differently, Galma Liban does not have words for these concepts, but when we operationalize them, he can bring forth an abundance of evidence for or against each concept. He can, for instance, present many observations showing how the overlapping authority of Qallu and Gada plays out in the crises they face in the political arena. Hence, what is presented is a lived-in, not a thought-of, aspect of Borana political life, derived from years of research, and verified through observation, case material, and eye-witness testimony.

What Arero Rammata said in 1963 and Galma Liban said in 1995 about the relationship between moieties, gada classes or between Qallu and Gada is that the institutions stand in opposition to each other and influence each other. The fact that one institution has authority that extends into the domain of the other institution is a fact well-known to them. It is a matter of heated debates. Abba Gada and Qallu both have authority over the same society but they exercise different kinds of authority. What one institution does significantly impacts on the other.

Indeed, until the constitutional change introduced by the Gumi in the gada of Jilo Aga in 1980, what the Qallu did had important and, in their view, excessive impact on gada leadership. That the Gumi stands in judgement of the Abba Gada is fully attested matter in their testimony. That the age-sets do what the gada leaders instruct them to do is also a normal and fully documented matter. The portrayal of these institutions as wholly independent of each other is, therefore, a complete misrepresentation of the reality.

What makes their political system "democratic" is not merely the pattern of division of labor and power-sharing between institutions, but, most importantly, the manner in which power is acquired, exercised, limited, expanded, or given up by one institution under pressure, criticism, or sanctions from other institutions. This is especially true of coordinate institutions such as Gada and Qallu or the co-equal moieties such as Sabbo and Gona.

Throughout the above analysis we have emphasized the balanced oppositions between Gada and Qallu, the unquestioned dominance of Gada in the political sphere and the equally unquestioned dominance of Qallu in the sphere of national political ritual. In combination the four institutions—the generation organization, the age sets, the National Assembly, and the Qallu institution—represent the society in complex ways that permit ample *individual freedoms.*

However, there is one sense in which the Qallu institution rises above all the other institutions. The senior Qallu's ritual dominions extend beyond his moiety, beyond Borana, beyond the allied nations who make up the Pax Borana, to the part of the extended Oromo nation, that has not yet plucked its roots and planted them elsewhere, adopted Islam and invented an Islamic genealogy for itself, and thereby erased much of its history and institutions.[3] Hence, in the domain of political ritual, the Qallu has great outreach. Much of the resilience of the Oromo nation is linked to its rituals, among which Muda plays a most important role. That is a fact that some Ethiopian rulers were very conscious of and tried to control.

## Fundamental Constitutional Change

The most important issue over which the Qallu and Gada institutions clashed in recent decades has to do with their domains of political, not ritual, authority. In recent decades there has been a sporadic power struggle between them. The conflict was over the relative authority of the Qallu and the Gada Assemblies in the electoral process.

In the 1960s and 1970s, gada leaders were saying that the authority to oversee the election of gada leaders is not properly the function of the Qallu and that this task should be returned to the Gada institution. This was the major constitutional issue that was hanging over Borana, and it was resolved in 1980, when the National Assembly decided to return that power to the Gada System. That is the most important piece of legislation passed by the Gumi since Dawwe Gobbo in the late 17th century. It will probably be remembered the same way that the institutional innovations of Dawwe Gobbo and Makko Bili are remembered in Oromo historical narratives. It is a fundamental piece of legislation that alters the mandates of their institutions and the basic relations between them.

It is worth remembering too that Jilo Aga, the Abba Gada during whose term of office this constitutional change was made (1976-1984), is the "eighth" cyclical successor of the great lawmaker, Dawwe Gobbo, Abba Gada (1696-1704), who is reputed to have created the exogamous rules governing the moiety system and the generational laws governing the Gada System. In the 360-year-long gada chronology, the cycle closes on the eighth generation: when that happens, *dhacc'i* returns: gada leaders are then under pressure to repeat the feats performed by their cyclical "luba ancestors."

By introducing this constitutional change, Jilo Aga and his Gada Assembly have *re-defined the division of labor and separation of powers between the Qallu and Gada institutions.* This issue was debated for three gada periods in the assemblies of Madha Galma, Jaldessa Liban and Gobba Bule, but did not come to a head until Jilo Aga's term of office, suggesting that *dhacch'i* was at work.

Those ethnographers, such as Paul Baxter, Marco Bassi, and Gudrun Dahl, who have never seen the Gumi at work, but, nonetheless, insist that the Borana "lawmakers" have *no legislative power,* and that all they do is to recite their customary laws every eight years, should now seriously re-think their position. The constitutional reform introduced during the gada of Jilo Aga (1976-84) has placed before us incomparably valuable evidence indicating that legislation does not deal only with minor issues, such as the treatment of horses or the laws about feminine modesty, but that it also deals with issues that *define and re-define the basic mandates of their institutions.*

The analysis of the Qallu and Gada institutions must now be taken to the next stage, to see how the legislative innovation will alter the relationship of mutual regulation that existed between the coordinate institutions. That is a task that must be left to the next generation of students of Oromo political life. All other aspects of the separation of powers between the two institutions remain unchanged. The balancing of ritual and political authority is still intact: the Warra Qallu still maintain their high ritual position. So too has their role as intermediaries between the people and the provincial government remained unaltered until the fall of the Communist regime in 1991. We do not know what the present regime has done with the institutions of indirect rule they inherited from the previous regimes.

It is important to remember that the houses of the Qallu had taken more political power than was their due, at the time that Borana territory was conquered by Emperor Menelik. They were given new powers as agents of the new system of administration and acquired the right to oversee the election of Gada leaders. The reduction in their power, in 1980, can, therefore, be seen as an attempt to redress the imbalance created by Menelik and his successors. The change was due to an internal legislative debate that had little to do with revolutionary, communist Ethiopia. The debate began long before the Dergue and will probably go on long after the Dergue.

The Warra Qallu themselves have also compensated for other difficulties created by the innovations introduced by Emperor Menelik. The Borana came to realize that the role of the newly appointed administrative intermediary *(balabbat)* and that of ritual leader *(Qallu)* are incompatible.[4] As a result the Qallu lineage has segmented into two separate lineages: the senior segment now maintains ritual leadership and the junior segment oversees relations with the central government, under the guidance of the National Assembly. The Qallu lineage is the node at which the clash between national and local institutions is most acutely felt.

We should not assume that the changes made by the Gumi of Jilo Aga, in 1980, will remain for all time and that the debate concerning this key aspect of the Oromo constitution has ended. The leadership of one *gogessa* has spoken on the matter, but there are four other *gogessas* that have yet to be heard from. Two National Assembly meetings have been held since then, and there is no evidence of any attempt to reverse the constitutional reform of Jilo Aga.

One the most important lessons that can be learned from the history of Oromo institutions is this: when something happens that throws the system out of balance on one parameter, the balance is restored on another parameter. The Oromo nation has great capacity for making dialectical changes in response to the historic challenges it faced.

Examples of such dialectic transformations are (1) the breakdown of moieties during the great migration and their replication and rebuilding in later stages, (2) the assimilation of aliens as rebellious second class citizens *(Gabaro)* and their ultimate incorporation into Oromo political life as a countervailing element of their dual organization, (3) the marginalization of the *ilman jarsa* through premature retirement, and their subsequent reintegration as the Junior Gada Council *(Garba),* (4) the decline of the Gada System due to the under-aging process and the rebuilding of the system as gada-cum-age-sets, (5) the recruitment of the Qallu into provincial government, the realization that Qallu and Balabbat do not belong together and the subsequent splitting of the lineage into ritual and administrative branches, and (6) the expansion of powers by the Warra Qallu, under Menelik, and the rebalancing of their powers through the constitutional reforms made by the Gumi.

All that is evidence that Oromo history is rich with examples of rational legislative transformations that allowed the society to overcome major internal and external challenges. Given this body of evidence, it is nonsense to suggest that Oromo have no legislative tradition and that all they do is recite their laws every eight years.

## Weaknesses of the Oromo Constitution

Oromo democracy is not perfect: if it were, it would not be democratic. Like all democratic institutions, it is the product of changing human thought that must always be re-examined in relation to changing historic circumstances. What then are the weaknesses in this political system?

### 1. Exclusion of women from political institutions

The single most important deficit in Oromo democracy is the exclusion of women from formal political participation and leadership. Borana say *Siqqe moti warri isin motu bade,* "Women's authority destroys the very people over whom it is exercised."[5] That is one of the many ways that Borana express their belief that women are not fit for political office. Women do, of course, take part in political life, in many subtle and informal ways. For instance, they use the medium of *karrile* songs to praise or parody the character of political leaders or those who have aspirations for high office.

Women who compose such songs often influence the course of elections, and the prospects of a lineage winning or holding political office. They celebrate great men, and criticize the weak or incompetent warriors, leaders, or lawmakers. The songs are remembered for generations. That is one kind of role that women play in the political life of their people. That, however, does not mitigate the fact that women are disenfranchised in the context of the formal political institutions. That is the situation that prevails in Borana today. All their principal institutions—Gada, Age-set, Moiety and Clan organizations—are headed by men.

There is only one significant exception: The Qallitti, the wife of the Qallu, or the mother of the Qallu—if he comes into the office during his minority—is reputed to hold an important place in their political life. According to Galma she is empowered to select one of the six Adula councilors. However, that claim needs to be corroborated.

On the whole, women are also excluded from judicial activities. In Oromo litigation, they are represented by their male patrilineal kin. That was the situation in the Gudru republic in Macch'a which d'Abbadie analyzed in the 1880s, and it is also the situation among the southern Borana today. Nonetheless, Borana women are very outspoken and have begun to make use of national laws and state courts to exercise rights they do not have in the traditional society, e.g., in matters concerning inheritance, separation, divorce or custody. There is great need to carry out research on the role of women in Oromo political life. In this regard, Belletech Dheressa has done pioneering work on Oromo women's role in history.

Furthermore, there is now a growing body of evidence from other branches of the Oromo nation, such as Arsi, indicating that the *Siqqe institution* played and continues to play an important role in protecting the *rights of women*. In particular the institution gives women important guarantees against male conduct that violates customary protections that are offered to them. The woman whose rights are violated can ululate in public, attract the support of other women, and proceed to take the offending male to justice. With such protections in place, it is unlikely that domestic injustice or violence will remain unchecked and unreported. (Arsi Elders, Nairobi, 2006.)

## 2. Rigidity of political structures

The second deficit in the Oromo polity has to do with the rigidity of the political structures underlying one of the four institutions, namely the Gada System. In particular, the requirement that the generations must follow each other in forty-year cycles, and that all brothers must belong to the same gada class regardless of their age, causes many cumulative demographic and structural problems which I have analyzed in great detail elsewhere (*Gada*, 1973, ch. 5). Hence, age groups, which are then re-grouped into chronological, not genealogical, generations could serve as more effective basis for a modern political system. With this adjustment, however, there is no reason why the institution could not serve as a viable political model. Alternatively, the generational system can be preserved by abridging the forty-year generation to something that approximates the average age span of generations.[6] In a modern state, demographers can easily furnish that information, and parliament can periodically change the generation interval to keep it in line with demographic changes, as is presently being done with retirement age in Europe and America.

### 3. Corruption in political life

One type of corruption in Oromo political life has been recorded by d'Abbadie in the Gudru Republic (Macch'a), where bribing jurors had become common practice. This was done by a juror arresting the litigation with a veto, and using the time out of court to ply other jurors with gifts. This resulted in what he calls an unhealthy practice of "buying the law." In contemporary Oromo society too it is likely that gift giving will continue to be a source of problems unless judges and electors are properly remunerated for their services.

An important deficit in Borana today has to do with the electoral process. In the absence of some type of voting procedure, it is difficult to see how the electors can reflect the public will in the manner they select candidates. Furthermore, the fact that candidates and their supporters give gifts to the electors is a source of major problems. Given this fact, the generosity of the wealthy candidate can easily warp the deliberation of the electors, and lead to the misrepresentation of the "will of the people." The many objective devices that modern democracies have invented, including polling and the ballot box, are major improvements over the traditional strategies for determining who is or is not the choice of the people. Having said that, however, it is necessary to add that the manner Borana assemblies reach consensus without counting "votes" is highly effective and that the introduction of voting and other aspects of *majoritarian democracy* into their deliberative assemblies may not be much of an improvement.[7] If the indigenous system of *consensus democracy* is to be preserved, the ingenious methods of consensus building and the ethical guidelines that govern conduct in assemblies must also be kept fully in force.

### 4. Traditional societies and modern states: the question of scale

The fourth problem emerges as an academic argument that claims that Oromo institutions may have been appropriate for the small scale society of a few tens or hundreds of thousands souls that the Oromo nation probably was when the institutions developed, but that the same institutions cannot serve the needs of a modern nation which is tens of millions strong. Admittedly, institutions must undergo a process of simplification and streamlining—and, on the bureaucratic side, considerable development—before they can become useful in that larger and more modern context.

Nevertheless, we do not know how much influence the scale of society has on the type of political institutions it develops: in this regard, there is room for much comparative research. Canton democracy in Switzerland, New England town-meeting democracy in the US, or the Magna Carta in England, were all institutions of small scale societies. That did not prevent the Swiss, the Americans and the British from reaching down to these deep traditions and using them as cultural, ethical and constitutional resources. As grass roots institutions, as systems of values, or as powerful historical memories they have survived until modern times. They have great motivational power. So too was Athenian democracy limited to a single city-state and thus small scale par excellence. That did not prevent modern nations from borrowing many of Athens' constitutional concepts including the concept of "democracy" itself.

The strongest, most stable, and most viable democracies today are those that developed from their own historic roots, e.g., Botswana, Morocco, or Swaziland, not those that were built on borrowed models, e.g., modern Kenya or Ethiopia. There is something fundamentally shaky about borrowed institutions. That is because the institutions are transplanted without the system of values and ethical roots on which institutions must grow. They cannot survive without those roots.

## On Functional Redundancy, Polycephalous Government, Bureaucracy and Succession

There has been some discussion among students of Ethiopian cultures concerning the character of Oromo political institutions and their strengths and weaknesses, compared with Western and other Ethiopian institutions. In my extended dialogue with Donald Levine, I drew explicit analogies between the separation of powers in the three branches of the American government and the division of functions between the three institutions of the Oromo. At a joint seminar we offered at the University of Chicago, I presented evidence that in both systems, there is a measure of functional differentiation but also a certain degree of overlap in functions, and that this latter property is the cornerstone of the system of "checks and balances"—as it evolved in the United States. It is clear that the separation of powers between the "co-equal branches" of government is not a simple division of labor in which the branches are assigned mutually exclusive spheres of authority, as happens in bureaucratic organizations, where sharp division of roles is the order of the day. The division of labor between co-equal institutions is, in fact, a system of partly distinct and partly overlapping domains.

I presented a similar property in the structure of Oromo democracy, which I described as a type of "functional redundancy" that enables each institution to regulate the other institutions. Levine responded by subsequently publishing his thoughts on Oromo democracy in a work titled *Greater Ethiopia: the Evolution of a Multiethnic Society*. In that work, he interpreted the factor of "functional redundancy" not as a positive attribute of a polycephalous democracy but as a negative property of an underdeveloped bureaucracy, that had failed to develop clear functional differentiation between its institutions and between the many roles within each institution.[8]

Granted that the historic weakness of the expansive Oromo nation was that it did not create an administrative system—a bureaucratic hierarchy—that could hold all the pieces of its widely dispersed branches together. The society kept breaking up into autonomous segments in each newly occupied territory. Granted also that the existing institutions do not have a well developed bureaucratic organization within them. It is, nevertheless, necessary to acknowledge that the Oromo political system is not a variety of bureaucratic government. Those who govern the system are not a hierarchy of officers with distinct tasks which they perform in the service of distinct institutions. Instead, the entire system is governed by councils and assemblies. Hence, the Oromo system shares some features with parliamentary governments in which assemblies and the constituent parties are poised against each other and regulate each other. Each Oromo assembly does have a modest degree of bureaucratic organization within it, and it is legitimate to ask, as Levine does, whether or not the roles in each organization are adequately developed. They are not. However, the relationship between the coordinate institutions of the Oromo cannot be understood in the language of bureaucracy.

In this analysis, it is important to acknowledge that two different kinds of leaders are needed in a modern democratic society: politicians who are *generalists* and bureaucrats who are *specialists*. Elected representatives are constantly called upon to deal with *any* societal, political, technical or economic issues raised by their constituencies. Hence, they cannot afford to develop narrow areas of specialization. At the same time they must rely on an *army of civil servants* for technical expertise. It is the "experts," not the "politicians" who make up the backbone of the governmental bureaucracy—the body that carries on from decade to decade, and continues to build up its store of information, knowledge and skills, as elected leaders come and go. It is clear that Borana has no "civil service" that can feed a bureaucracy. The few men of knowledge, such as Arero Rammata and Galma Liban, who perform a vital role as experts, are hardly comparable to the legions of experts available to the modernizing African state.

In his thoughtful analysis of contemporary Ethiopia, Levine considers many paths of societal evolution which the nation undertook in the past or might undertake in the coming decades. The place of Oromo democracy in this evolutionary process is yet to be properly re-evaluated. Levine's first attempt to do that in 1974 was useful for the middle decades of the 20th century, but it is no longer appropriate for the present era because of the immense changes that took place in Ethiopia during the last quarter of the 20th century. In particular, the new world of *ethnic federalism* in Ethiopia seems to have changed the fundamental premises of national integration.

But the immediate deficit of *Greater Ethiopia* that concerns us here is this: In reviewing the various paths toward societal evolution, Levine neglects one path that is of the utmost importance, i.e., the path toward *democratization*. One of the greatest handicaps that gets in the way of a modernizing African nation is not the lack of bureaucracy, which modern Africans adopt on a massive scale, albeit laced with corruption. The main hurdle has to do with that most difficult of all modern ideas—that government must be differentiated into autonomous entities that have special functions but also share some *overlapping responsibilities and reciprocal rights of oversight*.

In Western democracies this has taken the form of an independent parliament and an independent judiciary that constrain the executive branch. Without these constraints, the institutions of government can be easily reduced into a single monolithic state. That is a key problem that confronts the modernizing African state.

Virtually every state in Africa has created the mandatory "three branches of government," but it is often a mere façade. In most cases, parliament is not much more than a rubber stamp institution and the judiciary is a department of the Ministry of Justice, which can be readily dismantled by strong leaders. That defeats the very purpose of the tri-partite organization of the state and the great stability that can be achieved through the medium of mutually regulating institutions and by means of sensible, moderate, rational democratic discourse on which institutions must depend.

Over and above the institutions of democracy, the basic *attitudes, culture and language of democracy* is equally important. Oromo culture is devoid of the manic-depressive swings between the rebellious spirit that periodically sweep across the Abyssinian highlands, followed by deep feelings of guilt that crush the human spirit—all that constitutes so great a threat, that the society soon slides back to the comfort of knowing that a firm hand is in charge and the intra-psychic order is restored. The highly developed culture of obsequiousness before "king and country," respect for patriarchal authority, and loyalty to political leaders then re-surfaces and becomes the necessary condition for orderly political, familial, social, and psychic life.

It is wondrous to observe the complete equanimity, moderation, and confidence with which Oromo men and women criticize each other and their ritual or political leaders, and Oromo children criticize the parental generation supported of the alternate generation who are their grandfathers and their allies. Such cultural resources and modes of political socialization are extremely helpful, as the multi-ethnic society experiments with democratization on a national scale.

All new-born African democracies can benefit from a dictum derived from the centuries-old Oromo democracy —a motto that should be placed at the gate of every parliament in Africa: "Leave all cleverness behind, as you set foot on these blessed grounds!"

Yet another feature of Oromo democracy is the phenomenon of *orderly succession to positions of leadership*, which, as we have seen, is a fundamental feature of their political system. The British and Ethiopian monarchies—the two systems with which we have chosen to contrast this indigenous African democracy—reveal histories that are markedly different from Oromo history.

As indicated earlier, it took Britain nearly five centuries to complete the process of democratization. It was a violent history court intrigue, abdications, and civil wars. Similarly, the Christian kingdom in Ethiopia failed to institutionalize orderly succession to political office during most of its history. In the evolution of the Solomonid dynasty, the rules of succession were ill-defined and the number of potential heirs to the throne was very large, because of their rules of bilateral descent and succession, which allowed men and women to inherit or succeed through the male and the female lines. When a king succeeded to the throne, other claimants often had to be confined to mountain fortresses, sometimes for life.

During the past century and a half, nearly successions in Ethiopia were marked by conflict or civil wars. The relevant transitions were those from the Era of the Princes to Tewodros (1855), from Tewodros to Yohannes (1872), Yohannes to Menelik (1889), Lij Iyyasu (Menelik's heir) to Zewditu (another heir to Menelik's throne) with Haile Sellassie as regent, Haile Sellassie to Mengistu (1975), and Mengistu to EPRDF (1991). Which of these transitions can be said to have taken place in a predictable, orderly fashion and how much violence, bloodshed, and subterfuge was involved in each transfer of power? Tewodros and Yohannes were rebel chiefs who rose to positions of supreme authority by force, not by constitutional means. The last three transitions mentioned here were accompanied by full-scale civil wars: (a) the battle of Segele (1916) that led to the dethronement of Lij Iyyasu by Ras Tafari, whose crown name is Haile Sellassie, (b) the communist takeover (1974) that forced the abdication and subsequent assassination of Emperor Haile Sellassie, and (c) the overthrow of the Dergue (1991) by the Oromo, Tigrayan and Eritrean liberation fronts, after decades of armed struggle.

By contrast, during the past four centuries of Oromo history, traditional government changed hands regularly every eight years in accordance with constitutional provisions. Rarely did military leaders usurp political power by force. No leader was ever assassinated, beheaded, or poisoned. No potential heirs were placed in confinement for life, lest they rise to claim their ambiguous patrimony and put the incumbent, and the state, in jeopardy.

In Oromo society, some unfit leaders were, of course, impeached, but impeachment was a constitutionally mandated procedure, not an act of rebellion. In some areas, the Oromo did abandon their democratic institutions and adopted monarchic organizations, in which case they could have faced the same kinds of successional crises as the north Ethiopian monarchies. That, however, does not seem to have happened because the rules of succession in the male line by primogeniture were simpler and more practical, and, at the same time, grass-roots democracy continued to govern their lives at community level, through the medium of clan and village councils.

Oromo made laws to meet some of the great challenges that confronted them in history. They did so not because they had great lawgivers but an effective legislative assembly. This, I believe, is how we should understand Oromo societal evolution, as the capacity of the Oromo polity to re-invent itself by the longest and most arduous deliberations of the people and their representatives. The constitutional principles of Oromo democracy can serve as the foundation of a modern democratic political order, which distributes power *across institutions* and *across generations* while, at the same time, blocking the natural tendency of leaders to concentrate unlimited power in their hands, to disrupt the processes of peaceful political succession, and to eliminate all elements of popular participation. These are some of the principles that can serve as the cornerstones of a modern political system based on the egalitarian heritage of an indigenous African democracy.

# NOTES

1. In the earliest stages of my research, I had not begun to think of the National Assembly as a separate institution but as one of the assemblies of the Gada institution. However, the fact that all councils in Borana, including clan councils, take part in the deliberations persuaded me that the national assembly must be seen as an inclusive national institution in which all other assemblies and councils are, in varying degrees and in different forms, participants.

2. There are limitations on the manner and extent that the various councils are represented in the National Assembly. Oromo democracy is not a *direct democracy,* but a *representative democracy.* The argument often made by ethnographers that they have never seen "generation sets" or "age-sets" meeting "as sets" to make any decisions and that, therefore, do not have any political functions is a fallacious argument. *People participate through their representatives in the Gada assemblies.* The never have to meet "as sets." A "set" that numbers in the tens of thousands cannot be expected to meet as single body. That does not happen in any society, of a scale comparable to the Oromo.

3. All this was anticipated by the discussion of electoral politics, cross-cutting classes, functional redundancy in *Gada* (1973), 223.

4. Whenever conflict breaks out between the two lineages they typically go to national courts to resolve their differences. That is offensive to Borana because it diminishes the authority of the Gumi.

5. *Siqqe* is the staff that all married women hold on ritual occasion and is here used as a symbol of their authority. It is the equivalent of the staff, *Ororo*, men hold on similar occasions.

6. According to Christopher Hallpike, the Konso have experimented with their Gada System and have come up with a reasonable generation interval. See his "Origins of the Gada System, a discussion of 'Gada: Three Approaches to the Study of African Society,'" Africa, *Journal of the International African Institute,* 46(1976): 52.

7. See, in particular, Arend Lejphart's *Democracies: Patterns of Majoritarian and Consensus Government in Twenty-One Countries* (New Haven: Yale University Press, 1984).

8. Donald Levine, *Greater Ethiopia: the Evolution of a Multiethnic Society,* (Chicago: University of Chicago Press, 1974), 119-121, 136-137.

# APPENDIX I, Gada Chronology, as of 1963

| | | |
|---|---|---|
| 1. Sons of Jaldessa<br>2000-08<br>*Moggisa* | 2. Sons of Madha<br>1992-2000<br>*Sabbaqa* | 3. Boru Guyyo<br>1984-92<br>*Libasa* |
| 6. **Jaldessa Liban**<br>1960-68<br>*Fullasa* | 7. Madha Galma<br>1052-60<br>*Makhula* | 8. Guyyo Boru<br>1944-52<br>*Moggisa* |
| 11. Arero Gedo<br>1921-29<br>*Darara* | 12. Liban Kuse<br>1913-21<br>*Mardida* | 13. Boru Galma<br>1906-13<br>*Fullasa* |
| 16. Guyyo Boru Ingule<br>1885-91<br>*Sabbaqa* | 17. Dida Bittata<br>1876-83<br>*Libasa* | 18. Haro Adi<br>1868-76<br>*Darara* |
| 21. Liban Jilo<br>1845-52<br>*Makhula* | 22. Madha Boru<br>1837-45<br>Moggisa | 23. Sokhore Anna<br>1829-37<br>*Sabbaqa* |
| 26. Ingule Halakhe<br>1806-14<br>*Mardida* | 27. Boru Madha<br>1798-1806<br>*Fullasa* | 28. Wayyu Ralle<br>1791-98<br>*Makhula* |
| 31. Dhaddaccha Oda<br>Morowwa<br>1768-76<br>*Libasa* | 32. Madha Boru<br>Dadoye<br>1761-68<br>*Darara* | 33. Guyyo Gedo<br>1753-61<br>*Mardida* |
| 36. Sora Dhaddaccha<br>1730-37<br>*Moggisa* | 37. Wale Wacch'u<br>1722-30<br>*Sabbaqa* | 38. Jarso Iddo<br>1714-22<br>*Libasa* |
| 41. **Morowwa Abbayye**<br>1690-98<br>*Fullasa* | 42. Wayyu Uru<br>1682-90<br>*Makhula* | 43. Alle Kura<br>1674-82<br>*Moggisa* |
| 46. *Darara* | 47. Hindhale Doyyo<br>*Mardida* | 48. Yayya Ole<br>*Fullasa* |
| 51. *Sabbaqa* | 52. Doyyo Boru Lukku<br>*Libasa* | 53. Ososi<br>*Darara* |
| 56. *Makhula* | 57. Boboru<br>*Moggisa* | 58. Yayya Fullelle<br>*Sabbaqa* |

The most significant *dhacch'i* linkages in recent decades are boldfaced

| | | |
|---|---|---|
| **4. Jilo Aga**<br>1976-84<br>*Darara* | 5. Gobba Bule<br>1968-76<br>*Mardida* | **ACTIVE**<br>impacted by historic<br>*precedent* |
| 9. **Aga Adi**<br>1936-44<br>*Sabaqa* | 10. Bule Dabbasa<br>1929-36<br>*Libasa* | **INACITVE** (yuba)<br>partial retirement |
| 14. Adi Doyyo<br>1899-1906<br>*Makhula* | 15. Liban Jaldessa<br>1891-99<br>*Moggisa* | **INACTIVE** (jarsa)<br>final retirement<br>↓ |
| 19. Doyyo Jilo<br>1860-68<br>*Mardida* | 20. Jaldessa Guyyo<br>Debbasa<br>1852-60<br>*Fullasa* | |
| 24. Jilo Niencho<br>1821-29<br>*Libasa* | 25. Saqo Dhaddaccha<br>1814-21<br>*Darara* | |
| 29. Liban Wata<br>1783-90<br>*Moggisa* | 30. Bule Dhaddaccha<br>1776-83<br>*Sabbaqa* | |
| 34. Halakhe Doyyo<br>1745-53<br>*Fullasa* | 35. Dhaddaccha Wayyu<br>1737-45<br>*Makhula* | |
| **39. Dawwe-Gobbo**<br>1706-14<br>*Darara* | 40. Gobba Alla<br>1698-1705<br>*Mardida* | **ACTIVE**<br>has impact on<br>*lubas in power* |
| **44. Abbayai Babbo**<br>1667-74<br>*Sabbaqa* | 45. Abbu Lakhu<br>1659-67<br>*Libasa* | **INACTIVE:**<br>antecedents of<br>yuba |
| 49. Babbo Horro<br>*Makhula* | 50. Bidu Doqqe<br>*Moggisa* | **INACTIVE**<br>has no relevance<br>for the present<br>↓ |
| 54. Horro Dullaccha<br>*Mardida* | 55. Kura Dhalla<br>*Fullasa* | |
| 59. Gadayo<br>*Libasa* | 60. Urgumessa<br>*Darara* | |

# Appendix II,
## Chronology of Abba Gadas
## with moiety, clan, lineage affiliation
## Source: Galma Liban, 1995

G=Gona   S=Sabbo

### The First Gogessa

| Abba Gada | | Moiety | Clan/lineage | | G | S |
|---|---|---|---|---|---|---|
| Jaldessa liban | 1960-68 | Gona | Galantu/Berritu | | 1 | |
| Arero Gedo | 1921-29 | Gona | Dambitu/Warra Gussa | | 1 | |
| Guyyo Boru Ingule | 1885-91 | Gona | Gelantu/Berritu | | 1 | |
| Liban Jilo | 1845-52 | Gona | Dambitu | | 1 | |
| Ingule Halakhe | 1806-14 | Gona | Galantu/Berritu | | 1 | |
| Dhaddaccha Oda | 1768-76 | Gona | Galantu/Berritu | | 1 | |
| Sora Dhaddaccha | 1730-37 | Gona | Warri Jidda | | 1 | |
| Morowwa Abbayye | 1690-98 | Gona | Galantu/Berritu | | 1 | |

### The Second Gogessa

| Abba Gada | | Moiety | Clan/lineage | | G | S |
|---|---|---|---|---|---|---|
| Boru Madha | 1992-00 | Gona | Nonitu/Ammoyye | | 1 | |
| Madha Galma | 1952-60 | Gona | Nonitu/Ammoyye | | 1 | |
| Liban Kuse | 1913-21 | Sabbo | Digalu/Daddo | | | 1 |
| Dida Bittata | 1876-83 | Gona | Nonitu/Ammoyye | | 1 | |
| Madha Boru | 1837-45 | Gona | Nonitu/Ammoyye | | 1 | |
| Boru Madha | 1798-06 | Gona | Nonitu/Ammoyye | | 1 | |
| Madha Boru D. | 1761-68 | Gona | Nonitu/Ammoyye | | 1 | |
| Wale Wacch'u | 1722-30 | Sabbo | Digalu/Udumtu | | | 1 |
| Wayyu Uru | 1682-90 | Sabbo | Matt'arri/Metta | | | 1 |

> **The total number of times that the moieties won the office of Abba Gada during the last three and a half centuries is, Gona 27 (60%) and Sabbo 18 (40%).**

## The Third Gogessa

| Abba Gada | | Moiety | Clan/Lineage | G | S |
|---|---|---|---|---|---|
| Boru Guyyo | 1984-92 | Gona | Galangu/Beritu | 1 | |
| Guyyo Boru | 1944-52 | Gona | Galangu/Beritu | 1 | |
| Boru Galma | 1906-13 | Gona | Galangu/Beritu | 1 | |
| Haro Adi | 1868-76 | Sabbo | Digalu/Titti | | 1 |
| Sokhore Anna | 1829-37 | Sabbo | Matt'arri/Metta | | 1 |
| Wayyu Ralle | 1791-98 | Gona | Dambitu/Warra Gussa | 1 | |
| Guyyo Dedo | 1753-61 | Gona | Sirayyu | 1 | |
| Jarso Iddo | 1714-22 | Gona | Sirayyu | 1 | |
| Alle Kura | 1674-82 | Sabbo | Digalu/Titti | | 1 |

## The Fourth Gogessa

| Abba Gada | Dates | Moiety | Clan/Lineage | G | S |
|---|---|---|---|---|---|
| Jilo Aga | 1976-84 | Sabbo | Digalu/Titti | | 1 |
| Aga Adi | 1936-44 | Sabbo | Digalu/Titti | | 1 |
| Adi Doyyo | 1889-06 | Sabbo | Digalu/Titti | | 1 |
| Doyyo Jilo | 1860-68 | Sabbo | Digalu/Titti | | 1 |
| Jilo Niencho | 1821-29 | Sabbo | Digalu/Titti | | 1 |
| Liban Wata | 1783-90 | Sabbo | Digalu/Walajji | | 1 |
| Halakhe Doyyo | 1745-53 | Gona | Galantu/Lukku | 1 | |
| Dawwe Gobbo | 1706-14 | Gona | Qarch'abdu/Buyyama | 1 | |
| Abbayyi Baddo | 1667-74 | Gona | Dambitu/Obitu | 1 | |

## The Fifth Gogessa

| Abba Gada | | Moiety | Clan/Lineage | G | S |
|---|---|---|---|---|---|
| Guyyo Gobba | 2008-16 | Sabbo | Digalu/Emmaji | | 1 |
| Gobba Bule | 1968-76 | Sabbo | Digalu/Emmaji | | 1 |
| Bule Debbasa | 1929-36 | Sabbo | Digalu/Emmaji | | 1 |
| Liban Jaldessa | 1891-99 | Gona | Qarch'abdu/Buyyama | 1 | |
| Jaldessa Guyyo | 1852-60 | Gona | Qarch'abdu/Buyyama | 1 | |
| Saqo Dhaddacha | 1814-21 | Gona | Macch'itu/Jawwitu | | 1 |
| Bule Dhaddacha | 1776-83 | Sabbo | Digalu/Emmaji | | 1 |
| Dhaddacha Wayyu | 1737-45 | Sabbo | Digalu/Emmaji | | 1 |
| Gobba Alla | 1698-05 | Sabbo | Digalu/Nurtu | | 1 |
| Abbu Lakhu | 1659-67 | Gona | Qarch'abdu/Ebitu | | 1 |

269b

**APPENDIX III, MOIETIES COMPARATIVE CHART**

| BARENTU | | BORANA + BAHREY | | ORMA |
|---|---|---|---|---|
| **QALLO** | | | | BARETTUMA |
| OBORRA | Daga | | BARETTUMA | |
| OBORRA | Dorani | **Mattarri**/Doranni | BARETTUMA | **MATTARRI** |
| OBORRA | Billi | | BARETTUMA | |
| OBORRA | Akichu | Akachu | BARETTUMA | |
| NOLE | *Oromo* | | BARETTUMA | |
| NOLE | **NOLE** | **Nole** | BARETTUMA | |
| NOLE | Mutcha | | BARETTUMA | |
| BABILE | Gondala | | BARETTUMA | |
| BABILE | Karala | **Mattarri**/Karara | BARETTUMA | Waya |
| | | Maliyyu | BARETTUMA | Maliyyu |
| | | **KARRAYYU** | BARETTUMA | **KARRAYYU** |
| | | Hajeji | BARETTUMA | Hajeji |
| | | Sunqanna | BARETTUMA | Sunqanna |
| | | Wayyu | BARETTUMA | Wayu |
| | | **DIGALU** | BARETTUMA | **DIGALU** |
| HUMBANNA | | Humbanna | | Bworan |
| **ANIA** | | | BORANA | **IRDIDA** |
| KODELI | *Bidu* | | BORANA | Bworan |
| KODELI | **Anna** | Jillitu-Anna | BORANA | |
| KODELI | **Macha** | Macch'(itu) | BORANA | Manchitu |
| KODELI | Loke | | BORANA | |
| KODELI | | Guji | BORANA | Guji |
| KODELI | | Galantu | BORANA | Jalantu |
| SADACHA | Malkata | *x-over Mattarri* | BORANA | Mattarri-manqata |
| SADACHA | Babbo | | BORANA | |
| SADACHA | **Dembi** | Demb(itu) | BORANA | |

# A NOTE ON THE COMPARATIVE CHART

The middle column is a combination of the data from Borana, Ethiopia and from Bahrey's ancient moieties BORANA & BARETTUMA. Although they are merged here to serve as a parent society framework for the other societies, they were compared separately on page 165.

The chart on the opposite page shows that the same kinds of linkages occur when we compare Barentu* and Orma with the          parent system. Most of the evidence shows that Qallo of Barentu and Barettuma of Orma have ethnogenetic connections with BARETTUMA.

Ania of Barentu and Irdida of Orma show direct linkages with BORANA of Bahrey and Gona of Borana. In this latter case, the Matt'arri, who have a number of marginal characteristics show up mainly on the BARETTUMA, but sometimes on the BORANA, side of the divide.

The word "Oromo" is the name of a clan in Nole. Here is one of the many situations in which the name of the great nation also appears as the name of a clan. A similar word "Oromtitti" (not shown on the chart) also appears in Boran clan list. It is a lineage counterpoised with another lineage called "Gabartitti." This is the second instance when the term Oromo appears in Borana (South), but as the name of a clan or lineage.

Finally, in the shaded area we have Humbanna appearing at the top of the genealogy of the Barentu, i.e. above the BORANA/BARETTUMA divide. Similarly Borana or Bworan, which is the name of one of the ancient moieties appears here as a clan name in Orma.

The Tulama case which has not been presented in chart form is most interesting. Their genealogical formula runs as follows.

| | | |
|---|---|---|
| *Sagaltam **Gabra**,* | *Saglan **Borana**,* | *Torban **Barentuma**,* |
| Ninety Gabra, | Nine Borana, | Seven Barentuma, |
| | | |
| *Jihan Hora Galan,* | *Afran Abbicchu, Gimbicchu,* | |
| Six Hora Galan, | Four Abbicchu, Gimbicchu | |
| | | |
| *Saden  Ada'a,* | *Saden Sooddo* | |
| Three Ad'aa, | Three Sooddo | |

The formula contains the classic BORANA/BARETTUMA division as well as the Borana/Gabra division analogous to Borana/Gabaro of Macch'a or Borana/Gabra in Borana (South). This indicates that the ancient moieties have been preserved in Tulama, but that the Gabra assimilation process is also going on. Unlike Macch'a, however, it is added on to the system and does replace it. As often happens, the Gabra are here honored by being listed first, though they are junior.

---

*Note: Barentu data are derived from Trimingham who is the only author who presents genealogical data that reveal the dual organization. Arsi are not included in the chart because the data are incomplete.

# BIBLIOGRAPHY

Abbas Haji Gnamo. "Egalitarianism, Justice and Democracy in an Oromo Polity." In *The Oromo Republic: Decline under Imperial Rule.* (Forthcoming)

———."The History of the Arssi 1880-1935." B.A. thesis, Addis Ababa University, 1982.

———."Le pouvoir de bénir et de maudire: cosmologie et organization sociale des Oromo-Arssi." *Cahiers d'études africaine* 146 XXXVII no. 2 (1997): 289-318.

——— "Les Oromo-Arssi: continuité et évolution des institutions d'une societé éthiopienne." Thèse de Doctorat de l'Université de Paris I, Pantheon-Sorbonne, 1990.

Abèles, Marc. "Générations et royauté sacré chez les Galla d'Éthiopie." In *Production pastorale et societé.* Cambridge: Cambridge University Press, 1976.

Abbadie, Antoine d.' "Sur les Oromo, grande nation africaine." *Annales de la Societé Scientifique de Bruxelles* 4 (1880):167-92.

Adams, George Burton. *Constitutional History of England.* New York: Henry Holt, 1938.

Andrzejewski, B.W. "Ideas about Warfare in Borana Galla Stories and Fables." *African Language Studies* 3 (1962): 116-36.

*Anthropology and the Colonial Encounter.* Edited by Talal Asad. New York: Humanities Press, 1973.

Ascher, Marcia, "Mathematics Elsewhere." An unpublished paper that examines the logical-mathematical principles underlying the Gada System. A book is forthcoming. The author is a professor emerita of mathematics at Ithaca College.

Asmä Giorgis, *History of the Galla and the Kingdom of Shäwa.* Edited by Bairu Tafla. Wiesbaden GMBH, Stuttgart: Franz Steiner, 1987.

Asmarom Legesse. "Adaptation, Drought and Development: Boran and Gabra Pastoralists of Northern Kenya." In *African Food Systems in Crisis*, Part 1. Edited by Rebecca Huss-Ashmore. New York: Gordon and Beach Science Publishers, 1989.

———. "Age-sets and Premarital Sex: A Controlled Cross-cultural Test." *Ethos*, 1977.

———. "Age-sets and Retirement Communities: Comparison and Comment." *Anthropological Quarterly.* Special Issue on Ethnography of Old Age 52 (1979): 61-69

———. "Borana under British and Ethiopian Empires." In *The Oromo Republic: Decline under Imperial Rule* (forthcoming).

———. "Boran-Gabra Pastoralism in Historical Perspective." In *Rangelands: A Resource Under Siege.* Edited by P.J. Joss et al. Cambridge: Cambridge University, 1986, 481-482 [summary].

———. "Class Systems Based on Time." *Journal of Ethiopian Studies* 1 (1963): 1-19.

———. "The Design of Community and its Sociological Consequences: Marsabit, Borana, Kenya." In *Rural Settlement Structure and African Development.* Edited by Marilyn Silberfein. Boulder, Colorado: Westview Press, 1988, 229-250.

———. "Ethiopian Colonists and Frontier Peoples: The Borana Case." Paper presented at the conference on Society and History of Imperial Ethiopia. Organized by Donald Donham and Wendy James, Moterey, California, 1982.

———. *Gada: Three Approaches to the Study of African Society.* New York: Free Press, Macmillan, 1973.

———. "Kenya Boran: Flexibility and Change in a Pastoral Society." New Hampshire: American Universities Field Staff, n.d.

———. "La mort du soleil: signes naturels, tabous et authorité politique." In G. Francillon and P. Menget. *Soleil est mort, L'ecplise totale de soleil du 30 Juin 1973.* Nanterre, 1979.

———. *A Pastoral Ecosystem: Field Studies of the Borana and Gabra of Northern Kenya.* (Forthcoming.)

———. "Post-Feudal Society, Capitalism and Revolution: The Case of Ethiopia." *Leo-Froebenius Symposium.* Dakar, Senegal: Deutche UNESCO Commission, 1975.

———. "Prophetism, Democharisma and Social Change." In *Religion in Africa: Experience and Expression.* Edited by Thomas D. Blakeley et al. Portsmouth, NH: Heinemann, 1994.

Bairu Tafla. *Atsmä Giorgis and His Work: History of the Galla and the Kingdom of Shäwa.* Wiesbaden GMBH, Stuttgart: Franz Steiner, 1987.

Baissa Lemmu, see Lemmu Baissa

Bartels, Lambert. *Oromo Religion.* Berlin: Dietrich Reimer, 1990.

Bassi, Marco. *I Borana: Una società assembleare dell'Etiopia.* Milano: Franco Angeli, 1996.

_____. *Decisions in the Shade: Political and Juridical Processes among the Oromo-Borana,* translation of *I Borana* by Cinthia Salvatori, Trenton, NJ: Red Sea Press,

Baxter, Paul. "Absence Makes the Heart Grow Fonder." *In The Allocation of Responsibility.* Edited by Max Gluckman, Manchester: Manchester University Press, 1972.

_____. "Acceptance and Rejection of Islam among the Boran of the Northern Frontier District of Kenya." In *Islam in Tropical Africa.* Edited by I.M. Lewis. Oxford: Oxford University Press, 1966, 233-50.

_____. "Boran Age-sets and Generation-sets." In *Age, Generation and Time: Some Features of East African Age Organization.* Edited by Paul Baxter et al. New York: St Martin Press, 1978.

_____ "Boran Age-sets and Warfare." *Senri Ethnological Studies* 3 (1979): 69-95.

_____. "Ethiopia's Unacknowledged Problem: the Oromo." *African Affairs: A Quarterly Journal of the Royal African Society* 77, 308 (1978): 283-296.

_____. "Repetition in Certain Boran Ceremonies." In *African Systems of Thought.* Edited by M. Fortes and G. Dieterlen. London: Oxford University Press, 1965, pp. 54-78.

_____. "The Social Organization of the Galla of Northern Kenya." D. Phil. thesis, Lincoln College, Oxford University, 1954.

_____. "The Social Organisation of the Boran of Northern Kenya," London, 1954, [summary of the dissertation].

_____. "Stock Management and the Diffusion of Property Rights among the Boran." In *Proceedings of the Third International Conference of Ethiopian Studies* 3 (1966): 126-127.

Baxter, Paul, et al., ed. *Age, Generation and Time: Some Features of East African Age Organization,* London: C. Hurst, 1978.

Beguinot, Francesco. *Chronaca Abbreviata.* Rome, 1901.

*Being and Becoming Oromo: Historical and Anthropological Enquiries.* Edited by Paul Baxter, Jan Hultin, and Alessandro Triulzi. Lawrenceville, N.J.: Red Sea Press, 1996.

Beckingham C. F. and G.W.B. Huntingford. *Some Records of Ethiopia, 1593-1646.* Nendeln, Lichtenstein: Kraus Reprint, 1967.

Blackhurst, Hector. "Continuity and Change in Shoa Galla Gada System." In *Age, Generation and Time.* Edited by Paul Baxter and Uri Almagor. London: C. Hurst, 1978.

Bureau, Jacques. "Compte Rendue" *L'Homme* 3-4 (1974): 154-57.

Bieber, Friedrich J. Kaffa: *Ein Altkuschitiches Völkstum in Inner-Africa.* Anthropos Bibliothek. Vol. 1 and 2, 1923.

Cerulli, Enrico. *Etiopia Occidentale.* Vol. 2, Rome: Sindacato Italiano Arti Grafiche, [1930]-1933.

_____. *Folk Literature of the Galla of Southern Ethiopia,* Harvard African Studies, III. Edited by E.A. Hooton. Cambridge, Mass., Harvard University Press, 1922.

Dahl, Gudrun. *Suffering Grass: Subsistence and Society of Waso Borana.* Stockolm Studies in Social Anthropology. Department of Anthropology, University of Stockholm, 1979.

_____. "Ecology and Equality: the Boran Case." In *Pastoral Production and Society.* Edited under the direction of L'Équipe écologie et anthropologie des societés pastorales. Cambridge: Cambridge University Press, 1976, 261-281.

Dinsa Lepisa Aba Jobir. "The Gada System of Government." LL.B, thesis, Addis Ababa University, 1975.

Doyle, Laurance. "The Borana Calendar Reinterpreted." *Current Anthropology* (June 1986): 286-287.

Ensminger, Jean, and Jack Knight. "Changing Social Norms: Common Property, Bridewealth, and Clan Exogamy." *Current Anthropology* 38,1(1997):1-14.

Evans-Pritchard, E.E. *The Divine Kingship of the Shilluk of the Nilotic Sudan.* Cambridge: Cambridge university Press, 1948.

_____. *The Nuer: A Description of Modes of Livelihood and Political Institutions of a Nilotic People.* Oxford: Clarendon, 1940.

_____. *The Azande: History and Political Institutions.* Oxford: Clarendon,1971.

Fortes, M., and E. E. Evans-Pritchard, eds. African Political Systems. London: Oxford University Press, for the International African Institute of African Languages and Cultures, 1940.

*Freedom and Constraint: A Memorial Tribute to Max Gluckman.* Edited by M.J. Aronoff. Assen: Van Gorcum, 1976.

Foidevaux, Henri. "Antoine Thomson D'Abbadie." *Dictionnaire de Biographie Française.* Paris: Librarie Letouzey, 1933, 36-42

Goto, Paul S. G. "The Boran of Northern Kenya: Origins, Migration and Settlements in the 19th Century." B.A. thesis, Nairobi, Kenya: University of Nairobi, 1972.

Gluckman, Max. *The Judicial Process among the Barotse of Northern Rhodesia.* Manchester: Manchester University Press, 1955.

Haberland, Eike. *Galla Süd Äthiopiens.* Vol. 2, *Völker Süd Äthiopiens.* Stuttgart: W. Kohlhammer verlag, for Frankfurt am Main University, Fröbenius Institute, 1963.

Hallpike, Christopher. "The Origins of the Borana Gada System: A Discussion of '*Gada: Three Approaches to the Study of African Society,* by Asmarom Legesse.'" *Africa, Journal of the International African Institute,* London 46 (1976): 48-56.

Hinnant, John, "The Gada System of the Guji of Southern Ethiopia." Ph.D. diss., University of Chicago, August 1977.

Hobbes, Thomas, *Leviathan,* New York: Dover Publications, 2006, a reprint of *Leviathan: The Matter, Forme, & Power of a Common-Wealth Eclesiasticall and Civill,* London: Andrew Crooke, 1651.

Hocart, A. M. *Kings and Councilors: An Essay in the Comparative Anatomy of Human Society.* Foreword by E.E. Evans-Pritchard. Chicago: University of Chicago Press, 1970.

Hodson, Arnold. *Seven Years in Southern Abyssinia.* Westport, Connecticut: Negro Universities Press, 1970.

Holcomb, Bonnie and Sisay Ibsa. *The Invention of Ethiopia: the Making of a Dependent Colonial State in Northeast Africa.* Trenton, N.J.: Red Sea Press, 1990.

Hultin, Jan. " 'Sons of Slaves' or 'Sons of Boys,' the Premise of Rank Among the Macha Oromo." *Proceedings of the 8th International Conference of Ethiopian Studies.* Addis Ababa: University of Addis Ababa, 1988, 809-81

_____. *The Long Journey: Essays on History, Descent and Land among the Macha Oromo,* University of Upsala, 1987

Huntingford, G.W.B. *The Galla of Ethiopia, the Kingdoms of Kafa and Janjero.* Ethnographic Survey of Africa, Northeastern Africa, part 2, London: International African Institute, 1955.

_____. *Historical geography of Ethiopia.* Oxford: Oxford University Press, c1989.

Huxley, Elspeth. *White Man's Country: Lord Delamere and the Making of Kenya.* Vol. 1. New York: Praeger, 1967.

James, Wendy, "The Anthropologist as a Reluctant Imperialist," in Asad, Ed. *Anthropology and the Colonial encounter,* 1973.

_____. "Kings Commoners, and the Ethnographic Imagination in Sudan and Ethiopia," in *Localizing Strategies: Regional Traditions in Ethnographic Writing,* ed. Richard Fardon. Edinburgh: Scottish Academic Press, 1990.

Kelly, Hilarie Ann, "From Gada to Islam: The Moral Authority of Gender Relations among the Pastoral Orma of Kenya." (Ph.D. diss., Los Angeles: UCLA, 1985), 59-69, 361, 431.

Krige, E.J. "The Military Organization of the Zulu." *Social System of the Zulus.* Edited by E.J. Krige, London: Longmans, 1936, 261-279.

Knutsson, Karl Eric. *Authority and Change: A study of the Kallu institution among the Macha Galla of Ethiopia.* Göteborg: Ethnografiska Museet, 1963.

Lemmu Baissa. "Gada Government in Wallagga: The Rise of War Chiefs and the Shoan Conquest." In *The Oromo Republic: Decline under Imperial Rule,* forthcoming.

Lemmu Baissa. "The Democratic Political System of the Oromo (Galla) of Ethiopia and the Possibility of its Use in Nation-Building." M.A. thesis, George Washington University, 1971.

Leenco Lata. *The Ethiopian State at the Crossroads: Decolonization and Democratization or Disintegration?* Lawrenceville, NJ: Red Sea Press, 1999.

Levine, Donald. *Wax and Gold: Tradition and Innovation in Ethiopian Culture.* Chicago: University of Chicago Press, 1965.

_____. *Greater Ethiopia: the Evolution of a Multiethnic Society.* Chicago: University of Chicago Press, 1974.

Lévi-Strauss, Claude. *Structural Anthropology.* New York, Basic Books, 1963.

Lewis, Herbert S. *A Galla Monarchy: Jimma Abba Jifar, Ethiopia, 1830-1932.* Madison: University of Wisconsin Press, 1965.

_____. "Aspects of Oromo Political Culture." *Journal of Oromo Studies* 1 (1994): 53-58.

Lijphart, Arend, *Democracies: Patterns of Majoritarian and Consensus Government in Twenty-One Countries*, New Haven: Yale University Press, 1984.

Lugard, Frederick, D. The Dual Mandate in British Tropical Africa. Edinburgh: Blackwood, 1922.

_____. *Representative Government and "Indirect Rule" in British Africa.* Edingurgh: Blackwood, 1882.

_____. *The Rise of our East African Empire,* 2 vols. London: Frank Cass, 1968.

Lynch, B.M., and L. M. Robbins. "Namoratunga: the First Archaeoastronomic Evidence in Sub-Saharan Africa." *Science* 200 (1978): 766-78.

Mahteme-Sellassie Wolde-Mesqel. *Zikre Neger.* Addis Ababa: Government News Office, ca.1942 (Eth. Calendar.), ca.1949.

Marcus, Harold. *The Life and Times of Menelik II.* Oxford: Clarendon, 1975.

Mesfin Wolde Mariam. *An Introductory Geography of Ethiopia.* Addis Abeba: Berhanenna Selam, H.S.I Printing Press, 1972.

Mohammed Hassen. *The Oromo of Ethiopia: A History 1570-1860.* Trenton, N.J.: Red Sea Press, 1994.

————. "The Pre-Sixteenth-Century Oromo Presence within the Medieval Christian Kingdom of Ethiopia." In *A River Blessings.* Edited by David Brokensha. Foreign and Comparative Studies, Series 44, Syracuse University, 1994, 53-54.

————. "The Relation between Harar and the Surrounding Oromo." B.A. thesis, Addis Ababa University, 1972.

Nelson, Benjamin. *The Idea of Usury: From Tribal Brotherhood to Universal Otherhood.* Chicago: University Press, 1969.

Oberg, K. "The Kingdom of Ankole in Uganda." In *African Political Systems.* Edited by M. Fortes and E.E. Evans-Pritchard. London: Oxford University Press, 1940.

Pankhurst, Richard. *An Introduction to the History of the Ethiopian Army.* Addis Ababa: n.p, 1959.

_____.*The Ethiopian Borderlands: Essays in Regional History from ancient Times to the End of the 18th Century.* Lawrenceville, NJ., Asmara, Eritrea, Red Sea Press, 1997.

Pecci, Domenico. "Note sul sistema delle Gada e delle classi di età presso le popolazioni Borana." *Rassegna di Studi Etiopici,* 1 (1941): 305-21.

Pereira, Esteves F.M. *Chronica de Susenyos, Rei de Ethiopia.* Lisboa: Impresa Nacional, 1900.

Perham, Margery. *Lugard.* Hamden, Conn.: Anchor Books, 1968.

Philipson, J.H. "Notes on the Galla." *Man* 16 (1916): 177-81.

Plowman, Clifford H.F. "Notes on the Gadamoch ceremonies among the Boran." *Journal of the African society* 18 (1918): 114-21.

*River of Blessings: Essays in Honor of Paul Baxter.* Edited by D. Brokensha. Syracuse, N.Y.: Maxwell School, Syracure University, c 1994.

Salviac, P. Martial de. *Un peuple antique au pays de Menelik, Les Galla: grande nation africaine.* Paris: H. Oudin, [1901].

Sampson, Anthony. *Anatomy of Britain.* Liverpool: Hodder and Stoughton, 1962.

Schlee, Günther. *Identities on the Move: clanship and pastoralism in Northern Kenya.* Manchester: The University Press, 1989.

_____. "Inter-ethnic clan identities among Cushitic speaking pastoralists." *Africa* 55 (1985): 17-38.

_____. "The Oromo Expansion and its Impact in Northern Kenya." *Proceedings of the Eighth International Conference of Ethiopian Studies.* Vol 2. Edited by Taddesse Beyene. Addis Ababa: University of Addis Ababa, 1984.

Scholler, Heinrich. "Letters Exchanged between Ethiopian and German Emperors." *In Proceedings of the Fifth International Conference of Ethiopian Studies.* Apr. 13-16, 1978, Chicago: University of Illinois, Office of Publication Services, 1979.

Shongolo, Abdullahi A. "The Gumi Gaayo Assembly of the Boran: A Traditional Legislative Organ and its Relationship to the Ethiopian State and the Modernizing World." *Zeitschrift für Ethnologie* 119 (1994): 27-58.

Smith, Donaldson. "Expedition through Somaliland to Lake Rudolf." *Geographical Journal,* London 8 (1896).

*The Southern Marches of Imperial Ethiopia.* Edited by Donald Donham and Wendy James. Cambridge & New York: Cambridge University Press, 1986.

Stuart, James. *History of the Zulu Rebellion.* London: Macmillan, 1913.

Tablino, Paolo. *I Gabbra del Kenia.* Bologna: Tipografia Novastampa di Verona, 1980.

Taddesse Tamrat. "Feudalism in Heaven and on Earth: Ideology and Political Structure in Medieval Ethiopia." *Proceedings of the Seventh International Conference of Ethiopian Studies.* Lund, 26-29, April, 1982, pp. 195-96.

Tesemma Ta'a. "The Political Economy of Western Central Ethiopia: From the Mid-16th Century to Early 20th Centuries." Ph.D. diss., Michigan State University, 1986.

Torry, I.W. "Subsistence Ecology among the Gabra." Ph.D. diss., Columbia University, University Microfilms, 1973.

*Tribes without Rulers: Studies in African Segmentary Systems.* Edited by J. Middleton and D. Tait. London: Routledge, 1958.

Trimingham, J.S., *Islam in Ethiopia.* London: Frank Cass, 1965.

Triulzi, Alessandro. "Center-Periphery Relations in Ethiopian Studies: Reflections on Ten Years of Research on Wellega History." *Proceedings of the Seventh International Conference of Ethiopian Studies.* University of Lund, 26-29 April, 1982. Edited by Sven Rubenson.

_____. "Toward a Corpus of Historical source Materials in Wallagga: a Preliminary Report," *Proceedings of the Eighth International Conference of Ethiopian Studies,* Vol. II, 319-329, ed. by Taddese Beyene, University of Addis Ababa, 1984

_____. "United and Divided: Boorana and Gabaro among the Maccha Oromo in Western Ethiopia." In *Being and Becoming Oromo.* Edited by Paul Baxter et al. Lawrenceville N.J.: Red Sea Press, 1996, 251-264.

_____. "The Gudru Oromo and their Neighbours in the two Generations before the Battle of Embabo." *Journal of Ethiopian Studies* 13 (1975): 37-63

_____. "The Saga of Makko Bilii: A Theme in Mac'a Oromo History." *Paideuma,* 36 (1990): 319-327.

Turner, Victor. *The Ritual Process.* Chicago: Aldine, 1969.

Ullendorf, Edward. *The Ethiopians: An Introduction to Country and People.* London: Oxford University Press, 1960.

*Warfare among East African Herders.* Edited by Fukui Katsuyoshi and D. Turton. Osaka: Senri Ethnological Studies, 1979.

Werner, A. "Some Galla Notes," *Man,* 15(1915):1-22.

Whiteway, R. S. *The Portuguese Expedition to Abyssinia in 1541-1543.* Hakluyt Society, 1902; Lichtenstein: Krauss Reprint, 1967.

Zewde Gabre-Sellassie. *Yohannes IV of Ethiopia: A Political Biography.* Oxford: Clarendon, 1975.

# INDEX

This is a detailed index which can serve as a useful tool for further research. The literature on Oromo is vast. Systematic computer indexing can make it more accessible and transparent if it is used judiciously. For all words that have multiple meanings, each index entry was checked page by page. Alternate spellings are given in parentheses. There is some redundancy in the index designed to permit researchers to approach the material from a variety of perspectives, mainly sociological, political, legal, ethnographic and historic.

I completed this work at the age of 75, in the sixth year of the gada of our sons, the sons of Jaldessa Liban, *moggisa* (2000-2008). I belong to the luba of Jaldessa Liban, *fullasa*, Abba Gada of all the Borana (1960-1968), who made me a member of his luba in jest, though I have hardly taken this kind gesture lightly in my life and career. I have lived vicariously through all the stages of their adult life cycle and we are now about to leave Gada Mojji, the stage of peace, and render unto our peers an account of the lives we lived.

All the mistaken ideas in this book—such as inserting numbers and dates into their logical system of thought—are my own and will be corrected, in due course, by better scholars than I. All the wonderful ideas are those of Oromo men of knowledge who took me into their confidence and taught me the concepts, values and laws that govern their society.

During the last forty years, when I have been learning, thinking, and writing about the Oromo and their institutions, not a single Oromo elder has ever asked me, 'Why have you studied our culture?' The reason is clear: Oromo culture is a culture built on trust and on the presumption that people have no hidden or evil motives for doing what they do. That presumption continues as long as the individual does not commit an act that violates their trust. That is also the ethical premise of their democratic way of life.

Asmarom Legesse,
Philadelphia, PA,
30 December, 2006